W9-BEC-604

T R A V E L E R ' S

PORTUGAL

C O M P A N I O N

The 2000–2001 Traveler's Companions
ARGENTINA • AUSTRALIA • BALI • CALIFORNIA • CANADA • CHILI • CHINA • COSTA RICA •
CUBA • EASTERN CANADA • ECUADOR • FLORIDA • HAWAII • HONG KONG • INDIA •
INDONESIA • JAPAN • KENYA • MALAYSIA & SINGAPORE • MEDITERRANEAN FRANCE •
MEXICO • NEPAL • NEW ENGLAND • NEW ZEALAND • PERU • PHILIPPINES • PORTUGAL •
RUSSIA • SOUTH AFRICA • SOUTHERN ENGLAND • SPAIN • THAILAND • TURKEY •
VENEZUELA • VIETNAM, LAOS AND CAMBODIA • WESTERN CANADA

Traveler's PORTUGAL Companion
First published 2000
The Globe Pequot Press
6 Business Park Road, PO Box 833
Old Saybrook, CT 06475-0833
www.globe.pequot.com

ISBN: 0-7627-0361-X

By arrangement with Kümmerly+Frey AG, Switzerland
© 2000 Kümmerly+Frey AG, Switzerland

Created, edited and produced by
Allan Amsel Publishing, 53, rue Beaudouin
27700 Les Andelys, France.
E-mail: Allan.Amsel@wanadoo.fr
Editor in Chief: Allan Amsel
Editor: Anne Trager
Original design concept: Hon Bing-wah
Picture editor and designer: David Henry

All rights reserved. No part of this publication may be reproduced, stored in
a retrieval system, or transmitted in any form or by any means, electronic,
mechanical or otherwise without the prior permission of the publisher.
Requests for permission should be addressed to Allan Amsel Publishing,
53 rue Beaudouin, 27700 Les Andelys France outside North America;
or to The Globe Pequot Press, 6 Business Park Road, PO Box 833,
Old Saybrook, CT 06475-0833 in North America.

Printed by Samwha Printing Co. Ltd., Seoul, South Korea

TRAVELER'S

PORTUGAL

COMPANION

by Laurel Hirsch

photographs by Nik Wheeler and Bruno Barbier

Kümmerly+Frey

The Globe Pequot Press

OLD SAYBROOK

Contents

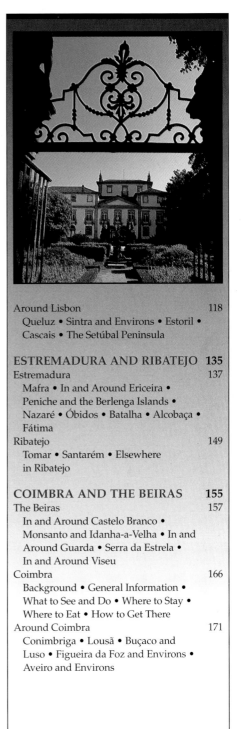

T R A V E L E R ' S
PORTUGAL
C O M P A N I O N

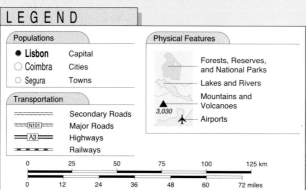

LEGEND

Populations

- **Lisbon**   Capital
- ○ Coimbra   Cities
- ○ Segura   Towns

Transportation

═══════	Secondary Roads
═══N101═══	Major Roads
═══A3═══	Highways
▬▬▬▬	Railways

Physical Features

	Forests, Reserves, and National Parks
	Lakes and Rivers
▲ 3,030	Mountains and Volcanoes
✈	Airports

0	25	50	75	100	125 km
0	12	24	36	48	60	72 miles

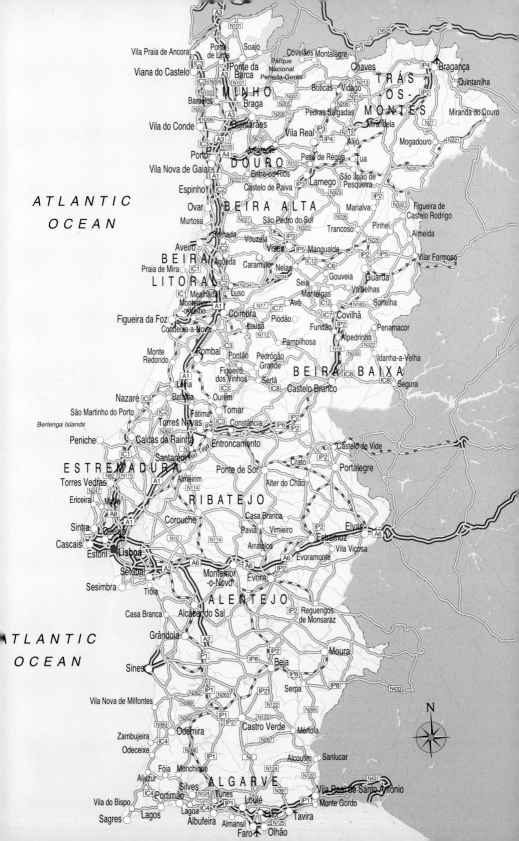

TOP SPOTS

Cruise the Douro

THE RIO DOURO ("RIVER OF GOLD") IS THE GRANDEST RIVER IN PORTUGAL, snaking east for some 200 km (125 miles) from Porto to Barca d'Alva on the Spanish border. And in keeping with some unwritten European rule, the Douro, just like the Rhône and the Rhine and the Loire and countless other rivers, is lined with great sprawling vineyards. All along the upper reaches are Portugal's renowned port vineyards, covering the steep surrounding hillsides and creeping right down to the water's edge. Occasionally you may spot a bright white *quinta* among the serried ranks of vines — a farm house belonging to a wine grower or, perhaps more likely now, one of the port companies, many of which have been in operation for centuries.

You might well find nothing more enchanting in all of Portugal than to take a cruise from Porto into the heart of the port country at Pinhão, sipping the delectable quaff as you go. Endouro Turismo ((22) 332-4236 FAX (22) 205-7260 in Porto organizes regular day-long outings, as well as weekend cruises that include a night at the luxurious Hotel de Lamego. There are shorter 50-minute jaunts, cruising beneath the city's four bridges, and although these give you a little taste of Douro delight, the river's real drama — deep gorges and expansive calm stretches between a series of dams — only starts in earnest further inland.

For true indulgence, spend a week living aboard the *Invicta* and sail your way into Spain, disembarking, of course, to visit the sites en route. Along with this route, Douro Azul ((22) 339-3950 FAX (22) 208-3407 in Porto offers several other tours as well.

Organized cruises aren't your only option: if you want to go it alone, take the train (two and a half hours) to Peso da Régua, a center for the port industry with a couple of port lodges to visit: the Casa do Douro and Ramos Pinto. Even better, take the train all the way to the end of its river-hugging route at Pocinho (four and a half hours from Porto). You won't find much here except the very best that the Douro offers: the lull of flowing water and the sweet aroma of wine.

Mosteiro dos Jerónimos OPPOSITE in Lisbon, the quintessential example of Manueline architecture.
ABOVE: Iron bridge over the Douro River at Pinhão, a main center of the port trade.

Wallow in *Fado*

LOVE IS A FIRE THAT BURNS UNSEEN,
A WOUND THAT ACHES AND IS NOT FELT
IT IS CONTENTMENT MALCONTENT,
A MADDENING PAIN WITHOUT GRIEF.
            — LUÍS VAZ DE CAMÕES

If there is one uniquely Portuguese art form it is *fado*, which simply means fate. Camões, Portugal's sixteenth-century lyric poet might well have been its Godfather.

There's lots of new music in Portugal, but everyone still loves *fado*, and when the Mother of all *fado* singers, the late Amalia Rodrigues, sings on the radio, cars pull off to the side to listen until her song is finished (and then all try to get back on the road at once). No visit to Portugal could possibly be complete without an evening spent listening to this dark music. Intensely nostalgic songs, unapologetically fervent in their melodrama, they are sung both by soberly dressed men and black-shawled women who ostensibly are all in perpetual mourning for the first famous *fadista*, a gypsy girl called Maria Severa. Of course, there's no need to understand the words to get the meaning — they're all about lost love, jealousy, the fate of death. The *fadista's* voice is powerful, the accompanying 12-string guitars haunting.

Fado was born in the Alfama district of Lisbon in the eighteenth century, and it is there where it still truly reigns. A slightly different, more cerebral variety emerged in Coimbra, which is not surprising knowing the city is home to one of Europe's most ancient universities, and eternal youthful sorrow permeates its narrow streets. Although much of the current *fado* performed in Lisbon is slickly touristic (and laughably overpriced), you can still hear the real thing in the smaller clubs where it is as earthy as it should be. Lisbon friends, of varying generations, concur regarding the Parreirinha de Alfama ((21) 886-8209, Beco do Espírito Santo No. 1, which is in the heart of where it all began. In Coimbra you can grow misty-eyed and dream the evening away at the Diligencia Bar ((239) 827667, Rua Nova No. 30, which is a popular haunt for both experienced and up-and-coming *fadistas*.

Travel the Trams

TRAMS ARE TO LISBON AND PORTO WHAT VAPORETTI ARE TO VENICE. Yes, convenient — if slow — city transportation, but even to the jaded local commuter, they serve as a reminder that getting there is part of getting there. Hop aboard an old *electrico* and snake up some of Lisbon's steepest hills, or labor along a stretch of Porto's coast. Antiquated with wheels that squeal and gears that groan (even louder than the doubting tourist), their polished mahogany and brass will seduce you.

In Lisbon, tram number 28 is the best one to sample. One terminus is up in the Chaido at Praça Camões, the other all the way on the other side of town in the Alfama. Stay on the line for the entire

A *fado* singer ABOVE touches the soul of the nation with heart-wrenching themes of fatalism and lost love. A tram RIGHT pushes past Lisbon's cathedral.

journey and you'll travel through several neighborhoods, some residential, some commercial, getting a taste of contemporary Lisbon living in the shadow of its past. Also just past the Sé, as the tram climbs into the Alfama, look right if you dare. The Téjo is just off the precipice you seem just barely on.

In Porto, don't miss tram number 1, which starts near the waterfront in the Ribeira and works its way along the coast to Foz. En route, you can stop at the recently-opened Tram Museum at Cais do Bicalho, with its displays of restored trams dating from the turn of the century to the 1970s. There's also an exhibit of wonderful old photos of Porto from the days when trams ruled the road.

Check into a Private Palace

FEEL LIKE SPENDING A NIGHT AT HOME? How about a seventeenth-century manor house where a king once slept, or a baronial mansion where your host is a count? Or even better, a country home with a welcoming family. Thanks to a scheme called *Turismo de Habitação* or TURIHAB (as well as two other organizations, see ACCOMMODATION, page 279 in TRAVELERS' TIPS), dozens of select private houses now offer some of the finest accommodation to be found in Europe from about US$50 a night.

TURIHAB was established by the owners of the houses with the idea of providing a novel service: you're not merely a casual "hotel" visitor, but a personal guest. Your hosts can also give you unique insight into the region — their personal tips on sights to see, the best restaurants (and the worst!), as well as anecdotes of the local history (and more often than not, on their ancestors who were instrumental in forming it), while your room is likely to be lavishly furnished with the family's antiques, perhaps dating back to the fifteenth century. Not all TURIHAB accommodation is in this kind of baronial league: you can choose a simple *casa rustica* (country cottage) if it's more to your taste, or a

rambling farmhouse or *quinta* (manor house). Many owners have created small apartments with fully-equipped kitchens, making the accommodation ideal for families. Most homes are set in rolling gardens, if not on vast estates with private vineyards, and almost all have installed swimming pools. Contact the main TURIHAB organization ((258) 741672 FAX (258) 741444, Praça da República, 4990 Ponte de Lima, for their full brochure. Far more complete and informative is the *Guide for Tourism in the Country* published by the Portuguese tourist office and well worth its price of approximately US$15.

Discover *Manuelino*

ORNATE, ORIGINAL, EVEN BIZARRE, YOU CAN'T HELP BUT MARVEL AT THE GNARLS OF MANUELINE ARCHITECTURE. Getting its name from King Manuel I who reigned during Portugal's fifteenth- to sixteenth-century heyday — the Age of the Discoveries — the style is a direct product of Portugal's seafaring conquests. Not only are the motifs a mélange of nautical and religious symbolism, with more than subtle hints of oriental exoticism, the huge edifices could not possibly have been built without the new-found fortunes, and the new-found sense of grandeur. And nor for that matter, could the Portuguese have otherwise hired skilled artisans from Italy, Spain, and the Low Countries.

This wealth and confidence gave rise to magnificent cathedrals, monasteries, and churches — all of which were, for this brief period, adorned with the unique Manueline touch: elaborate sculpted stonework of knots and globes and shells, of laurel leaves and poppies and acorns.

Two supreme architectural examples are to be found in Belém, just outside of Lisbon. The Torre de Belém, considered to be the sole truly authentic *Manuelino*

The Igreja de Santa Maria in Belém houses the neo-Manueline tomb of the navigator Vasco da Gama and a monument to the poet Luís Vaz de Camões.

building, as it was constructed within the king's reign, looks as if it could have been plucked from an ornate Moorish chessboard. The vast, vaulted Mosteiro dos Jerónimos with its columns carved to replicate the rigging of a Portuguese caravel, is a classic example of the period.

Two other stunning works certainly worth the trip off the beaten tourist route are the chapter house window of Tomar's Convento de Cristo, and the Unfinished Chapels of Batalha. The decoration of the justly famous window sprouts from the root of a cork tree that sits upon the bust of a sea captain. The root then spawns framing masts encrusted with coral and lashed with knotted ropes and cables. Uncharacteristically somber, the intricately carved pillars of the Unfinished Chapels reach into the open air as if an omen to the end of an era.

Eliminate those Evil Humors

BEING STRESSED OUT IS NOTHING NEW. WHEN IN PORTUGAL, WHY NOT DO AS THE ROMANS DID? A visit to a Portuguese spa will not be shrouded in the grandeur you might find in France and Switzerland, but claims to cures are certainly grand. And the egalitarianism itself is quite refreshing. Predominantly in the north of the country, although you'll find a few in the Algarve, some of the spas date from the time of the Romans, and all specialize their treatments in accordance with the elemental properties of their waters.

Even skeptics will agree that therapies at the Termas da Curia ((231) 512185 FAX (231) 5158383, Sociedad das Águas da Curia, Curia, 3700 Anadia, perhaps Portugal's most famous spa, will lower your blood pressure. How could they not? The bucolic setting is deep in the heart of the Bairrada region, home to my unequivocal favorite *vinho tinto*. And for an element of luxury, check into the elegant turn-of-the-century Grand Hotel da Curia ((231) 515728 FAX (231) 515317 E-MAIL hbelver@mail.telepac.pt, Curia–Tamengos, 3700 Anadia, with its own health center that is replete with mud

and Turkish baths, two swimming pools, and most important, a qualified masseuse.

All the information you could possibly want regarding each of Portugal's 41 spas, including the temperature and pH-level of the waters, and an exhaustive list of neighboring hotel accommodation, is included in the Portuguese tourist authority's *Official Guide to Spas*. Request a copy from your local Portuguese tourist office, and be sure to arrange a well-earned break from the travails of traveling.

Scale the Medieval Walls

GUARDING OVER PORTUGAL AND ITS PAST STAND ITS WALLS OF PROTECTION. Dozens of hilltop forts and castles, once Portugal's frontline of defense against the Moors, and later, the Spanish and French, were used right up until the nineteenth century. Linked to many of them is the name of Dom Dinis, the "Fortress King" of Portugal, who during his reign from 1279 to 1325 built or rebuilt over 50 castles, particularly along the strategic eastern border with Spain.

Climbing the walls is a great way to glimpse Portugal's past, as well as see some of the most picturesque corners of its present landscape. Hugging the safety of the castle are often old villages, many little changed from the days of Dinis himself. Arguably the prettiest and most romantic walled town is Óbidos (which Dinis gave his fiancée as a bridal gift) while Elvas, just 13 km (eight miles) from the Spanish border, still ranks as one of the best-fortified towns in Europe.

Don't miss Castelo de Vide and nearby Marvão either — the latter perched so high on a rocky hilltop, it's a wonder it was ever defeated. Stay the night if you can when you visit these fortified villages and in the windswept silence of the narrow lanes you'll catch a real sense of the indomitable spirit that helped preserve Portugal's independence for centuries.

Ancient ruins at the Citânia de Briteiros.

Catch a Country Market

PORTUGAL STILL KNOWS HOW TO HOLD A GENUINE OUTDOOR COUNTRY MARKET — the sort where you can find everything from clucking hens and squealing pigs to handmade ceramics, baskets, and carved wooden ox yokes. These are markets that are most definitely not staged for the passing tourist, and some of the country's best are to be found in the northern Minho district. The grandest of all takes place in Barcelos, every Thursday from morning until dusk. This huge country fair, sprawling across the town's inordinately vast central square, is a microcosm of Portuguese rural life: small farmers with their mounds of tantalizingly fresh fruits and vegetables, potters displaying their brightly-colored wares, gypsy women selling clothes and shoes. This is the place to pick up your typical Portuguese gifts and souvenirs, or simply to mingle with the locals.

Other good markets to take in on your tour include the Saturday fair at Estremoz in the Alentejo (great for terracotta dishes and water jugs as well as fine little homemade wooden toys); the daily market at Caldas da Rainha in Estremadura, which is famous for its whimsical cabbage-leaf ceramics (a national ceramics fair is held here in early July); and then most definitely the one at Ponte de Lima held every other

Monday, where if you're not in the market to buy an ox, you can watch others do so as you sip a locally produced *vinho verde*.

Dine, Eat, Snack

INDULGE! WHO EVER COMES HOME FROM A VACATION HAVING NOT OVEREATEN? This is most definitely not the time to count, neither calories nor *escudos*. But in all truth, neither of the two will pile up all that quickly in Portugal.

Now doubt, you've already heard of the freshness of the produce, of the fish caught in the morning and served the same evening. And have already just about smelled the breads baking, and

have been on the verge of savoring the cloud-like almond desserts. The cuisine here, its variety notwithstanding, can be some of the most complex found on the Iberian Peninsula. Yes, there are the ubiquitous grilled meats and fish (which also should not be missed), but a good five centuries after the spice trade, and who knows how many since the inception of grape cultivation, refinement has certainly been attained.

Lisbon, Porto, the Algarve, the *pousadas*, all have their renowned dining spots (some more worthy of their name than others), but by all means, do not hesitate venturing into the small, unknown restaurant in the even smaller out-of-the-way town.

Trust your instincts, your sense of smell, or better yet, your sense of adventure. The startling green soup *will* belie a luscious creamy coriander. Just as the herbed roasted pheasant *will* be as tender and sweet as its chestnut stuffing. (A dinner of slow-baked lamb marinated in red wine should be a visa requirement.)

Yes, there are Portuguese restaurants throughout the world, but what truly marks its cuisine is the quality and freshness of its ingredients. And for that, you must voyage to the Old World.

Open-air market LEFT at Viana do Castelo in the Minho. ABOVE: Cafés and restaurants take to the streets in Lisbon's Rossio district.

(A few places to mark on your map: Solar Bragançano in Bragança; Terr' à Terra in Lisbon; Jonas Bar on the beach between Estoril and Monte Estoril; any little café with fresh little curry chicken pastry puffs that look irresistible — they are.)

Hunt for the Best *Azulejos*

STEP INTO ALMOST ANY CHURCH OR PALACE IN PORTUGAL AND YOU'LL NOTICE ONE RECURRENT FEATURE — the extravagant use of *azulejos*, blue and white or polychrome wall tiles.

The Portuguese have been refining the art for over 500 years, starting with mainly blue (*azul*) tiles after the Moors originally introduced a geometric style of tilework into the country.

Some of the most striking *azulejos* are in places where one might least expect them — as at the São Bento train station in Porto, where amid the frenzy of commuter traffic and urban existence, Jorge Colaço's neoclassic blue and white panels depicting much of Portugal's history present a juxtaposed calm. But undoubtedly, superb examples also emblazon the churches, in particular Almancil's Igreja de São Lourenço in the Algarve and Évora's Igreja de São João in the Alentejo. And then Lisbon even honors the craft with the Museu Nacional do Azulejo. Housed in the Madre de Deus church, its cloisters boasts a 37-m (120-ft) ceramic panorama of the city that dates from the eighteenth century.

The real fun, of course, is to discover the old in the new. And when you can, to touch it, to live it. A stay in Porto's Pensão Castelo de Santa Catarina is always delightful, and not least of all, for its (perhaps, over) adoration of *azulejos*. Falling in love with its fully tiled (somewhat kitsch) exterior, only barely prepares you for the fatty blues cherubs in the bathroom. More staid is the Casa da Pérgola in Cascais. Blue and gold *azulejos* frame its windows, and the drawing room of this nineteenth-century villa is elegantly tiled.

Azulejo tiles adorn Portugal's public buildings.

YOUR CHOICE

The Great Outdoors

With so much attention given to Portugal's splendid architectural sights and well-developed southern seaside resorts, the country's great outdoor attractions further north are often overlooked. But if you're a hiker, nature-lover, or even just in the mood for a respite in the countryside, you'll find Portugal has some of the best-kept outdoor secrets in Europe, ranging from rambling forests and gardens to rugged mountain ranges.

On the wild side, there are 21 officially protected areas, including the Peneda-Gerês National Park in the north and some 15 *parques naturais* and *reservas naturais* scattered throughout the country.

Information on these sites is available from the National Parks Services' headquarters ((21) 352-3317 in Lisbon at Rua Ferreira Lapa No. 29.

The highest mountain range in the country is the northeastern **Serra da Estrela**, which features Portugal's tallest peak, the 1,991-m (6,532-ft) Torre. With its superbly varied landscape, from deep ravines to lush forests, this is the area to head for if you're after some challenging hiking. Penhas da Saúde, near Covilhã, is a good spot to base yourself — there's even skiing in the winter. In the Serra da Estrela Natural Park, you can choose from several major trails, but be sure to get the guidebooks and maps that are available from the information offices in Manteigas, Covilhã, or Seia. Alternatively, you can contact the Club Nacional de Montanhismo ((275) 323364 to find out about organized weekend expeditions.

Less demanding trails are found in the popular **Peneda-Gerês National Park** in the far north of the country, though here, too, there are plenty of tough hikes for those who want them. The sleepy spa town of Caldas do Gerês is the park's main base with a good range of accommodation available, and a park office that sells maps detailing roads and major trails.

The basilica on the Monte de Santa Luzia OPPOSITE above Viana do Castelo affords expansive vistas of the Minho coast. ABOVE: The Costa da Caparica has some of the finest Atlantic beaches near Lisbon.

You can do easy day-trip walks into the hills from here — a favorite is to follow the old Roman road (complete with Roman milestones) past the Vilarinho das Furnas reservoir. Further afield, trails through the forests lead to the simple hamlets of Ermida and Cabril, and on again to the mountain village of Paradela. This last 23-km (14-mile) section is part of an official long-distance footpath that is continuously being extended throughout the park, mostly following traditional routes.

If you'd rather someone else show you the way, contact Trote-Gerês ((253) 659343 in Cabril for information on organized walks, horseback riding, and canoeing in the area. The park administration ((253) 600-3480 can also help out with information.

Down from the mountainous north, you can enjoy some wonderfully relaxing rambles in the verdant hills of Sintra near Lisbon, and in the 1,185-hectare (480-acre) Buçaco Forest near Coimbra. **Sintra**'s charms were frequently praised by British poets and travelers of the eighteenth century, most famously by Byron, who used "Cintra's glorious Eden" as an opening setting for his poem, *Childe Harold*. Today, the town center's Royal Palace and hilltop Pena Palace draw groups of tourists, but it's still easy to find your own Byronic Eden in the romantically unkempt Monserrate Gardens or Pena Palace Park. Nearby, Colares makes another fine starting-off point for walkers, and as everywhere in Portugal, you'll find several good campsites in the vicinity. The helpful Sintra tourist office can provide information on these and other types of accommodation in the area.

But there is absolutely nothing like the **Buçaco Forest**. Benedictine monks built a hermitage here as long ago as the sixth century — and the religious presence persisted. A good millennium later, in 1622 to be precise, a papal bull was issued forbidding women to enter the forest. (Ostensibly, so as not to tempt the purity of the monks.) And then in 1643, another was pronounced threatening anyone who

damaged the trees with excommunication. Carmelite monks who settled in the forest during the seventeenth century built boundary walls and planted new and exotic varieties of trees including Mexican cedars and Austrian oaks. The Carmelites remained in the forest right up until 1834 when religious orders were abolished throughout Portugal.

Buçaco is now open to everyone, with its rich variety of over 700 different types of trees making it an extraordinarily lush little haven. At the heart of the forest are the remains of the Carmelite monastery with its cork-clad cells, and the more eye-catching pseudo-Manuèline Royal Palace Hotel, once a royal hunting lodge. But the forest's best attractions are its trees. Paths

meant just for ambling meander among them and lead to panoramic summits past tiny chapels and crosses, waterfalls and streams. On weekends the forest can be packed with local picnickers, but linger here on a weekday and you'll capture some of Buçaco's special quality of tranquillity and reverence.

Sporting Spree

Wherever you go in Portugal — whether it's the sparkling south or the mountainous north — you'll find plenty of challenging sports to keep your adrenaline pumping. Your best destination if you're a golf or tennis

enthusiast is the southern Algarve region, which has long been famous for its 18 superb **golf** courses. There are, however, now 49 courses throughout all of Portugal to choose from, many designed by such international experts as William Mitchell, Henry Cotton, Frank Pennink, and Robert Trent-Jones II. All of them are complemented by stunning settings of pines, lakes and flowers, often against a backdrop of sea and sky. The *crème de la crème*? By almost universal consensus, it's the Mitchell-designed Quinta do Lago course in Almancil just west of Faro, built on a 800-hectare

Fighting bulls are bred on the plains of the Ribatejo. Unlike in Spain, the beasts are not killed in the ring.

(2,000-acre) luxury estate. You can contact the management directly ((289) 390700 FAX (289) 394013.

Serious golfers who want to be sure of enjoying their game should consider booking a package that includes green fees and pre-booked tee-off times — dozens of tour operators in both the United States and the United Kingdom offer these specialized vacations. In the United States, contact Golf International ((212) 986-9176 TOLL-FREE (800) 833-1389 FAX (212) 986-3720 in New York City, which offers tailor-made luxury vacation packages that even cater to the needs of couples who might not both be utterly enamored with golf. Another reliable tour operator is Golf Getaways Ltd. ((818) 991-7015 TOLL-FREE (800) 800-4028 FAX (818) 991-9270 WEB SITE www .golfgetaway.com in Oregon, which arranges an array of vacations including fly/drive golfing packages to Estoril and the Algarve. In the United Kingdom, three choices are Golf Holidays International ((44-1480) 433000; Longshot Golf Holidays ((44-1730) 268621; and Sovereign Golf ((44-1293) 599911. Alternatively, get a hold of the beautifully illustrated brochure

published by the Portuguese tourist office. It's replete with photos, diagrams, and contact information for every course in the country.

In July and August you may find the Algarve too hot for golf (many courses reduce their fees at this time) but that's when **tennis** becomes the most popular sport. You can find excellent tennis centers in the Algarve at Vilamoura, Vale do Lobo, and Carvoeiro — and if you're heading for Lisbon, check out the sophisticated Clube de Ténis do Estoril ((21) 466-2770 FAX (21) 468-6669 at Avenida Conde de Barcelona, 2765 Estoril, where you can enjoy complete tennis vacations.

Package tennis vacations to the Algarve including coaching by international professionals are good value: try the United Kingdom-based Roger Taylor Tennis Holidays ((44-081) 947-9272, or the Travel Club of Upminster ((44-1708) 223000 who can also arrange mixed sporting weeks of tennis, golf and riding.

Water sports, of course, are another Algarve specialty: water skiing, scuba diving, sailing, and big game fishing are all available through the major resorts

here, though serious windsurfers should head north, to Praia do Guincho (near Cascais) for some really awesome Atlantic rollers (world championships have been held here).

Canoeing and fishing are delightful on Portugal's northern rivers. Once you've received your **fishing** license (available from Instituto Florestal, Avenida João Crisóstomo No. 26, Lisbon) you can fish on any of Portugal's rivers. In the north, the Minho, Mouro, Castro and Douro rivers are particularly good for salmon, trout, and barbel.

But if the fish aren't biting, you can always spend a day **canoeing** instead. When you're in Coimbra, contact O Pioneiro do Mondego ((239) 478385 for a paddle on the Mondego River. Even further north, in the mountainous Peneda-Gerês National Park, Trote-Gerês ((253) 659343 can set you canoeing on the tranquil Cávado. They also have **horseback riding** facilities — another popular sport in Portugal that you can find almost everywhere (ask at the local tourist offices for contacts), with horses ranging from Anglo-Arab to the famous Lusitano variety, known as the "Royal Horse of Europe."

Several country homes in the TURIHAB scheme have horseback riding on the premises, or hosts can arrange outings in the vicinity. The proprietors of **Casa de Sezim** ((253) 523000, Casa de Sezim (see WHERE TO STAY, page 211 under GUIMARÃES), for example, are members of an equestrian circuit and maintain their own stables, offer horseback riding tours, and hold periodic equestrian exhibitions.

The extensive plains of the Alentejo province are particularly enjoyable for horseback riders. In Évora, Mendes & Murteira ((266) 703616 can make arrangements for horseback riding excursions as well as for fishing, **walking** and **bicycling** tours in the region. Or why not get a new perspective and take off in a **hot-air balloon** while you're here? Or an off-road, drive-yourself **jeep safari**? Contact Mendes & Murteira or TurAventur

((266) 743134 for these novel ways of looking at the countryside.

Mountain-biking is catching on fast in Portugal, though you'd be advised to bring a bag of spares as roads and trails can be a bit rocky. If you just want to rent a bike for the day, ask at the local tourist office. You might be surprised, but virtually every little town has taken to the craze and bicycle rental shops are everywhere. A word to the wise: the Alentejo and coastal Algarve are relatively flat. The same cannot be said for the rest of the country. For an organized cycling vacation, try Easy Rider Tours ((978) 430-000 FAX (978) 463-6988 TOLL-FREE (800) 782-2424 WEB SITE www.easyridertours.com, in the United States, which offers a selection of biking and walking tours (degrees of difficulty well indicated) throughout the spring and fall. The groups are small, and despite the prices being quite reasonable, accommodation is often at *pousadas* and

The golf courses of the Algarve OPPOSITE TOP are renown for their manicured greens. BOTTOM: Prince Henry the Navigator stands at the prow of the Monument to the Discoveries. Fishing boats ABOVE are pulled up on the sand at the Algarve resort village of Albufeira.

manor homes. All tours are accompanied by both an American and a local guide, providing a true insider's perspective.

And if you've still got energy to burn, you might fancy a weekend's **canyoning** (tackling a river canyon on foot: a combination of swimming, abseiling, and rock climbing) or **hydrospeed** (a form of whitewater rafting using individual floats — and crash helmets!). These are action-packed, high-thrills adventure sports for those neither weak of body nor mind. If you are game, these are the people to contact: Turnatur ((21) 207-6886 in Lisbon; and Trilhos ((22) 520740 in Porto.

SPECTATOR SPORTS
Soccer is Portugal's national obsession. When the football season is on, people talk about little else: televisions in cafés and bars are on during important matches (and they all seem to be). Don't be surprised — or even worse, insistent — if your waiter is delayed in bringing your *bacalhau* or *vinho verde*.

The other sport associated with Portugal is **bullfighting**. The main center is the province of Ribatejo where the bulls are bred, although there are rings throughout the country. The season lasts from April to October and bullfights take place mainly on Sundays. Costumes are elaborate, and the whole affair takes on a festive theatrical atmosphere. Everyone will tell you how much more humane the sport is here than in Spain, but it must be said that this is merely self-assuaging. It is true that the bulls are not killed in the ring, however I remain unconvinced that this is preferable. Regardless, they are finished off after the spectacle, and just as in southern France, a butcher van awaits at a back exit.

Auto racing is also popular in Portugal, the major races taking place at the *autodromo* in Estoril and attracting huge crowds. There is also the Rallye de Portugal do Vinho de Porto, held for a week each March on country roads: it begins and ends at Estoril as well.

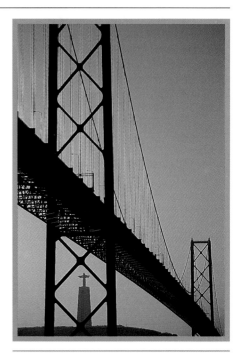

The Open Road

Certainly one of the main attractions of a trip to Portugal is Portugal itself. It is an extraordinarily beautiful land that has, for the most part, managed not to destroy itself. There's no better way to explore the real Portugal than by meandering by car (or by foot) in the countryside. Leave the *auto-estrada* or highways (especially those most lethal along the Algarve and between Lisbon and Porto) and follow the minor roads wherever possible. The Michelin 1:400,000 map of Portugal, or the Euro-Mapa 1:300,000 Portugal and Galicia map are two of the best guides for this kind of touring. In fact, the national maps distributed by the car rental companies, as well as those you get from the *Turismos*, are also quite detailed and unusually easy to read. Please note that during the past few years major rehabilitation and rerouting has been undertaken, and an up-to-date map is crucial for a good journey.

Unless you're trying to see as much of the country as possible, you'll probably find it more enjoyable to stick to one region and make day-trips from a long-term base rather than worry about finding new accommodation every night. My rule of thumb for all travel is to cover as little distance in as much time as possible. And if you do choose the subsidiary routes (which again, are infinitely preferable to the highways), don't be fooled by Portugal's small size: distances may look easy to accomplish in a day but you'll find minor roads can become blocked when an ox-cart heads a line of traffic on an impassable road. Distractions are frequent, too — ruined forts or deserted beaches, meadows of wildflowers or a good wine at lunch. But of course, if you remember that you have no reason to be in one place more than another, just relax and breath in the eucalyptus.

Even in high season you should be able to find a place to stay in a small town or village without reserving ahead (the local tourist offices can always help), or if you can, try to plot out an itinerary a few days in advance. The following are merely some suggestions for great scenic discoveries in Portugal, but as a Portuguese friend of mine said, "Get out of Lisbon and just get lost."

The obvious attraction in the **Algarve** is the coastline and its beaches, but if you're after something a little less crowded and more unusual, head inland to the foothills of the Serra de Monchique. If you're based in or near Faro, it's worth following a route that takes in the ruins of the Estói Palace, the historic town of Loulé, and the picturesque riverside castle-town of Silves, on the N269. A perfect place for a lunch-stop, Silves is just 21 km (13 miles) from your goal at Monchique, but leave time to stop first at Caldas de Monchique, an atmospheric little spa deep within the woods. Monchique itself is a lively market town, with acceptable accommodation if you choose to stay the night, and a panoramic view of the whole Algarve coastline from nearby Fóia.

Heading out of the Algarve, into the **Alentejo** plains, the easiest route is to

follow the main IP2 to Beja and on to Évora. But for lovers of snaking country roads rich with atmosphere, I highly recommend the minor N122 that sticks close to the Spanish border from Castro Marim to Mértola. The first part of this route, with a little side-trip to Alcoutim and its fourteenth-century castle, is one of the most dramatic in the Algarve, following the Guadiana River past villages right on the water's edge. The old walled town of Mértola with its remote and mysterious air, perched high above the Guadiana, makes a wonderful stopover. The atmosphere lingers long after you leave, especially if you continue on the back-roads N265 and N255, meandering through classic Alentejo scenery, to the attractive towns of Serpa

The 25 de Abril bridge LEFT spans the Tagus at Lisbon. *Azulejos* ABOVE adorn a Braga façade. RIGHT: Rooftop scenes of Viana do Castelo.

and Moura. From here you're about 70 km (44 miles) from the spectacular walled hilltop village of Monsaraz. The route from Mourão, 12 km (seven miles) south provides a magical approach, through fields of wildflowers, cork and olive trees (keep a lookout, too, for hoopoe birds). A night's stopover here could well be a highlight of your Alentejo tour, a calm interlude before you reach Évora some 82 km (51 miles) to the northwest.

There are several excellent day-trips possible from Évora. The most obvious is to head for the beautiful marble town of Estremoz, 46 km (28 miles) to the northeast (and home to the country's most spectacular *pousada*), stopping at the hilltop fort of Évoramonte en route. Coming back, you can take a different route via

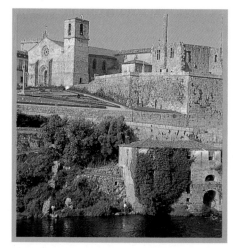

Arraiolos, famous since the seventeenth century for its carpets. A day-trip to Monsaraz is also a must if you haven't dropped in already during your travels.

A favorite Évora excursion is to set out on a quest in search of dolmens. There are over a dozen megalithic sites in the area that date from around 3000 BC. Pick up the special *Guide to Megalithic Monuments* from the Évora tourist office and you could find yourself blithely combing the countryside for days on the hunt for standing stones and circles. The nearest are about 14 km (eight miles) away, near Guadalupe, off the N114 to Montemor, and also southwest of Évora, near Valverde, off the N380. The strangest is the dolmen-cum-chapel at Pavia, 29 km (18 miles) north of Arraiolos, on the N370. These dolmen hunts make ideal day-trips for cyclists, too.

It's hard to beat the Alentejo for dreamy touring. From **Lisbon to Porto** (317 km, or 197 miles) you'll inevitably find the roads more crowded. But the coastal route between these cities is splendid, becoming quieter the further north you go, and ideal in many places for seaside stopovers. From Sintra, stick to the minor N247 and you'll find the beach calling all the way to Peniche, a fine place to base yourself and less touristic than Nazaré further north, though the Pinhal de Leiria pine forest near Nazaré is also tempting for stopovers, with its excellent beaches and campsites. From here you can skirt the coast, avoiding major roads nearly all the way to Aveiro, though an inland diversion to Coimbra is highly recommended if you've got the time. The nearby Forest of Buçaco is a worthwhile day-trip from Coimbra, too (see THE GREAT OUTDOORS, page 23). But if it's sea breezes you're after, the Praia de Mira, 29 km (18 miles) to the south of Aveiro, offers some great stretches of sand. Furadouro, near Ovar, 25 km (16 miles) north of Aveiro, is another pleasant little spot for a

An Alentejan farmer takes a break from his labors. ABOVE. Barcelos LEFT is home to the Minho's largest weekly market. RIGHT: A frigate moored at the docks of the Parque dos Nações in Lisbon.

beach stopover before you hit the traffic mayhem of Porto.

The most scenic tour from **Porto** is along the Douro River, following the river-hugging and extremely snaking N108 north of the river, or the even prettier N222 to the south. The glossy *Rio Douro* map (available in Porto bookshops) makes a good companion for this tour, with detailed notes about places of interest en route.

The provincial town and port center of Peso da Régua, 100 km (62 miles) east, makes a good first night's stop — or two nights if you have time for a day's sightseeing trip to the attractive town of Lamego nine kilometers (five miles) south. Filling a day's excursion itself in the vicinity of Lamego are a trio of curious, half-forgotten treasures: the twelfth-century São João de Tarouca Cistercian Monastery, the medieval fortified bridge of Ucanha, and the derelict Cistercian monastery of Salzedas.

Back on the **Douro**, the further east you go, the deeper you will find yourself in port country (see CRUISE THE DOURO, page 11 in TOP SPOTS) and the wilder the N222 seems to become. Roller-coaster fans will love the dramatic crossing of the Douro east of Pinhão at São João da

Pesqueira, where the road plunges down and up again so steeply your ears pop. Faithfully, the N222 sticks within sight of the river almost to the very end — the quiet border town of Barca d'Alva, where you can hear Spanish sheep bleating from across the border while the river babbles along. A night spent in nearby Freixo de Espada a Cinta is a memorable experience in remoteness. From here, you're at the back entrance to Trás-os-Montes, the least-known region of Portugal, worthy of days of desultory rambling.

Another touring alternative from Porto is to leave your car behind and take the train on the Douro line to Peso da Régua. From here you can make a day's excursion to Vila Real on the spectacular Corgo line before continuing eastward to Pinhão from where the narrow-gauge Tua line (one of the last of its kind in Portugal) meanders up to Mirandela. The Douro line itself ends at Pocinho, about as isolated a place as you'll find on the river. From Porto direct to Pocinho by train takes about four and a half hours.

The northern **Minho** district is a perfect place to pass some time. As long as you're not after any great nightlife or shopping facilities, the little town of

Ponte de Lima, 23 km (14 miles) east of Viana do Castelo, could make an ideal base, conveniently close both to the coast at Viana and to inland places of interest such as Braga, Barcelos and Valença do Minho, on the northern Spanish border. Another distinct advantage of setting up base here is the preponderance of country homes, *quintas*, and estates offering accommodation. From Braga you can head off into the Serra do Gerês mountains and base yourself at Caldas do Gerês for a few days' hiking in the hills (see THE GREAT OUTDOORS, page 23).

Finally, for the adventurous explorer who's after the unknown, there's the vast, remote **Trás-os-Montes** region. Montalegre, Chaves, Bragança, and Miranda do Douro are recommended for stopovers, but be prepared for long, isolated drives and frequent distractions: I found myself delayed even before I reached Chaves by the extraordinarily remote villages around Montalegre, little changed for centuries. Even the Portuguese themselves know little about this area, and if you ask a city person to recommend a route, invariably the answer will be to stick to the highways. Weather permitting, graciously ignore the advice.

YOUR CHOICE

Backpacking

Despite rising prices, Portugal remains one of the least expensive places to travel in western Europe. Living frugally by using trains and buses, staying in campsites or youth hostels and self-catering, you could get by on about US$40 a day. Moving up a notch, staying in cheap *pensãos* and enjoying reasonably-priced restaurant meals will cost you about US$60 to US$75 a day. If you're a student you can also take advantage of discounts on admission prices to museums as well as on long-distance bus and train fares. Off-season, you'll find accommodation prices drop considerably — and even in high season it's always worth asking at the reception desk for cheaper rooms (for example, without a bathroom or windows) since these are often not mentioned initially.

There are dozens of authorized campsites in Portugal — the *Roteiro Campista* booklet available in Portuguese

---

Aveiro OPPOSITE is called the "Venice of Portugal." ABOVE: The vast plaza of Lisbon's Estação de Oriente at the Parque das Nações.

Traveling solo works out to be more expensive if you stay anywhere other than at a youth hostel. Single-room rates are more than half the double-room rate. Traveling in a pair you should be able to afford to splurge on the occasional *pensão* (see ACCOMMODATION, page 279 in TRAVELERS' TIPS) or two-star hotel. It's worth considering that in late fall and winter prices often drop so low you could stay in a palace hotel for the price of a summertime *pensão!*

Getting around Portugal by public transportation is quite economical, and although trains are generally cheaper than buses, they are slower and don't delve into the countryside as deeply as the buses. You can get pretty much anywhere in Portugal by bus as long as you've got the time. Hitchhiking is perfectly acceptable, but not very common. In remote areas you're likely to find that your driver is only going to the next farmhouse. (Although Portugal has an extremely low crime rate, and traveling as a single woman is not remotely dangerous, I do not suggest women should hitchhike alone.) Bringing your own bike is a great alternative, as long as you avoid the sweltering Alentejo summers and the mountainous north. Bikes are allowed on trains and buses (certain services only) for a small fee — and several hours' tedious paperwork at the station.

The lively Algarve resorts of Lagos and Albufeira are popular starting places for many young budget travelers — many don't go any further! Lisbon, of course, is another magnet but its expensive and crowded accommodation scene soon drives backpackers westward to Cascais or Sintra, or northward to Coimbra (another major university town) and Porto. The Serra da Estrela and Peneda-Gerês mountain ranges are where the energetic ones head for, leaving their backpacks to hike across the hills or taking them with them to camp in the wilderness.

bookstores gives full details, or you can ask at the local tourist offices. Another good bargain is the chain of 20 youth hostels, although the most popular ones (for instance, those in Lisbon and Lagos) get booked up quickly in high season. For advance reservations or further details, including how to purchase the obligatory IH card, contact Movijovem, Central de Reservas ((21) 355-9081 FAX (21) 352-1466, Avenida Duque de Ávila No. 137, Lisbon.

Some of the best budget accommodations are rooms (*quartos* or *dormidas*) in private houses rented out by the owners. Similar to the bed-and-breakfast system (although breakfast is rarely included in the price, or even available), the rooms are invariably immaculate (frilly bed-covers and lace curtains are popular) and at around US$25 a double in high season are a good value. You can find these rooms either through the local tourist office, or more likely, they'll find you: *dormidas* owners often accost prospective customers at bus or train stations in the more popular resorts. And don't be alarmed if your host speaks nothing but Portuguese: you'll generally find they understand you anyway, and once prices are settled, make charming hosts.

Colorful *azulejos* ABOVE in the narrow streets of Lisbon's Alfama district. RIGHT: Cooling off the Lisbon way.

Living It Up

The Portuguese aren't shy of living it up: bars and discos in Lisbon, Porto and the major Algarve and Estoril resorts stay open until at least 2 AM, and most much later. No self-respecting night-owl would consider appearing before midnight. But then again, he'd probably just be ordering dessert at that point. There are old standbys, but part of the fun is seeking out the new ones. And not to worry, they're always popping up. With entry into the European Union and the emergence of a young mobile (and mobile-phoned) class, Portugal has seen an inordinate upsurge in reveling.

You'll have no trouble spotting the Algarve's hottest night spots in Lagos and Albufeira — the bars and clubs are great proponents of self-advertising. And anyone you run into knows them anyway. Reliably lively bars in Lagos are **Mullens**, Rua Candido dos Reis No. 86, **Stones**, Rua 25 de Abril, and **Phoenix** at Rua 5 de Outubro No. 11; while in Albufeira you can start a high-decibel evening at **Classic Bar**, Rua Candido dos Reis No. 10, and continue on to **Silvia's Disco**, Rua São Gonçalo de Lagos. Casinos, for those with money to burn, can be found at Alvor, Monte Gordo, Vilamoura and Albufeira (and beyond the Algarve, at Figueira da Foz, Póvoa de Varzim, and Estoril).

The Algarve's most chic restaurants and hotels are largely found in the coastal resorts, concentrating in the deluxe resort complexes of **Quinta do Lago** ((289) 396666 TOLL-FREE IN THE UNITED STATES (800) 223-6800 FAX (289) 396393 E-MAIL hqdlago@mail.telepac.pt WEB SITE orient-expresshotels.com, and **Vale do Lobo** ((289) 393939 FAX (289) 394713. But for sheer exclusivity, and I might add class, head for **La Réserve** restaurant and hotel near Estói (sufficiently far from the seaside resorts to maintain its elevated status); while Faro's little **Cidade Velha**

The sun-filled Algarve offers year-round luxurious vacations with its numerous seaside resorts and golf complexes.

restaurant can make for a romantic hideaway for special celebrations. Far to the west, on a windswept cliff top near Sagres, the **Fortaleza do Belixe** *pousada* annex (with just four rooms) is as close to the sea and wind of this rugged end of Portugal as you can get. Enjoy the luxurious accommodation, and long after the last sightseers have straggled off, you can continue to sip your apéritif sitting on the precipice of Europe.

Traveling north through Portugal you'll find that these government-run *pousadas* offer some of the country's most sophisticated accommodation. In fact, *pousada*-hopping has recently become a world-class sport, and I have met travelers of many origins who can declaim the assets of one over another with the ease of comparing a Rolex with a Monvado.

Throughout Portugal, but particularly in the northern Douro and Minho regions, perhaps Portugal's gem indulgences are its exquisite private manor-houses available under the scheme called Turismo de Habitação or TURIHAB (see CHECK INTO A PRIVATE PALACE, page 14 in TOP SPOTS, and ACCOMMODATION, page 279 in TRAVELERS' TIPS). Here, you will pleasure in a more personal moment of deluxe living, with the owner-host treating you as a private guest.

Remember, *pousadas* are often housed in the restored castles, keeps and palaces (brimming with antiques), and the best of them — in Évora, Estremoz, Óbidos and Guimarães — require reservations months ahead for stays during high season. I have, however, breezed into a few of them during spring on only a day's notice.

For an intimate change of pace from a stay at a *pousada*, ask at the local tourist office about Turismo de Habitação villas or mansions in the region. I have found few places more enchanting than the **Quinta da Capela**, a seventeenth-century manor house overlooking the lush Monserrate Gardens near Sintra; except perhaps, for the **Casa de Sezim** just outside of Guimarães, which rates as one of my all-time favorite lodgings.

In Lisbon, some might, of course, consider the most sophisticated hotels to be the modern extravaganzas like the **Hotel Ritz** and the **Meridien**, but none of them can possibly approach the elegant grandeur of the **Hotel Avenida Palace** or the luxury of the **Palácio de Seteais** in nearby Sintra. Until, of course, you consider the nineteenth-century **Lapa Palace**, formerly the private residence of a count.

Also in Lisbon is the more modest but quite unique **York House**, a former sixteenth-century monastery with rooms around a courtyard. It makes an eccentric contrast to late nights on the town — and you'll have plenty of those in Lisbon if you want to savor some of the best restaurants and clubs in the country.

One of the city's choice restaurants is **António Clara**, where you dine in a turn-of-the-century villa on exquisite cuisine. But do I prefer it over **Gambrinus**, with its supremely delicious seafood? Avoid having to make the decision and spend an evening dining at each.

The nightlife highlights are even harder to choose: Lisbon rocks, bops and drinks hard all night, though you can swoon to traditional *fado* (see WALLOW IN FADO, page 12 in TOP SPOTS) if that's more your scene. The Bairro Alto area is the traditional center of all nightlife activity with dozens of bars, old and new — nose around here and you'll soon find something to suit your taste. Favorite watering holes are the **Procópio** bar near Largo do Rato, the live jazz venue **Hot Clube de Portugal** in Praça da Alegria, and **Lontra** on Rua São Bento where they have live music mostly from the Cape Verde islands. Newest on the Lisbon scene are a rash of designer bars in the Alcântara docks area and along the nearby Avenida 24 Julho (the velvet-decor **XXIV Julho** and **Alcântara Café** are the trendiest). For discos, try the latest and most hip **FrágiLUX** on Avenida Dom Henrique just across from the Santa Apolónia train station.

Not to be outdone, Porto boasts its own brand of opulence on the hotel and restaurant front: **Hotel Infante de Sagres**,

A resort club on the beach at Albufeira, in the Algarve.

Praça Dona Filipa de Lencastre No. 62, has the most luxurious restaurant and rooms in the city, though the exclusive lunchtime restaurant in **Taylor Fladgate & Yeatman's** port lodge, Rua do Choupelo No. 250, Vila Nova de Gaia, has undoubtedly the finest view of the city and the Douro. Sophisticated soirées sipping port is best done in the **Solar do Vinho do Porto**, Rua Entre Quintas, **Jardim do Palácio de Cristal**, a civilized setting where you will be offered a choice of over 150 varieties of port.

For an evening of pure opulence and esthetic pleasures, start out with a three-course dinner at **Telégrapho** ((22) 332-2019, Rua Ferreira Borges, a grand formal restaurant in the stately *Bolsa*, where the cuisine is are delicately prepared and elegantly presented. Then, without even leaving the building, merely pass to the Sala Árabe for a chamber music recital, or perhaps even a jazz concert in a setting of Moorish splendor. Do bear in mind that although concerts are frequently presented, schedules are somewhat erratic.

Nightlife in Porto revolves around the riverside Ribeira area: the trendy **Cosa Nostra** at Rua de São João No. 76 has some of the city's best live music, while **Meia Cave** at Praça da Ribeira No. 6 is a current favorite, attracting a well-dressed set. Across the river at Rua Rei Ramiro No. 228, Vila Nova de Gaia, **Rocks** is worth visiting for its atmospheric setting of old port cellars and lively rock music,

Family Fun

You won't have to worry about keeping the kids happy in Portugal: there's an abundance of outdoor activities and a happy-go-lucky atmosphere that is infectious and can even help to relax stressed-out parents. The Portuguese are child-friendly (if not downright adoring), welcoming kids into hotels and restaurants, cooing over chubby babies and, given the slightest excuse, handing out candies or gooey cakes.

The most suitable family accommodation is in simple pensions that are used to coping with young children. Campsites and youth hostels (see BACKPACKING, page 33) are great meeting grounds for kids of all nationalities and good value if you've got a large family. If you're not the roughing it type, however, an ideal choice would be to stay at some of the country homes, particularly those with independent self-catering apartments (see under ACCOMMODATION, page 279 in TRAVELERS' TIPS). Most have swimming pools, sprawling gardens, and families with kids of their own. The three sons of the host at Quinta da Boa Viagem, for example, hold summer-long international soccer tournaments with their new friends. And at some of the larger resorts in the Algarve there are special children's clubs with organized activities for three- to eleven-year-olds.

You'll probably find the best family fun in the **Algarve**, with its fine beaches, unending supply of simple cafés and restaurants, wide choice of water sports and other outdoor activities, and the overriding informal and "less foreign" air about the place. Two amusement parks to bear in mind that adults (or at least those accompanied by children) will also enjoy are **Zoomarine** ((289) 560300 FAX (289) 560308, N125 west of Albufeira in the town of Guia, and **Krazy World** ((282) 574134, just north of Guia in the town of Algoz.

while the best disco in town, **Swing**, is across town in the other direction, at the Centro Comércial Brasilia, Avenida da Boavista.

Beyond Porto, luxurious accommodation is best found through the TURIHAB scheme — top of the line are the flagship **Paço de Calheiros** in Ponte de Lima, the elegant family home of TURIHAB's president, Count Francisco de Calheiros (the "Paço" indicates a king once stayed here).

For unimaginable Manueline extravagance and architecture, head for the Forest of Buçaco near Coimbra where you can wine, dine, and stay the night in the glorious **Palace Hotel** at the very heart of this ancient forest.

The fifteenth-century Paço dos Duques de Bragança in Guimarães is a great setting for kids to burn energy.

Zoomarine is a huge complex with park areas that presents dolphin and sea lion shows and offers more interactive presentations, as well as an aquarium, a nature museum, and a film center, along with swimming pools and restaurants. Krazy World not only has playgrounds and swimming pools, but it also maintains a petting zoo with inhabitants significantly more cuddly than those you'll find at their alligator and crocodile parks. For kids (and parents) a little less bestial, there is also a 36-hole mini-golf course and a four-wheel dirt-bike range.

If the children are old enough, you might want to go on some family day-trips by bicycle (these days, rental outfits are even available in almost every small town — ask at the *Turismo*), a good option

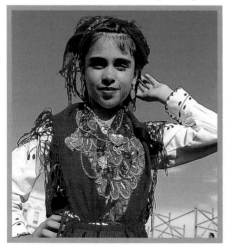

almost everywhere in Portugal, but particularly in the Algarve and Alentejo where the terrain is relatively flat.

Lisbon and **Porto** pose more problems because their major sights — churches and museums — aren't exactly a kid's idea of a fun time. But some of the museums could go down very well, such as Lisbon's **Maritime Museum** with its wonderful displays of ships and seafaring paraphernalia, with models of vessels dating from the fifteenth to the nineteenth centuries, and the **Ethnological Museum** where displays of Portugal's former African colonies are coordinated with an imaginative use of audiovisuals. Both of these museums are in Belém on the outskirts of Lisbon, and the journey there by tram is fun in itself. Lisbon's other forms of transportation — the **Gloria funicular** and **Santa Justa elevator** — are so popular with kids that I've met families who have admitted to riding them several times a day! If your kids can deal with another museum, consider taking them to the **Toy Museum** ((21) 910-6016, Rua Visconde de Monserrate, Sintra, where they have an exhibit of over 20,000 toys. In the **Parque dos Nações**, the site of Expo '98, there is a particularly well-staged aquarium that will give parents a moment of fun as well. The **Oceanário de Lisboa** ((21) 891-7002 is open daily from 10 AM to 7 PM. This ex-Expo site actually provides a good break from the urbanity of Lisbon for all ages, and you might want to consult their WEB SITE www .parquedasnacoes.pt for information on activities scheduled during your visit.

When restlessness sets in and the strains of Lisbon's cityscape take hold, hop on a train to the lively seaside resort of **Cascais** for the day, or take a break in nearby **Sintra**. Forget the serious tour of Sintra's Royal Palace, and head for the hilltop **Pena Palace** and castle instead — the energetic can clamber up to the castle from the town center in about an hour.

Trams are a highlight in **Porto**, too, including the **Tram Museum** (See TRAVEL THE TRAMS, page 12 in TOP SPOTS), but an aquatic alternative popular with children is the little jaunt down river by boat (trips

leave regularly from the Ribeira waterfront). Throughout the summer the lively *Feira do Porto* funfair is held nightly at the Palácio de Cristal.

Portugal's **castles** are perfect for families: you can walk the walls, play hide and seek in the old keeps, and picnic in the shadow of history. The best fun are those in Silves, Óbidos, Castelo de Vide, Marvão, Valença do Minho, and Elvas. Most of these have accommodation facilities right within the walls, which gives you a chance for some atmospheric evening explorations.

Even miniature castles provide entertainment: in the northern town of Coimbra there's the **Portugal dos Pequenitos Park**, where Portugal's most famous monuments (including some from the former colonies) have been recreated in miniature. The kids scramble in, on and over them to their hearts' content. Older children would probably prefer canoeing down the river instead (see SPORTING SPREE, page 25 for details) or horseback riding in the nearby park (for information call the Coimbra Riding Center ((239) 837695).

Horseback riding is an increasingly popular family activity in Portugal, particularly in the Algarve, Alentejo,

and Peneda-Gerês National Park. The local tourist offices have contact numbers for stables that offer both training sessions and guided tours into the countryside.

For the family with seriously active teenagers, you might consider throwing yourselves into a weekend of canyoning or hydrospeed (see SPORTING SPREE, page 25), or sending off the kids for their own adventure vacation with a week's potholing or rafting organized by Movijovem ((21) 355-9081 FAX (21) 352-1466, the youth hostel head office at Avenida Duque de Ávila, No. 137, Lisbon. A less dramatic action-packed option is to base yourselves in a place like Cabril in the **Peneda-Gerês National Park** and take advantage of the horseback riding, canoeing, and hiking possibilities in the area. Nearby Rio Caldo, on the edge of the Caniçada reservoir, is another attractive base, with windsurfing, motorboats, canoes and pedal boats available.

OPPOSITE TOP: Children dress up for the *festas* held on saints days throughout Portugal. LEFT: The tradition continues at the Festa de Santo Antonio. ABOVE: Performance pieces for audiences of all ages are on show at the Parque dos Nações.

Cultural Kicks

The great thing about Portugal's cultural attractions is their variety. Churches, palaces and museums may be the obvious highlights but just as memorable and not to be missed on your cultural itinerary are medieval hilltop castles, railway stations "wallpapered" with *azulejos*, and even the eccentric art deco cafés and their customers.

But an aside. Please don't fall into the age-old tourist trap of the age-old! Portugal is moving into the twenty-first century along with everyone else (in fact, one hour earlier than most of the rest of Europe). Contemporary art galleries, modern dance performances, and theater

art pieces are on show year round. Not just during festivals, and not just in Lisbon and Porto. Coimbra, with its student ardency, is a prime example. Ask at the *Turismos* for their monthly "what's on" brochure. You might be pleasantly surprised.

Back to the past. And a few must-sees. For museums, the giant towering over all is the **Gulbenkian** in Lisbon, a minimum two-day indulgence if you want to do it properly. Others that are worth going out of your way to visit are the **Machado de Castro** in Coimbra, the **Alberto Sampaio** in Guimarães, and **Évora's Municipal Museum**. Évora itself is one huge open-air museum, arguably the most cultured city in the country with everything from a Roman-era temple to beautiful seventeenth-century *praças* and mansions.

But you must move nearer to Lisbon to find Portugal's greatest architectural monuments: the **Alcobaça Cistercian Monastery**, which represents the finest creation of Portuguese Gothic architecture; the nearby **Batalha Monastery**, a stunning achievement of Manueline design; and, above all, the Mosteiro dos **Jerónimos** in Belém, the country's undisputed Manueline masterpiece. See these, and you will have had a taste of the gamut.

That still leaves a few notable points along the cultural itinerary. Uniquely Portuguese are the *azulejo*-decorated stairway at **Bom Jesus**, near Braga, the **São Bento railway station** in Porto, and the superb *azulejo*-rich churches of Almancil, Évora and Barcelos. Staggering examples of the country's heavily **gilded chapels** are those of São Roque in Lisbon and Santo António in Lagos. And then there are always the **historic walled towns** of Óbidos, Monsaraz, and Marvão. The extravagant **palaces** of Queluz and Pena…

More immediately threatened by urban development are Portugal's wonderful **art deco cafés** such as Nicola

ABOVE: A young "bishop" at *festa* time. LEFT: The Igreja da Graça in Lisbon dates from the thirteenth century. RIGHT: A stained-glass window in one of Portugal's finest architectural monuments, the Mosteiro dos Jerónimos in Belém.

and A Brasileira do Chiado in Lisbon, Café Aliança in Faro, Café Brasileira in Braga, and Café Majestic in Porto. These fragile relics of an elegant past, however, may just survive urbanization because we do all visit them.

Shop till You Drop

In Portugal, every region has its specialties, best bought where they are made.

The northwestern province of **Minho** is famous for its beautiful traditional costumes. The port lodges of Vila Nova de Gaia, in **Porto**, are the best places to shop for port, arguably Portugal's most famous product. In the northeast province of **Trás-os-Montes**, woven goods, tapestries, black pottery, wrought-ironwork, and painted furniture are all good buys. In the neighboring provinces of Beira Alta and Beira Baixa, black pottery and wrought-ironwork remain favorites, with the **Serra da Estrela** region famous for the excellent cheese called *queijo de Serra*, and **Castelo Branco**, also a cheese producer, noted for embroidered bedspreads.

The coastal province of **Beira Litoral** makes some of the most attractive Portuguese pottery, and the famous old porcelain factory of Vista Alegre near **Aveiro** produces the expensive and sought-after dinner services and figurines sold in shops not only in Lisbon and Porto, but worldwide. The fishing towns here and throughout the country sell traditional clothing and are usually good places to buy lace, particularly in **Peniche** where the delicate bone lace is displayed outside the houses. In inland **Estremadura**, the town of Caldas da Rainha is famous for its quirky bright green pottery made in the shape of cabbage leaves, vegetables, fruits and animals, and seen in shops throughout the world. **Lisbon** is a showcase for regional craftwork from all around the country and has some good bargains in gold and silver filigree jewelry. Jewelry shops still line the Rua Aurea ("Gold Street"), but many cluster around the Praça da Figueira. Some rather chic antique shops that are visited by dealers from around the world are to be found on Rua de São José.

In **Porto**, the best area for jewelry shopping remains Rua das Flores. Continue to the bottom of Rua das Flores and you will come upon a small *praça* that boasts a large wine store, with selections from all regions of Portugal and a knowledgeable English-speaking staff.

The southern province of the **Alentejo** sells all sorts of goods made of cork that won't pose too much of a problem in baggage weight. Other good buys are goatskin goods, peasant-style clothing, woolen capes, wickerwork, and copperware, with the area around Évora particularly noted for its painted furniture. Most precious of all are the rugs from Arraiolos that the town has been producing since the seventeenth century.

Folkloric Barcelos cocks ABOVE are sold as souvenirs throughout Portugal. OPPOSITE: Open-air market TOP in Viana do Castelo. Spaniards cross the border to shop at Valença do Minho BOTTOM.

In the **Algarve**, one of the most distinctive features of the houses are the latticed chimney pots that are sometimes sold as souvenirs. They may, however, prove to be far more attractive on the spot than when you get them home and try to figure out what to do with them. One rather useful item is the copper *cataplana*, a Moorish invention for steaming food that is both practical and attractive. Copper and brass ware is generally a good buy here, as is palm and wicker work.

Non-European Union residents are entitled to VAT refunds on certain goods purchased in Portugal. Europe Tax-free Shopping now operates a tax refund system that does the bulk of the paperwork for you, so look for the Tax-free for Tourists sign in shop windows, and when making your purchase ask for a tax-free shopping voucher. When you leave the country, you can take the vouchers to the Tax-free counter in the airport transit hall where you will be given a refund. You will need to carry your purchases in your hand luggage as customs officials will want to see the goods.

Short Breaks

Short-stay trips are perfect for Portugal, as within a few days you can soak up enough sun and atmosphere, culture and good times to make you feel you've lingered for weeks. Of course, if you're traveling from afar, with the exhaustion of long flights and jetlag, keeping near the Lisbon region makes the most sense, as most likely this is where you'll fly into.

Lisbon and **Sintra** make an ideal partnership: after a few days in the big city seeing the sights, you'll find nearby Sintra a pleasantly relaxing rural retreat. Walking in the hills or through the rambling Monserrate Gardens will give you a fine taste of Portuguese countryside, while the Pena Palace and Capuchos Monastery will provide the touch of eccentric culture for which Sintra is famous.

For a different kind of break, after visiting Sintra and perhaps Óbidos and Batalha, make a jaunt to the Estoril Coast and combine city and historic touring with a golf and water sports escape.

If you are flying into Lisbon and your time permits, consider flying off to **Faro**

for a day or two as well: rent a car when you arrive and visit the still pristine beauty of Sagres and Monchique. For a (protracted, if you can) moment of luxury accommodation and elegant dining, take refuge at Hotel La Réserve in Santa Bárbara de Nexe just west of Faro.

Porto and the **Douro Valley** is another obvious city-country combination. Lively Porto and its port center of Vila Nova de Gaia have depended for centuries on the Douro River that runs through it. Cruising the Douro (or taking the train — see CRUISE THE DOURO, page 11 in TOP SPOTS) is a trip through the country's port history and an ideal way to see one of the most scenic parts of Portugal. If you have the time, you may want to stop en route to explore Lamego, Amarante, or the area around Pinhão. Porto by train is never far away. (Getting from Lisbon to Porto for those pressed for time is quite simple as there are several flights a day between the two cities.)

A more unusual but attractive option for hikers would be a trip from Porto to the Peneda-Gerês National Park, basing yourself at Caldas do Gerês for a few days and stopping on the way back at Braga for a dose of culture.

Festive Flings

Portugal, particularly during the summer months, is a procession of colorful and flamboyant festivals. Every city, town, and village holds a festival to honor its patron saint and often another for the Holy Virgin. The larger the place, the longer and more elaborate the celebrations. These festivals are naturally founded on religious origins, but for many local participants they have become more irreverent celebrations entailing song, dance, fireworks, traditional costumes, eating, and drinking. They are wonderfully colorful occasions and you should try to experience one if you can. Country fairs (*feiras*) selling handicrafts and local produce are often held in conjunction with the festivities.

In addition to these classic, folkloric affairs, contemporary Portugal has its galas as well. Film, music, and theater festivals generally take place in the spring and summer, and although they tend not to be as showy as some other European

OPPOSITE: A detail of the ornately carved exterior of the Hotel Palácio de Seteais. ABOVE: Women at the annual June Festas dos Santos Populares enliven the typical Portuguese mosaic motif.

events, they still attract quite a spectrum of performers and performances. Along with great performances, partaking in Portugal's current scene will obviously afford you a more balanced perspective of the country as a whole.

Here is a selection of some of the more interesting festivals, but it is by no means a complete list. The Investimentos, Comércio e Turismo de Portugal ICEP (see TOURIST INFORMATION, page 274 in TRAVELERS' TIPS, for addresses) publishes a booklet giving exact dates and details of fairs, festivals, and folk pilgrimages. They also have information on the contemporary art scene, with specifics of who will be where when. To get a pulse on the land, do try to see the spectrum.

Early spring is perhaps Portugal's greatest festival season, as **Holy Week** spawns celebrations throughout the country. The most renowned of these takes place in Braga, where in true medieval fashion, penitents take to the streets in hooded garb and march barefoot in a torch-lit procession.

If a bacchanalia is more to your taste, try to catch the **Carnival** festivities leading up to Mardi Gras. The most ecstatic of them all, without question, is hosted by Loulé. Something of a quiet town, or as much of one as one finds in the Algarve, it explodes with round-the-clock celebrations, and flaunts some of the more outlandish costumes found anywhere outside of Brazil.

In early May, the **Festas das Cruzes**, or Miracle of the Cross, in Barcelos is particularly beautiful to observe. Locals dress up in resplendently colorful folkloric outfits, and carpets made of flower petals are paraded through the streets.

Should you find yourself in Tomar the first weekend of July (even years only), the **Tabuleiros festival** is something not to be missed. A procession of hundreds of young women (ostensibly virgins), dressed completely in white, parade through the city balancing towering headdresses made out of loaves of bread and adorned with flowers. The festival's origins are said to hearken back to a pagan fertility rite, and the contemporary atmosphere is in keeping with tradition.

More carpets of flowers can be found during Viana do Castelo's **Senhora da Agonia festival** held in mid-August. Here, amid blasts of fireworks, the local bishop leads revelers through the town and down to the port, where he bestows his annual blessing upon the fishing boats. The official celebrations continue for three days, but remember, even throughout the year, Viana is a town known for its love of leisure.

Of the more contemporary festivals, there are two that are most outstanding. One is the springtime **Festival Internacional de Cinema de Tróia** in Setúbal, which although (or perhaps, because) it is less famous than other European film festivals, often screens some of the finer, less commercial films. Taking place in the same region of the country, the summer time **Festival dos Capuchos** presents an extraordinary contemporary array of theater pieces, musical concerts, and dance performances, many of which are onetime, site-specific events. For information, contact the regional *Turismo* in Setúbal, Lisbon, or your home country prior to leaving.

There are also numerous summer **jazz festivals** strewn throughout the beach spots along all of Portugal's coastline.

Fiddler OPPOSITE at a folkloric festival in the Minho. ABOVE: Costumed dancers bring heat to a summer festival in Lisbon.

Galloping Gourmets

A culinary tour of Portugal is like taking little tastes of the country's history, from the time of the Romans and their love of wine to the days of the Moors and their fondness for sweets. But above all, it's the Age of Discoveries and the country's colonial experience that have provided most of the flavor of Portuguese cuisine. In your travels around the country you'll soon notice the Portuguese love of spices, most of which originally hail from Asia and Africa: cinnamon, chili, nutmeg, cloves, coriander, chocolate, and on and on and on.

Onions, garlic and olive oil reign supreme, as they do in all Mediterranean cooking, but here they are distinctly and surprisingly accented. And certainly, while there is an identifiable Portuguese cuisine, cooking remains a provincial affair. Delicious seafood is everywhere, but if you're inland or happen to be traveling near a river (and it's hard not to be), enjoy a meal of freshwater fish such as trout or salmon. Anywhere and everywhere, fruits and vegetables are locally grown and the meats come from

herds naturally grazed. Both are invariably fresh. My only complaint is that, generally speaking, half the amount of salt used would still be two times too much. Risking a few looks of utter incomprehension, I have taken to asking for absolutely no salt. This is somewhat akin to asking for Turkish coffee with no sugar. Most often, I get a fairly properly salted meal.

Seafood forms the basis of many local dishes. Freshly caught sardines, *sardinhas*, are excellent, as is swordfish, *espada*: the latter can be smoked in the Sesimbra fashion, or eaten raw with a little olive oil and vinegar, once a popular dish in Mozambique. The best I had was simply charbroiled over an open flame. Octopus (*polvo*) and spider crab (*sapateiro*) are often served stuffed, as are freshwater fish such as salmon, lamprey, and trout (*salmão, lampreía,* and *truta*), while around Lisbon and in the north, eel (*enguia*) is considered a delicacy.

When you're in the Algarve or Alentejo, don't miss sampling the regions' famous *cataplana* dish — shellfish or fish cooked with ham, tomatoes, peppers, and onions (servings are usually for a minimum of two people). The name *cataplana* actually refers to the kind of casserole in which the dish is cooked: similar to a Dutch oven, or really, a Moroccan *tajine*, it's a Moorish derivative used for slow cooking stews and still favored by the Portuguese. (If you enjoy cooking, a *cataplana* makes for a great souvenir.)

With all these sea creatures readily available pretty much throughout the year, it may seem strange that the most popular dish of all is dried, salted cod (*bacalhau*). Once a staple for the poor, it can now be rather more pricey depending upon the establishment. Every restaurant seems to carry *bacalhau*, and there are said to be 365 ways of preparing it. Try *bacalhau à Brás*, in

Pastries ABOVE are a tradition in Lisbon. Stone-carved arches OPPOSITE are a feature of towns in the Minho.

YOUR CHOICE

which flakes of cod are fried in olive oil with garlic and vegetables, or *bacalhau à Gomes de Sá*, a casseroled version topped with black olives and egg slices. As an hors d'œuvre try *bolinhos de bacalhau*, little deep-fried balls of cod mixed with potato.

Another popular fish dish is *caldeira*, a stew that can be eaten as a very filling soup. By the way, Portuguese soups like these are good news for hungry budget travelers. You can eat rather well for very little if you order a *caldo verde*, which is a dark green potato soup with shredded cabbage and a slice of spiced sausage; or *sopa alentejana*, a garlic bread soup.

Bread itself — usually white bread (*pão*) served with butter at every meal — is one of the simple pleasures of eating in Portugal. In your travels around the country, you'll encounter several other types of bread, such as rye bread (*pão de centeio*), or the rougher-textured breads often served in the north.

Pork is the staple red meat, and its quality is excellent. *Presunto*, a cured ham, is available almost everywhere but is especially good in Lamego (it makes a great picnic sandwich together with the local sparkling wine). Spiced and smoked sausages such as *chouriço* or *linguica* are also well worth trying. They're often served as appetizers or to add flavor to soups, omelets, and sandwiches. And in your **Alentejo** wanderings, you will most definitely come across the traditional *carne de porco à alentejana*, a pork stew first marinated in wine and herbs and then slowly cooked with baby clams. *Borrego* or *cordeiro*, lamb, is another Alentejan specialty — you'll find the restaurants of Évora all feature a *borrego* dish or two (a favorite is the *feijoada à alentejana*, essentially a very filling lamb and bean stew).

As you might imagine, the cuisine of the northern mountainous regions of the Alto Minho and Trás-os-Montes include a few meat specialties that are perfect on a chilly winter's night. In Ponte de Lima, you'll find it almost obligatory to order the local *arroz de sarrabulho*, a highly-

seasoned stew composed of several different meats and sausages, with potatoes and vegetables, and served on a bed of rice. Another local delicacy is *cabrito asado*, which is tender roast kid often served with saffron rice.

When you reach Porto, however, your culinary bravado might well be put to the test. The local specialty is tripe. If you dare, set aside your prejudices and try the admirable *tripas à modo do Porto* — tripe with haricot beans and belly pork. This way of preparing it (one of many) is particularly delicious and gives a new perspective on tripe.

Turning to deserts, these vary by region, but most tend to be very sweet. Try *pudim de flan*, a kind of caramel custard, and *arroz doce*, a rich, cinnamon-flavored rice pudding. There are also egg-rich sweets, collectively known as *doces de ovos*, often incorporating fruit or almonds. Some originated in convent kitchens and have tongue-in-cheek names, such as *toucinho de céu* (bacon from heaven) and *barrigas de freiras* (nun's bellies.)

There are some fine cheeses to sample, mainly made of goat's or ewe's milk, which are often served as an appetizer. The most famous is probably *Queijo da Serra*, a soft but slightly firm and quite strong cheese produced from ewe's milk from the Serra da Estrela. Made between October and May it should be eaten young, but an aged variety called *Serra Velho*, is considerably more pungent, and quite delicious.

WINE AND OTHER BEVERAGES

Wine connoisseurs will be in for a pleasant surprise as they travel round Portugal: whites, reds, rosés, and fortified wines are all produced here and are often of such high standards that they are winning increasing recognition worldwide. There is no question that the reason Portuguese wines are not better known abroad is solely due to marketing, and has nothing to do with quality. Within Portugal itself, you'll soon notice how enthusiastic the locals are about their

wine: it's as much a part of the daily lunch and dinner menu as bread or *bacalhau*. Prices, even in most restaurants, are remarkably reasonable, and the choice is so broad that sampling a regional wine wherever you are might qualify as a traveling priority. Even the cheapest and humblest *vinho da casa* is usually quite palatable. To control production and quality there are 10 demarcated regions in continental Portugal designated by the National Wine Council. The wines produced within these must conform to certain specifications regarding the variety of grape, the alcohol content, and the length of time the wines are aged. These regions carry the *selo de garantia*, a seal

of approval similar to the French *Appelation d'Origine Contrôlée*.

When buying wine, whether you are ordering in a restaurant or making a purchase at a private shop, try to sample bottles from the smaller producers. As everywhere, a few large corporations are gobbling up these smaller houses, and although the resulting wine is clean and consistent, subtlety and character are often forsaken. Sogrape is a prime example. This is the corporation that governs the Mateus empire and is even more far-reaching. Their better wines are perfectly acceptable, but somewhat bland

Outdoor dining in Albufeira ABOVE is a classic way to start the night.

and "industrialized." Once you make your preference known, most people in the business, whether it's a wine steward or a shop owner, can and will advise you well.

Vinho Verde accounts for a quarter of Portugal's production and is made from grapes grown in the northeast of the country, mainly in the Minho region with its damp climate and temperate summers. *Verde* (green) refers to the youth of the wine, not its color, and although a red version is produced, you'll generally just come across the white (which is for the better). These light, crisp wines are not complex and have a low alcohol content and a natural gentle effervescence. Despite new efforts to export *vinho verde*, it is generally agreed upon that the wine does not travel well. So even if you think you're familiar with it from home, be sure to taste a few while in Portugal. I assure you, those you will find here are far superior. And if you do stay at Casa de Sezim just outside of Guimarães, be sure to sample the *vinhos verdes* produced on the premises, they are particularly clean and crisp and you can rest assured that nothing befell them during transport.

The other well-known exports are two **rosés**, Mateus Rosé and Lancers, both of which are light and when chilled can make a pleasant summer apéritif. But there is no way around it, in this case their popularity is due far more to marketing ploys than quality.

Further south, the Dão Valley in the Viseu area of central Portugal is the home of the **Dão wines**. These are large, full-bodied reds, matured for a minimum of 18 months in the cask; the whites are drier and matured for a shorter period. A red Dão will be a ruby color, and *very* broadly stated, more similar to a French Burgundy than a Bordeaux. Regardless, although there's no need to go crazy, these wines truly should be aged at least five years before drinking, and you would do better ordering a less expensive wine from another region than a young Dão.

Near the coast, the **Bairrada** region around Coimbra produces some excellent strong, well-rounded deep-red reds that age well, and I must say, drink even better. I have fallen wholeheartedly in love with these wines. Again, as they are complex, they do need to age, but although 1989 and 1991 were superb years, so was 1994 and, slightly less so, 1995. The region also produces some sparkling white wines that are more than acceptable. Two names to look for are Luís Pato (a medium-sized enterprise) and Casa Saima (a tiny producer undoubtedly worth the search).

Near Lisbon, there are four old demarcated regions that have been greatly reduced in size because of both urban development and the creation of several newer regions. In the Trancão Valley north of Lisbon the small Bucelas region produces **whites** under the Caves Velhas label, and in the Colares region west of Sintra the vines planted in sand produce rare and a distinctive red wine that is at its best after years of maturing.

South of the Téjo, the Setúbal region is the origin of Moscatel de Setúbal, one of the best **Muscat** wines in the world. This is an ever-so-slightly less sweet version of a sweet wine. Without being a devotee of the genre, I must say I do find it made for a pleasant chilled apéritif, the sweetness well balanced by olives or tastes of salty cheese.

A word of caution. You need not feel compelled to search for the stray older bottle, whether a Dão, Bairrada, or Colares. Even if price is not a factor. (As anywhere, greater cost does not necessarily correlate with greater quality.) Ultimately, one of the most important questions regarding aged wine is, "where has this bottle been in the interim?" I must say that I have always encountered a great degree of integrity among wine sellers and restaurants with wine lists worth speaking of — items are appropriately priced, and I am almost never steered to the pricier bottles. On the contrary, as I frequently travel solo, I often have to insist to solicitous waiters that I truly prefer to choose a bottle from the list, as wine by the glass never offers a comparable choice.

Turning to fortified wines, the country's most famous product is, of course, **port**, made by adding brandy to wine in order to arrest the fermentation of the sugar. The result is to raise the alcohol content to between 18% and 20% by volume while retaining the sweetness. Although port is found absolutely everywhere in the country, the best place to sample it is in its eponymous home of Porto, as well as across the river in Vila Nova de Gaia where the wines are matured in casks in the famous port lodges. This area was once the province of English shippers. Port became so popular in England that it became an English institution, as the brand names still testify: Sandeman, Dow, Cockburn, and Croft. If you're a port novice (and even if you're not) you should drop in to one of the lodges while you're in Porto for a free port-tasting tour — one of the best ways to get a taste of how port is produced and how best to drink it. There are really four categories of port: top of the list is vintage port, followed by late-bottled vintage, then ruby and tawny ports, and finally white port.

Vintage port is made from the wines of especially good years and the grapes of one harvest only, matured for two years in the vat and then at least ten in the bottle. Vintage port improves as it gets older and is the most expensive. It is drunk as an after-dinner wine.

Late-bottled vintage is made from grapes of a good year — usually not vintage years — and matured for about five years in the cask to speed up the process. Once bottled, it is ready to drink and requires no decanting; the result is a lighter, sharper wine.

The remaining ports are all aged in the cask and are ready to drink when bottled; vintage dated tawny comes from a single year, with a minimum of seven years in the cask, while others are known by their age, 10, 20, 30 or over 40 years old, and are blended with different vintages. Ruby port matures for three

years in the cask and is the most widely drunk of all the ports.

And finally, white port, which lacks the body of the others, is usually dry and served chilled as an apéritif.

A wide range of **brandies** is also made, called *aguardente* or *aguardente de vinho*, the older ones being *aguardente velhas*. Beware of *aguardente de bagaceira*, a ferocious spirit made from grape skins, seeds and stalks, which is firewater that bears some resemblance to Italian *grappa*.

Some interesting **liqueurs** are also produced: *Brandymel*, a mixture of brandy and honey, *Amênoa Amargandoa*, made from almonds, and *Medronha*, made from arbutus berries. If wine or port isn't to your taste, you can always stick with *Sagres*, the most popular local **cerveja** (*beer*). It's produced by a state-run brewery that also makes two stronger brews called *Superbock* and *Cristal*. Similar to English lager, these beers are served cold. There's a low-alcohol lager, too, but you may have trouble finding it beyond the major cities.

Common everywhere are Portugal's excellent brands of **mineral water** (either still, *sem gas*, or carbonated, *com gas*). And if you're a coffee freak, you'll be very happy: the ubiquitous cafés and *pastelarias* serve excellent coffee day and night. Similar in flavor to the French or Italian beverage, Portuguese **coffee** can be consumed in a variety of ways. If you want a small strong cup, like an espresso, ask for *uma bica*. A popular breakfast brew of hot milk with a *bica* tipped in and served in a glass is called *um galão*, while a cup of half milk and half coffee is *um meia de leite*. In the mood for an iced coffee? Order *um café gelado*. Simplest of all is *um café*, an ordinary black coffee. If you want milk with it, ask for *um café com leite*.

Tea, *cha*, is also widely drunk; you can have it with milk (*com leite*) or a slice of lemon (*com uma rodela de limão*). And for an elegant ambience in which to drink your afternoon tea, keep an eye out for the lovely old *casas de cha* scattered across the country.

Special Interests

RELIGIOUS SIGHTS

On May 13, 1917, three young shepherd children, aged 10, nine and seven, claimed they saw the Virgin Mary while tending their flocks of sheep near Fátima. The apparitions recurred five times, all on the thirteenth of the month, but only one of the children could converse with the Virgin and hear her warnings against sinful living and her

entreaties for prayer to ensure world peace. By October 13, some 70,000 people had gathered to witness — or refute — the miracle, which was accompanied this time by strange celestial distractions.

Fátima is now the most important religious venue in Portugal, the ultimate goal if you are interested in making a tour of the country's most notable religious sites. Like every Roman Catholic country, Portugal is rich in grand churches, cathedrals and monasteries (see CULTURAL KICKS, page 44 for the architectural highlights) and it would be easy to drift from town to town discovering impressive religious art and devotion wherever you go.

But there are several other specific pilgrimage points worth visiting en route to Fátima: **Bom Jesús do Monte** near Braga, and **Nossa Senhora dos Remédios** at Lamego with their dazzling black-and-white baroque stairway zigzagging up hills and culminating in churches at the top. The most fervent penitents climb the stairways on their knees, pausing to pray at little chapels along the way. Visit Bom Jesús at Pentecost and

Nossa Senhora dos Remédios in early September if you're interested in observing or participating in the largest pilgrimages.

The city of Braga at Easter time is also quite extraordinary for witnessing a contemporary demonstration of serious religious fervor. The climax is the **Ecce Homo** procession on Easter Thursday night, in which hundreds of barefoot penitents dressed in black-hooded robes march carrying flaming torches. Easter Sunday witnesses processions and pilgrimages at dozens of places in Portugal, most famously at Braga and at Loulé in the Algarve.

Even in the farthest corner of the country — at Miranda do Douro in Trás-os-Montes — there's an annual pilgrimage (in early September) to Our Lady of Nazo at Póvoa. But the Fátima pilgrimages to commemorate those first apparitions are still the largest and most impressive. Tens of thousands of pilgrims converge on Fátima on the twelfth and thirteenth of every month and up to 100,000 pilgrims in the months of May and October. Many of them literally crawl on bent knee toward the great white neoclassical basilica that dominates the vast esplanade below. If you are not a fellow pilgrim, but rather a curious tourist, you might prefer to arrange your visit for another time, as those who participate take it quite seriously and your observation might be considered (by all parties) as somewhat voyeuristic.

To partake in organized Catholic pilgrimages, contact **206 Tours** ((516) 361-4644 FAX (516) 361-3682 TOLL-FREE IN THE UNITED STATES (800) 206-8687 WEB SITE www.206tours.com, who arrange itineraries that visit several religious sites in Portugal including Santarém and Fátima, as well as Lourdes in France. Longer tours include extensive travel in Portugal, Spain, and France. For travelers in the United Kingdom, **Destination Portugal** ((01993) 773269 FAX (01993) 771910 E-MAIL info@witney.itsnet.co.uk offers several tours with a religious focus, in addition to their extensive roster of more general vacations.

GARDENS

Gardens in Portugal come in two verdant varieties: romantic and rambling, or formal and trim. And you don't have to travel far from the center of Lisbon to find both. The city's **Estufa Fria** (Cool House), a botanic garden in the Parque Eduardo VII, is a delightful place to start a garden tour of Portugal. Established over 60 years ago, there's an abundance of exotic plants, ferns, and flowers that tumble under canopies of wicker and glass. The park is also home to the **Estufa Quente** (Hot House) which, replete with several species of orchids (and despite its cacti), resembles a tropical rainforest. Less exotic, but equally enjoyable as a respite from city traffic, is the **Jardim Botânico** whose paths meander through corridors of royal palms.

Leaving Lisbon, a garden-lover's first port of call should be **Queluz**, whose pink rococo eighteenth-century palace is complemented by an inspired formal

OPPOSITE TOP: Santo António processions in Lisbon's Alfama district. LEFT: Penitents marvel at baroque fountains and balustrades as they make their pilgrimage up to Bom Jesús sanctuary. Botanical curiosities ABOVE in one of Lisbon's many gardens.

garden, with cascading bougainvillea and *azulejo*-tiled fountains, and dotted with statues. A wonderful setting to relax and wander.

Rambles become even more enchanting in the **Monserrate Gardens** of Sintra. The abandoned *quinta* here was originally built for the Englishman Sir Francis Cook in the 1860s, but the garden and a previous Gothic house had already attracted several notable English visitors. Among them was the eccentric gay author, William Beckford who, having fled England in the wake of a scandal, lived at Monserrate from 1794 to 1808 and even imported a flock of sheep to roam in the English landscaped garden. A year after Beckford's departure, the poet Byron dropped in, planting a tradition for visiting the place.

But the garden's present attractions — fabulous Himalayan rhododendrons, plants from Australasia and Mexico — are due to the efforts of a painter, William Stockdale, who planted this ambitious botanic collection in the 1850s. Today, after decades of neglect, it's mostly a magical shambles, though the pathways and flower beds in the immediate vicinity of the *quinta* are well-maintained, but still where you can lose yourself for hours.

Moving further north, nature lovers absolutely should not be too rushed to skip a visit to the ancient stupendous **Buçaco Forest** near Coimbra (see THE GREAT OUTDOORS, page 23) before heading for Vila Real and the nearby **Palácio de Mateus**. Built in 1743, this flamboyant little palace is recognized the world over from the picture represented on bottles of Mateus Rosé wine, now manufactured by the Sogrape company headquartered down the road. The tour of the palace might be disappointing for some, but the formal gardens behind it are enchanting, with their prim little statues that guard tiny box hedges, and the perfectly-hewn tunnel of trees. Cool and dark, it is irresistible.

WINES AND PORTS

Wine buffs and port aficionados have two tasty options in Portugal: either wander at random, sampling local wines as you go, or head for the famous *quintas* and wine estates for some serious wine-tasting.

The obvious choice when it comes to **port** is the Douro Valley, home to the port estates. The best place to start a Douro Valley tour is in Porto: across the river is Vila Nova de Gaia where the valley's port is stored and matured in the lodges' huge cellars. A dozen of the lodges offer free port-tasting tours: it's worth visiting one of the smaller, more personal lodges such as the old British firm, Taylor Fladgate & Yeatman, as well as the larger more obvious tourist oriented ones, such as Sandeman (now owned by Seagrams, a Canadian company).

Taking the train (or a cruise — see CRUISE THE DOURO, page 11 in TOP SPOTS) up the Douro, you'll reach Peso da Régua, a major transport center for the Douro Valley's wine industry through which the wines pass on their way to Porto. There are two lodges here you can visit without advance reservations —

Exquisite eighteenth-century formal gardens ABOVE on the palace grounds of Braga's Museu dos Biscaínhos. Ornamental lakes, intricate granite stonework and *azulejos* RIGHT are features of many country estates.

YOUR CHOICE

Casa do Douro and Ramos Pinto — both of which offer excellent tours.

But Pinhão, further east, is the real heart of the port estates. If you base yourself at the lovely seventeenth-century Casa de Casal de Loivos, or the Casa das Pontes, you'll be right at the heart of port activity: both these mansions (part of the Turismo de Habitação scheme) are on active port estates near Pinhão. The tourist office in Porto can provide details for reservations — essential months in advance if you want to visit during the lively harvest season (mid-September to mid-October). This is a far better time for a visit than the summer months when the Douro Valley can experience scorching temperatures.

When it comes to discovering Portugal's table wine districts, you've got a far wider choice of regions. Best known are the *vinho verde* wines of the northern Minho area, a fine place for touring. One of the best of the cooperatives' *vinhos verdes* is the Alvarinho of Monção but more famous abroad are those of Aveleda at Penafiel, east of Porto, a major operation that welcomes visitors. While you're visiting Viana do Castelo, Vila Real, or Braga, make sure to stop in at the regional *Turismo* and pick up a copy of their *Vinhos Verdes Route*, an attractive map with indications and contact information for 45 local producers who open their doors to visitors. For **rosés**, of course, you should head for the Palácio de Mateus near Vila Real and the nearby Sogrape modern winery, which now produces the internationally merchandised wine. You can also visit the wineries of Lancer's rosé operation at Vila Nogueira de Azeitão near Lisbon.

But one of the treats for an œnophile in Portugal is discovering the lesser-known houses and varieties. The smooth, full-bodied red Dão wines of the Beira Alta region are some of the country's best — although they remain largely unknown abroad. The sparkling Raposeira wine of Lamego near Peso da Régua is unexpectedly enjoyable (you can visit the factory for tours and tastings). And in the eastern part of the Alentejo, Portugal's most recent demarcated region, is now producing some very tasty reds.

Finally, for something unique, you might want to try the *vinho dos mortos*, "Wine of the Dead." Produced by the residents of Boticas, a rather unremarkable village near Chaves in the region of Trás-os-Montes, this wine is literally buried for a year or two. The custom dates from 1809 when villagers concealed their wine underground from the invading French troops, and afterward, discovered that the burial had improved the taste. The Café de Armindo near the main street of Boticas usually has some *vinho dos mortos* on hand, but don't be surprised if it tastes a little gritty.

Taking a Tour

As Portugal becomes an increasingly popular vacation destination, the availability of a wide array of tour packages and low-cost flights has also been on the rise. Local travel agents will be able to offer you a variety of fly-drive options, both with and without hotel accommodation. A particularly qualified tour operator is **Magellan Tours (** (609) 303-9003 TOLL-FREE (888) 783-3432 FAX (609) 786-3338 WEB SITE WWW .magellantours.com, 100 East Broad Street, Palmyra, New Jersey 08065, which is run by a staff intimately familiar with the country and offers a wide range of options including fly-drive deals for the independent traveler, as well as deluxe specialized tours for a minimum of two people and a maximum of six. They also arrange river cruises with stays at some of the finer manor homes. Another highly reliable and

OPPOSITE TOP: One of the attractions at the Parque dos Nações is the new aquarium on the Olivais pier. LEFT: The balustrade at the Mosteiro dos Jerónimos. ABOVE: Bullock-drawn carts are still used in the Minho.

For those interested in a luxurious vacation comprised of *pousada* stays, contact **Marketing Ahead** ((212) 686-9213 TOLL-FREE (800) 223-1356 FAX (212) 686-0271. They can organize hotel accommodation and car rental but do not handle flights.

For a tantalizing taste of Portugal, consider dropping into Lisbon as a port of call. Most of the major cruise lines include it on their itineraries, and several include Porto and Funchal in Madeira as well.

Thanks to the popularity of the Algarve among British vacationers, package tours offered by British tour agencies to resorts in this area provide some of the best vacation deals available. You can find a wide range of tours from reliable companies such as **Thomson Tour Operations Ltd.** ((0171) 387-9321 FAX (0171) 387-8451, Greater London House, Hampstead Road, London NW1 7SD; **Caravela Tours Ltd.** ((0171) 630-9223 FAX (0171) 233-9680, Gillingham House, 38/44 Gillingham Street, London SW1V 1HU; or **The Magic of Portugal** ((0181) 741-1181 FAX (0181) 748-3731, 227 Shepherds Bush Road, London W6 7AS. These outfits also offer customized vacations throughout all of Portugal, whether they be fly-drive, self-catering, or more luxurious stays which could include river cruises.

highly experienced tour operator is **Abreu Tours** TOLL-FREE (800) 223-1584 FAX (212) 354-1840 WEB SITE www.abreu-tours.com, 25 West 45 Street, New York, New York 10036, which also has offices in Portugal. Along with the standard coach tours readily available, this outfit will customize tours around your interests — whether architecture, gastronomy, wine, religious history, etc. — and will provide a knowledgeable guide. They can tailor Douro river cruises to fit your plans. In the United Kingdom, contact **Abreu Travel** ((0171) 229-9905 FAX (0171) 229-0274, 109 Westbourne Grove, London W2 4UL, and in Spain, it's **Viajes Abreu** ((91) 700-4410 FAX (91) 319-6931, Calle Genova No. 16, 28004 Madrid.

Serious golfers and cyclists can take advantage of several good package tour offers (see SPORTING SPREE, page 25). Catholic travelers who are interested in participating in the religious festivals and pilgrimages can also join specialized tours (see SPECIAL INTERESTS, page 58).

Any major travel agency should be able to provide information on these and other package tours to Portugal. For a full listing of companies, including those catering to more specialized vacations, contact the Portuguese National Tourist Office for a copy of their *Tour Operators Guide*.

ABOVE: Presidential honor guard on parade in Lisbon. LEFT: Vasco da Gama bridge spans the Tagus River, defining Lisbon's skyline. RIGHT: A local gentleman enjoys a folk festival in Barqueiros.

Welcome
to
Portugal

PORTUGAL, IT SEEMS, HAS ALWAYS BEEN DEEMED AT THE END OF THE EARTH. Whether as the limit beyond which the Phoenicians dared not venture, or as a land defined by those same shores that tempted generations of its own seafaring navigators, or as a twentieth-century country never quite firmly within its time, cut off for a variety of reasons, not the least of which was four decades of dictatorship.

And save for the few adventurous travelers (and the numerous Northern European sun worshippers and golf fanatics), Portugal has never been a top spot on most tourists' itineraries. This is changing, as well it should.

Here is a country that is hurtling into the future—you'll find cybercafés, avant-garde theater festivals, state-of-the-art sports facilities, and of course, the ubiquitous mobile phone. But Portugal remains a country that also *is* its "folkloric" past. A true past. Not one staged for the meandering tourist, but rather one that naturally occurs in Portugal's daily present. A past constructed in massive fortresses and monasteries that seem to have escaped from a children's tale of the Middle Ages. An historic calendar filled with lavish saint-day festivals that still bring entire towns out onto the streets in a spirit of both celebration and religious devotion. A tradition of weekly open markets, of land tilled by beasts of burden, of villages whose winding cobblestone streets invariably lead to an open square adorned with at least a few cafés and even more than a few flowers. And perhaps best off, as far as we travelers are concerned, a tradition of meals. Meals that are in absolutely no hurry to end. Meals of several courses, all made from the freshest ingredients—vegetables from the garden out back, fish from the river across the road, and wine from the local vineyard, perhaps even the one in which you are drinking it.

And of course, a country of people justly proud of their heritage, and perhaps justly leery of the encroachment of modernity. The Portuguese can seem a bit standoffish, decrying their status as Europe's poorer cousins, but beneath the façade, you'll find an enormously generous people, with endless time to chat and share a glass, or more, of *vinho verde*. A certain sense of irony seems to infuse conversations, as if always to remind the visitor that here is a nation that has known the rise and the fall, and has gleaned from its knowledge enough wisdom to allow the inevitable next rise to take its time.

Today, Portugal's wealth is Portugal. And in physical beauty, it is overflowing in riches. All visitors will find their own Edens, as Lord Byron famously did just north of Lisbon in Sintra, but it is almost universally agreed that the sparsely populated mountainous northern region along the length of the border with Spain is virtually unequaled in beauty. Verdant, glistening with its mountain lakes, its roads as winding as the rivers they hug, a drive through this region in early spring when the dense forests are a rash of trees in blossom is pure escape. And it is here where you will also find so many of Portugal's manor houses that have been converted into bed and breakfasts. The grandeur of the estates, the privacy, the welcome, and the inside information the hosts readily bestow make for the ideal compliment to the landscape. The foreign observer gently metamorphoses into the intimate insider, dining with locals, taking roads less traveled, learning the life.

Of quite a different kind of beauty is the Alentejo region that stretches across central Portugal. Flat and arid, it's been said to be a cyclist's heaven. It is also home to one of the country's most extant Roman ruins — the Temple of Diana in Évora — which stands in the square that faces the town's *pousada*, itself a converted fifteenth-century monastery. The region is also known for its wealth of prehistoric dolmens, 5,000-year-old funerary markers. And in typical Portuguese fashion, past centuries stumble upon one another. But then, the region most certainly does not ignore our present. The Alentejo's Atlantic coast has some of the country's most pristine beaches, with conditions and facilities to enthrall even the most ardent windsurfer. There are also great restaurants, and without question, the absolute best *pousada*. Go to Estremoz. Yes, the structure and the furnishings are magnificently antique, but the service and the cuisine are up-to-the-minute, and guests luxuriate in the combined pleasure of the spanning centuries.

Opinions regarding the Algarve, Portugal's southern coast are rather polar — you love it or you hate it. It is extremely built-up, and getting more so by the minute, but clearly, the surging tourist population indicates that there are those who love it. The beaches stretch for miles, and the weather is ridiculously fine year round. Some of the world's most preferred golf courses are to be found here, and other sports enthusiasts — windsurfers, divers, equestrians, cyclists, hikers, and certainly party animals — will also find endless ways to assuage their desires.

As an urbanite, I find myself less inclined to suffer the trials of city life while traveling, but Portugal's two main city centers — Lisbon and Porto — have personalities that enchant and proportions that do not overwhelm. Both cities sport an elegance that is at once a bit faded, but also modern and polished. The past concurs with a contemporary scene that nudges the visitor to recall that Portugal is not merely home to relics, but a place on the move, and the direction is up.

OPPOSITE: Newlyweds pose on a promontory overlooking the Cávado River at Barcelos in the Minho. ABOVE: A tempting display of local food and wine on offer in Viana da Castelo.

Portugal and Its People

PORTUGAL LIES ON A NARROW STRIP AT THE WESTERN EDGE of the Iberian Peninsula, overshadowed in some respects by its larger neighbor, Spain. The two countries share more than their people might prefer to admit: their histories are intertwined, and the very existence of Portugal as a separate entity has, perhaps somewhat misguidedly, been described as an accident, rather than the result of uniqueness in culture, race, language, or history. Regardless, the Portuguese found themselves in an area of geographical importance in the westernmost part of Europe: the gateway to the Mediterranean Sea, Africa, and the lands beyond the Atlantic, and controlling southern Europe's maritime route to northern Europe. Having the only good natural harbors on the Iberian Peninsula, perhaps it was appropriate that the young kingdom's destiny should have been to turn Europe's face to the future and a new world, discovering and charting routes to far-off places known to exist but shrouded in the mists of legend. The spirit of adventure is but one thread that runs through the Portuguese character, which has long since been tempered by harsher realities.

As the spearhead of European exploration and conquest in the New World, Africa and Asia, Portugal had to defend itself against larger and more powerful nations who resented its success and new-found wealth. It also had to accept unfavorable political alliances, accommodate double standards in ethical matters, and to tread the tightrope of peaceful coexistence with its powerful and occasionally predatory neighbor, Spain. Descended from successive waves of prehistoric populations from Europe and Africa, the Portuguese national consciousness has, in more recent centuries, sustained invasion and subjugation by the Moors, the Spanish, the French and the English, engendering a certain fatalism in their psyche.

Their country has seen great riches at times, but much longer periods of privation. During periods of prosperity, the wealth rarely benefited anyone beyond the aristocracy, the Roman Catholic Church, the royal family, and a few merchants. The vast majority of the population lived in penury, eking out a meager existence from what was then rather inhospitable soil on tiny plots

of land in the north, or as tenants and hired labor on the great estates of the south. Nevertheless, the Portuguese maintain a sort of nostalgic collective memory of the days of imperial greatness, as well as a deep identification with the Church.

In some intangible way, it seems true that people who live close to the land mirror its qualities. Although Portugal is small, its topography and climate are extremely diverse, with its green, rolling hills and harsh, rocky mountains, arid plains, and hot Mediterranean-like expanses, along with cold, damp

mountain regions with a winter rawness typical of the Atlantic seaboard. It is also richly endowed with a range of architectural treasures of real splendor: castles, monasteries, fortified towns and villages, palaces, formal gardens, and great country houses. The Portuguese temperament is similarly complex and multifaceted. Here are a people of obvious warmth, who are brave and stoical; their unpretentious formality is not only courteous, but implies a wish not to encroach on another's privacy. And to their extreme credit, although the Portuguese are unequivocally industrious, they quite

The shrine of Fátima LEFT is one of Catholicism's most important pilgrimage destinations.
ABOVE: Capela dos Reis in Braga.

astonishingly exude a laid-back calm that is infectious.

THE MISTY PAST

In the Stone Age, the territory that is now Portugal was inhabited, and although we know little about those early hunters and farmers, they did leave us some mysterious megalithic burial sites. These people grew cereals, kept animals that they had tamed or were the ancestors of our domestic varieties, and fished in the sea. They made bone

carvings and rough earthenware pottery. The relationship between pottery and bronze casting implies a knowledge of ceramics to make the molds, pottery invariably being a precursor to the forging of bronze weapons and vessels. And just as with these somewhat unknowable ancestors, the Portuguese still make pottery to this day.

Over time, successive waves of immigrants came into the area. A people known as the Iberians crossed the Mediterranean from Africa and gave their name to the Iberian Peninsula, settling mainly in the south and what is now eastern Spain. The Ligurians came overland from Italy and settled largely in the north of the peninsula, as did the Celts who came by boat from northern France and

Britain. Excavations have uncovered settlements dating from those times. The best example in Portugal is the Citânia de Briteiros just outside Braga.

Over a thousand years before the birth of Christ the Phoenicians arrived, and these traders, metalworkers, and sailors were likely instrumental in leaving the Portuguese a tradition of nautical exploration and commerce.

Three hundred years later, it was the Greeks who found their way to the peninsula, establishing harbors on the Mediterranean coast, and introducing the grape vine and the olive tree. The Carthaginians also arrived, and like those preceding, left their mark. But in approximately 200 BC, it was the Romans. They came, they... etc.

THE ROMANS

After their conquest of Carthage and its territories, the Romans turned their attention to the rest of the Iberian Peninsula in 201 BC. Between the Tagus and Douro rivers they encountered a tribe known as the Lusitani. These ancestors of today's Portuguese could best be described as not prone to subjugation. It took the greatest military power in the world, their finest generals, and a hundred years to conquer them. Domination was finally achieved by Julius Caesar, and the Romans set about colonizing that region and elsewhere in the Peninsula. They brought magnificent architecture; they engaged in enormous hydraulic engineering projects, transporting water across the country and supplying it to the cities; they introduced a new and sophisticated artistic taste in gardens, the use of mosaics, and the sculpting of tombs. Perhaps their most important contributions were a legal system, the Romanization of the language and — without intending it—Christianity. Around this same time, it was Roman policy to resettle the troublesome Jews in far-flung corners of the empire, and thus many were exiled to Iberia. In centuries to come, the consequences of this banishment were to have a profound effect on both the Jews and their hosts.

The Romans used a system of municipal governments to administer the territory, minting their own coins and operating a complex code of financial and urban law that defined both rights and obligations; slavery was introduced, a practice the Portuguese were later to follow in their own colonies, and which lasted until the eighteenth century. Gold, lead, copper, and iron were mined; marble was quarried, and great farms flourished, producing cereals, fruit and olives, as well as where magnificent horses were bred. Fish was harvested from the sea and the coastal estuaries, textiles were woven and dyed, and salt was extracted in great marine pans.

Then, in the fifth century AD a German cloud appeared on the northern horizon.

man than God and not of the same essence, contrary to standard accepted scripture. In time, they returned to the standard, but first having established the precedent of uniting church and state. One group founded its capital and a major bishopric in Braga, where the Church held paramount ecclesiastical power for centuries in what was to become Portugal. They also began persecuting the Jews, with eventual serious consequences for the whole of Iberia, Portugal as much as Spain. In the meantime, a new force was gathering to the south, which early

THE GERMANIC PERIOD

For a considerable time, small groups of Teutonic people had been settling in the north of the Iberian Peninsula, and in the fifth century waves of their belligerent countrymen began attacking the disintegrating Roman Empire. A tribe called the Suevi conquered parts of Iberia, as did the Alans and the rapacious Vandals; the Visigoths followed, but differed from the others in that they adopted Christianity and many Roman customs and ways, administering much as the Romans themselves had. They expelled the Suevi and Byzantines and for a time introduced Arianism, a heretical Christian doctrine which held that Jesus was more

in the eighth century was poised to usher in five hundred years of a very different kind of order.

THE MOORS

Hailing from what at the time was generally referred to as Arabia, the powerful Islamic expansion swept across all of north Africa, conquering and converting as it went along. In 710 the Arabs (or Moors), aided by their inscripted Berber foot soldiers, crossed the Mediterranean to Spain. They

Celtic-Iberian ruins OPPOSITE at the Citânia de Briteiros in the Minho. Évora's Temple of Diana ABOVE is Portugal's most magnificent surviving monument from the Roman era.

continued on, sweeping through southern France, where they were stopped at the Battle of Pewters in 732. The Spanish had halted their advance at Covadonga in 718, but the Moors established a caliphate at Córdoba to administer the Iberian Peninsula. Theirs was an era of tolerance and order, commerce and wealth. Scholarship in mathematics, medicine, engineering, navigation, architecture, and philosophy flourished. Jews and Christians alike were allowed to practice their religions. Much has been written about the Christian resistance to Islam, however the documented truth is that the inhabitants of Iberia converted in swathes, and many churches were rededicated as mosques. When the *Reconquista* began, many of the defenders were Iberian Muslims, who fought along side the Moors themselves. Beyond the sublime architecture that they left, the Moors brought new agricultural methods, such as the mechanized milling of corn and the construction of enormous water-wheels to lift water from the rivers into cultivated fields. They had an influence on taste in music and in architectural ornamentation, not the least of which was the use of decorative tiles.

Still, there were parts of the northern Iberian Peninsula that had not been brought fully under Moorish control, and forays were made into the territory under their sway by small Christian armies. Encouraged by the Pope and promises of help from northern Europe, these Christians became increasingly aggressive. A long war of attrition ensued, in which Moorish strongholds fell to Christian forces, one after the other. The last to fall was Granada in 1492.

However, human history is necessarily as complex as those who make it, and removed from these battlegrounds, there was a Corsican in the throes of creating a new empire.

THE BIRTH OF PORTUGAL

The appeals of the Christian aristocracy to northern Europe for help in driving out the Moors met with varying degrees of success. One of those who did assist was Earl Henri from Burgundy, who had taken control of the town of Porto at the mouth of the Douro. On April 9, 1097, he staked a claim to the land between the Douro and Minho rivers, so-called *Portucale*. Within a short time, Henri's son, Afonso Henriques made his capital the city of Guimarães and proclaimed his earldom a kingdom. This did not sit well, neither with the Muslims in the south, nor with the kings in the north who had conquered Castile. For the first time, but not the last, a Portuguese king had to fortify his country against Castilian attack. Still, Portugal continued its southbound conquests, taking Lisbon in 1147 after terrible fighting, and later the Algarve. Its historic misfortune was that Castile developed at the same time, was every bit as ambitious, and had considerably more muscle.

Portugal's advances as a military power resulted in cultural and economic leaps backward. Famine and disease accompanied the fighting, and religious repression began to manifest itself. The succession of kings and the shifts in power are complicated and merit at least a book of their own, but one point is worth mentioning. At about this time, a fundamental conflict arose that endured for hundreds of years. The king faced opposition from his nobles, who sought to limit his power. This attempt was devoid of altruism. Indeed, at times the king attempted to institute reforms that the nobility found threatening and managed to prevent, ultimately to the country's detriment.

One could be forgiven for assuming that a country of Portugal's size had a fairly homogeneous socioeconomic structure: in fact it was divided into three different societies.

Portugal's mountain tops are crowned with rugged castles and forts, many built in the fourteenth century under King Dinis.

In the north was an agricultural economy worked by feudal lords. They provided their serfs with a little grain and a degree of protection from invading forces in return for labor. In the center, power resided in the municipal authorities, where wealth was generated by crafts, manufacture and trading. In the south were great estates, *latifúndia*, ruled by knights of the religious orders and worked by Moorish slaves and Christian immigrants. There was a constant shortage of labor on the land, as people preferred to try and make a better living in the towns,

despite opposition from the landowners; conversely, taxes were constantly being imposed in the towns for new fortifications.

As a result of these difficulties a revolution took place in 1383, bringing into prominence the House of Avis and ushering in a new era for Portugal. Chaos ensued. The peasants rose up against the feudal lords, the townspeople rose up against the king, and a number of contenders for power tried to make enough alliances to seize the throne. A palace revolt was led by Duke João of Avis, who was able to use his military contacts to get the support he needed. All of this was too much for Castile, which made a bid to wrest control, and by extension, Portugal. An outbreak of bubonic plague drove them

away from Lisbon. Two years later in 1385, a group of aristocrats, churchmen and municipal representatives elected Duke João as king, bestowing upon him the title of João I. Castile made the mistake of invading again, and was soundly beaten at the Battle of Aljubarrota that August. In thanksgiving, the monastery of Batalha was built, and Portugal entered an age of unprecedented power.

THE HOUSE OF AVIS AND THE VOYAGES OF DISCOVERY

João's priority was now to weld new alliances to protect himself from Spain, and in 1386, merely one year after the victory at Aljubarrota, he signed a perpetual alliance with England at Windsor, and sealed the deal with a marriage to Philippa of Lancaster. Their children were immensely successful: Duarte became king and won the support of the nobility, Pedro became a patron of commercial development in the towns, and Henrique — remembered by posterity as Henry the Navigator — became commander of the Order of Christ. He established a tradition of maritime exploration and conquest that brought Portugal to the height of its greatness. João also had an illegitimate son, Afonso, who married into great wealth and founded the ducal House of Bragança. That family came into prominence 260 years later.

In 1415, Henry led an expedition to expel the Moors from Ceuta in North Africa, an event that marked a decisive shift in the whole mentality of Europe, turning its eyes to horizons of unimagined conquests beyond the known world.

This was the beginning of Portugal's imperial age, in which it conquered Madeira, the Azores and the Cape Verde Islands, charted the route around Africa in the voyages of Bartolomeu Diaz, found the sea route to India in 1498 in the courageous voyage of Vasco da Gama, and established colonies in Goa, Angola, Mozambique, Guinea, Macau, Timor, and Brazil. Portugal came to dominate the trade in gold from west Africa — transporting by sea what the Moors had transported by land — and gained great wealth for itself. Quite outstanding when one considers the size of the Portugal and that at the time, its population was only one and a half million. Needless to say, so small a country could not sustain such an empire, and Spain did everything in its power to foment the downfall.

SPANISH RULE

There were fundamental weaknesses in the social fabric of Portugal. For a start, founding new colonies meant that significant numbers emigrated, reducing the population to

introduce the Inquisition from Spain into Portugal in 1536, establishing a reign of terror. Many of the professional and learned men were Jews, as were traders and bankers. (Following Spain's sudden conquest of the last Moorish kingdom on the Iberian Peninsula in 1492, religious tolerance disappeared. In 1497, Portugal followed Spain's example and forbade public worship by both Jews and Muslims.) Large numbers were expelled, impoverishing not only the cultural and scientific life, but also the country's economic health.

about a million. Secondly, an increasing number of men had to carry out the conquests and defend the newly-won territories, diverting them from productive enterprise. (The situation was not improved through the importation of black slaves, who clearly had suspect loyalties and were hardly a stabilizing factor.) Thirdly, the great wealth flowing into the country did not percolate down to the common people: it stayed in the hands of the crown, the aristocracy, the Church, and a few merchants. The fourth reason was that as the country's priorities had been diverted from the development of local industry, and it often proved to be more economical to import goods, rather than to buy them locally. Finally, João III had the stupidity to

Reducing the population was bad enough, but this qualitative loss almost destroyed Portugal. Furthermore, the Inquisition created tension with England, and although it had been Portugal's perpetual ally, it was not on the best of terms with the Pope and Roman Catholic authorities. When the young King Sebastião went off to Africa in a campaign against the Moors and got himself and 8,000 men killed, Spain seized its chance and annexed Portugal in 1580 on the pretext that the king had left no heirs. Philip II of Spain was now also

LEFT: Eyes cast to new horizons — a detail of the Monument to the Discoveries. ABOVE: The sixteenth-century Torre de Belém sits majestically overlooking the Tagus.

Philip I of Portugal, and promised to safeguard Portugal's language, currency, overseas empire, and its government. By and large he kept his word, but he did not stop the Dutch and the British from nibbling away at the empire, although he *did* expect Portugal to help foot the bill for his ruinous wars. After another two Philip had continued in the same vein, matters came to head in 1640 when there was a coup in Lisbon. An unwilling Duke of Bragança was proclaimed king by the nobility: João IV. His House, the last Portuguese dynasty to

date, continued to rule into the twentieth century.

THE FIRST BRAGANÇAS

The reluctant João IV struggled to maintain Portugal's independence, regain some of the lost overseas empire and make allies. This was a momentous time for all Europe: the great powers of England, France, and the Netherlands were all in the throes of civil, religious, and international wars. João finally had to sign a treaty with England, which was then under the sway of the Protestant Cromwell, an anathema to the deeply conservative Portuguese. Fighting continued with Spain for nearly 30 years, and it was

not until 1668 that Portugal's independence was finally recognized. Attempts were made again to stimulate the establishment of local industry, but once more these were set aside when gold and diamonds were discovered in Brazil in the 1690s. But as before, the newfound wealth was ill-advisedly used to build extravagant palaces and churches, leaving Portugal's basic infrastructure weak and vulnerable, and its people poor. Although a number of important public works were constructed, these were of little benefit to the general population.

A commercial landmark of the time was the signing in 1703 of the Methuen Treaty with England, in which the English — who had developed an unquenchable thirst for port — were granted preferential terms for the import of textiles into Portugal and her colonies (much to the disadvantage of the local weavers) in return for unrestricted access to England's wine market. The real effect was to give the British control of Portugal's port industry.

Fortunately for the country, which was about to experience the greatest natural catastrophe in its history, a ruthless, efficient, and in many ways innovative official became chief minister: the results of the appointment of the Marquês de Pombal are still visible, two and a half centuries later.

THE GREAT EARTHQUAKE

On All Saints' Day on November 1, 1755, a violent earthquake struck Lisbon and other parts of Portugal. It happened while many were at Mass, and the lighted candles started fires that compounded the horror. Some fled to the Tagus River and directly into the arms of a tidal wave. Ensuing epidemics completed the misery. The final death toll reached around 40,000.

Pombal swiftly restored order, using the opportunity to introduce and enforce administrative and economic reforms in the name of the king. Plans to rebuild Lisbon and other major cities, as well as smaller towns, along a practical grid pattern were drawn up and then implemented, industry was encouraged, the Jesuits were thrown out, slavery was abolished in metropolitan Portugal, the laws regarding wine production were revised to reduce the advantage the English had secured for themselves, and the excesses of the Inquisition were curbed. The institutionalized persecution of the Jews was officially terminated. Although he put an end to public executions by burning, Pombal did authorize the use of torture on his opponents, and ensured with savagery that his instructions were obeyed.

Having achieved such vast accomplishments and in possession of a great autonomy, Pombal attempted to usurp the throne in 1777. He failed and was banished. And

would be made available to the Braganças if certain conditions were met. The Portuguese colonies in the Americas were also on the shopping list, with Spain slated to be the primary beneficiary.

In the meantime, the royal family had been evacuated to Brazil by the British, and although the Portuguese authorities made no trouble for the French invaders, their welcome began to wear thin. An expeditionary force under the lead of the future Duke of Wellington was dispatched from Ireland in 1808, and it evicted Junot and then trans-

although the queen did reinstitute certain religious elements to the government that had previously been eradicated by Pombal, his legacy was of lasting benefit.

THE PENINSULAR WARS

In 1807, Napoleon's army invaded Portugal. He had demanded in vain that it close its ports to British shipping. Napoleon's force was under the command of General Junot, who had formerly been the ambassador to Lisbon. There had been a secret pact signed between France and Spain, in which Portugal would be divided into three parts, with the northern and southern regions to be awarded to Spain, while the central region

ported the invaders back to France with their booty. Further invasions increased the misery of the long-suffering Portuguese, who also had had their fill of the British military dictatorship under Viscount Beresford, who had been ruling the country for 10 years. In 1820 open revolt broke out and smoldered for another 31 years, going through the same destructive phases as the French revolution had. When the entire country was in a state of exhaustion, a constitutional monarchy was established. In the interim, however, Brazil in 1822, under one of the Braganças had become a politically independent empire.

Grand monuments throughout Lisbon honor past heroes. LEFT: Marquês de Pombal. RIGHT: Dom Pedro IV.

This had the effect of driving Portugal away from its traditional system of government.

Portuguese Liberals were divided into two groups, one more radical than the other, and amid acrimony and civil disturbances, they steered Portugal through the ensuing decades, slowly bringing reforms to the economy, judiciary, and administration.

THE END OF THE MONARCHY

The seeds had already been sown for a pluralist democracy in Portugal. When economic

recession struck Europe in the 1870s, the old question of import-substitution and developing local industry arose. On the other hand, since the final loss of Brazil in 1898 — when it threw out its last Bragança monarch and became a republic — there had been talk of reinforcing the African colonial empire, linking Mozambique and Angola and developing the territory between. This was rudely interrupted when the British demanded Portuguese withdrawal from the Zambezi heartland in 1890. Although humiliated, Portugal had little choice but to agree. Republican sentiment began to simmer, and erupted in 1908 after economic deprivation had embittered the peasantry and the military. The king had been begged to rule by

decree in those difficult times, but instead authorized his prime minister, João Franco to rule dictatorially, an unpopular decision. On February 1 of that year, King Carlos and his son were assassinated in the middle of Lisbon. His second son took the throne as Manuel II, but mounting pressure forced the unfortunate man to abdicate in 1910. So ended the power of the ancient House of Bragança, and after 813 years of monarchy, Portugal had become a republic.

THE FIRST REPUBLIC AND SALAZAR

In 1911 a new constitution was adopted, and the Law of Separation declared Portugal a secular state.

Unfortunately things did not go as smoothly as would be have been desired. Portugal underwent 45 changes of government in the first 16 years of its republican life. The arrival of the Great War did not help matters. Goaded by Britain, still its ally, and fearful of the fate of its African colonies, Portugal declared war on Germany in 1917 with neither the military might nor the political will for the conflict.

In 1926, under the charge of General Carmona, the army staged a coup and Portugal saw an end to its short-lived democracy, a luxury that would not return for almost another 50 years.

Then in 1928, António Salazar, who was a professor of economy at the University of Coimbra, was appointed by Carmona as his minister of finance. Salazar's condition for accepting the office was unrestricted control of the finances of all ministries. And from a certain perspective, through the implementation of harsh austerity measures, he could be considered to have been successful. Four years later, he became the prime minister, and then a mere year after that, he established himself as dictator. His rule has been termed fascist because, as is a dictator's wont, he opposed pluralism and was prepared to use force. Such definition, however, might be somewhat erroneous, at least when compared with his contemporaneous self-avowed fascists. There is no question that Salazar was able to impose his will on Portugal by riding the storm that first brought

Mussolini, and then Hitler and Franco to power, but some distinction might be made. Salazar did not attempt to rouse the masses (perhaps, he did not dare to), there were no grandiose parades, nor quests for new empires (although certainly, independence for existing African and Asian colonies was unthinkable), and perhaps most significantly, he did not partake in the racist dogma so routinely espoused at the time. Salazar even banned his own political party, but it is more than justly argued that he did so to prevent the fomenting of an opposition from within.

and imprisonment. Arguably, his main achievement was to give Portugal a measure of contrived stability, and to keep it out of World War II, thus avoiding the cataclysms that engulfed most of Europe from Spain to the Urals. A consequence of isolation, however, is of course isolation, and the people of Portugal remained impoverished, and except for the members of a still quite distinct aristocracy, uneducated. The ensuing results of this isolation continue to haunt the nation as it struggles to become a major player in the new united Europe.

He was a conservative man—much more so than his republican predecessors — and a deeply religious Catholic, although his faith did not stop him from using methods that Pombal would have admired. The working class and the peasants (who formed the vast majority of the population), not surprisingly, bore the brunt of the dictatorship. Rights were restricted, unions banned, and workers were forced into national organizations that were controlled by the employers. Intellectuals and members of the educated class also suffered, as all opposition was ferociously routed out. Censorship was imposed and order was maintained by the despised Polícia Internacional e de Defesa do Estado (commonly known as PIDE), who routinely used torture

THE CARNATION REVOLUTION

In 1968, Salazar suffered a stroke that left him mortally ill, and he was succeeded by Dr. Marcelo Caetano, who attempted to modernize and reform the government. It was too late. Hostility had grown, especially among the armed forces who had served in the colonies. They formed an organization called the Movimento das Forças Armadas and in the early hours of the April 25, 1974, troops moved into Lisbon and took control in a nearly bloodless coup. The event entered

LEFT: A windmill looms over a whitewashed terrace at Peniche, Costa da Prata, harnessing the Atlantic breezes. ABOVE: There can never be too many festivals.

the history books as the Carnation Revolution, because the soldiers placed red carnations in the barrels of their rifles.

A provisional government representing all political factions was established under the respected military leadership of António de Spínola as president, and Mário Soares as foreign minister. Their first problem was to deal with the question of the African colonies, a source of great dissent that lead to uprisings. In the first two years following the coup, the nation underwent six governments, as all players jostled for their place in the

to win the presidential election, appointing Soares as prime minister.

In a swing to the right in 1987, the first majority government since 1974 came to power, retaining Soares as president and Cavaco Silva as prime minister, with the two continuing to remain in power following the next national elections four years later. After much wrangling, Portugal was finally admitted into the European Union in 1986, and with the influx of European Union grants, the nation experienced unprecedented economic growth. This in turn enabled Silva to forge

evolving political system. Impoverished Alentejan laborers seized farms owned by absentee landlords and set up cooperatives, while many industries, banks, and insurance companies were nationalized.

Soares' plan for the careful dismantling of the colonies was ignored and the Portuguese government simply turned its back on them, leaving a state of violent chaos, with some of the ramifications persisting today. In 1975, there was a flood of refugees into Portugal after the South African government had restricted the number of immigrants it was prepared to accept, and the nation's population of 10 million swelled by 700,000. A major insurrection was crushed by General Eanes in the same year: he then went on

ahead with wide-reaching economic reforms that entailed the privatization of state-owned industries and the overall encouragement of private enterprise. Although massive investments — both foreign and domestic — occurred, so did worker unrest. In response to the government's attempts to reform labor laws, workers took to the streets. But despite the extraordinary 24-hour general strike of March 1988 and the massive rallies of early 1989, the legislation was approved.

Both seasoned politicians, Soares and Silva persevered and held on to power after the 1991 elections. However, along with the general economic slump experienced throughout western Europe, Portugal was clearly not on equal footing to compete with its partners. And as everywhere, there was party corruption and infighting. The long and short of it is that Silva lost the office of prime minister to the socialist António Guterres in the 1991 elections. Five years later, Silva ran for president (due to constitutional term limits, Soares' could not run again), but he lost to Jorge Sampaio, who at the time was Lisbon's socialist mayor.

Guterres has adhered to his promise of readying Portugal for admission into the European Monetary System and the single-currency community, thus mollifying some of the fears and concerns of the business community. He, however, remains a man of social commitment and continues to negotiate this rather perilous tightrope.

GEOGRAPHY AND CLIMATE

Situated in the southwest extremity of Europe, Portugal occupies an 88,500-sq-km (35,383-sq-mile) narrow strip on the Iberian Peninsula. From east to west it measures 220 km (137 miles) at its widest, and from north to south 560 km (348 miles). To the east, it is bound by a land border with Spain that extends 1,215 km (755 miles), and has virtually no natural barriers, and the Atlantic Ocean to the west. The four major rivers are the Douro and Minho in the north, the Guadiana in the southeast — which forms the border with Spain — and most important, the Tagus, which is the longest river in Iberia, with Lisbon at its mouth.

North of the Tagus lies Portugal's more mountainous region, the highest range being the Serra da Estrela in the northeast, which rises to an altitude of 1,991 m (6,532 ft). South of the Tagus is the alluvial plain of the Alentejo and Ribatejo provinces.

The northern coast, sometimes called the Costa Verde, is a land of exposed sandy beaches, forests, and green valleys. Its climate is temperate with warm, primarily dry summers and mild, wet winters, while the sea tends to be cold and rough year round. This is also the country's most densely populated region. Inland, the harsh-featured Douro valley, the country's most famous wine-making area, has a more extreme climate with cold winters and scorching temperatures in summer.

South of the Douro, the low-lying coastal belt is cooled by sea breezes and has heavy rain in winter. To the south lies Estremadura, the province stretching as far as Setúbal, south of Lisbon. Its coastline is edged with beaches and cliffs, and it is here that the Mediterranean Sea begins to affect the climate.

In the northeast corner beyond the Gerês and Marão ranges lies the isolated and sparsely populated region of Trás-os-Montes, an area of high mountains, large plateaus, and deep valleys. Less rain falls here but greater extremes of temperature occur than

elsewhere in the north, and can reach as high as 40°C (104°F) in summer, and fall to below freezing in winter.

South of the Douro, the northeastern provinces of Beira Alta and Beira Baixa form Portugal's most mountainous area, an extension of the high plateau of central Spain.

The central zone consists of the coastal area around Lisbon and the inland province of Ribatejo on an alluvial plain, where temperatures are warmer than in the north, the rainfall lower and the summers longer.

To the south lies Portugal's largest region, the Alentejo, which occupies nearly a third

LEFT: The Oriente train station offers a modern perspective of Lisbon. ABOVE: Seaweed is dried on beaches at Afife in the Minho and used as fertilizer.

of the country's area. Stretching from Spain to the Atlantic, it is an area of rolling plains and reddish-brown soil. This is the bread-basket of Portugal, and the land where half the world's cork comes from. Summers are long and can be cruelly hot on these airless prairies, while the short winters can be extremely cold.

Separated from the Alentejo by the Serra de Monchique and the Serra de Caldeirão, the southernmost strip of Portugal has a sub-tropical climate. Winter temperatures in the Algarve rarely drop below 12°C (54°F) and in summer they average 24°C (75°F). The coast is lined with long, sandy, inviting beaches.

RELIGION

Constitutionally, as decreed by the 1911 Law of Separation, Portugal is a secular state. However, roughly 95% of the population are Roman Catholics, albeit practicing the religion with an ardency that ranges from the profoundly fervent to the obligatory. As is evidenced by the many churches dating from the tenth and eleventh centuries, Portuguese Catholicism has roots that reach far into the religion's past and rituals with clearly pagan origins are still practiced in parts of the country. Appeals from Rome to stop painful acts of personal sacrifice — such as walking on the knees and self-flagellation — have by and large been thoroughly rejected.

In spite of the Church's initial disapproval, the cult of Fátima grew and flourished. This relates to a vision of the Virgin said to have been seen by three children in 1917, when they were given three secrets. In October of that year, although none but the children saw the Virgin, 70,000 people claim to have witnessed a miracle in which the sun moved and the sick were cured of their illnesses. Salazar made good use of the opportunity to focus popular attention on a Portuguese miracle, and had an extravagant basilica built there.

Sometimes Christianity's darker roots emerge, particularly in the remoter northern regions, where superstition and belief in magic prevail. People still sometimes visit the local *bruxa* or witch, and strange rituals surround birth, death, and fertility.

But the separation of Church and State seems to be passionately defended by all

parties, and perhaps surprising to the American tourist (and others as well), will be the ready availability of contraceptives. Even in the smallest towns, a coin-operated condom dispenser is located outside pharmacies. But still, the Portuguese love their traditions, and during the summer months there is a plethora of religious processions, called *romariás*, especially in the northwest. Each village and town has its own celebrations — a brochure is available from the ICEP (Investimentos, Comércio e Turismo de Portugal; see TOURIST INFORMATION, page 274 in TRAVELERS' TIPS

for addresses) with details of what takes place when. These festivals are an indelible part of Portuguese life.

A word on the subject of the Portuguese churches: many of the most important ones were built during the times of Roman and Visigoth occupation and display a remarkable diversity of styles, both architecturally and in their ornamentation. They range from the very simple and the starkly elegant to enormous structures, the extravagance of their sculpture and gold leaf inspiring awe in both the devout and mere visitors.

Mosteiro dos Jerónimos cloisters, Lisbon ABOVE and Capela dos Reis in Braga LEFT display the rich diversity of artistic and architecturals styles.

Lisbon
and
Environs

LISBON

Lisbon is a city with the stamp of past greatness. Overlooking the Tagus River, the gateway to the Atlantic, its weathered edifices are monuments to the days when Portugal was the vanguard of discovery of the world beyond the horizons of Renaissance Europe. Although they recall an era of untold wealth, the older cathedrals and fortresses were witness to the worst natural cataclysm in her history, when in 1755 this proud and glittering city was reduced to rubble by a shattering earthquake. But Lisbon never lost the soul of Portugal: its faded beauty reflects not only nobility, but also the tribulations of a people who have known better times.

BACKGROUND

Archaeological evidence suggests that the city was founded by the Phoenicians, who around 1200 BC colonized the hilltop where the Castelo São Jorge stands, naming their settlement Alis Ubbo, meaning Delightful Harbor. The Romans then made it their administrative center in 60 BC, building new fortifications around the hilltop, traces of which can still be seen.

In the fifth century AD, the city then fell to the conquest of the Visigoths and remained under their hand until 714, when the Moors took control of it, continuing to reign for over four centuries. Under Moorish rule, the city flourished and became a center of commerce and learning. Several attempts to capture Lisbon from them ended in failure, but in 1147 Afonso Henriques, aided by an army of Crusaders, laid siege to it. After a grueling 17 weeks, the Moors surrendered and the Crusaders pillaged what had been a cultured city. Members of the English contingent decided to stay on in the area and an English priest, Gilbert of Hastings, was made Bishop of Lisbon.

In 1256, after the Moors had been expelled from the Algarve, the capital was moved from Coimbra in the north, where shortly afterward the first university was founded, to the more centrally located Lisbon. The building of the city then began in earnest and Lisbon became an important trading port.

The fifteenth century brought the voyages of discovery, and by the sixteenth century, as the Spice Route to the Moluccas opened and Portugal began to exploit the wealth of its colonies, Lisbon became the hub of a great maritime empire and a major trading center, luxuriating in previously unknown wealth and glory. The population swelled to 165,000, making it the largest city on the Iberian peninsula. King Manuel I, who ruled from 1495 to 1521, launched a massive campaign of construction, enriching Lisbon with many beautiful and ornate buildings. Of those, fortunately the magnificent Convento dos Mosteiro dos Jerónimos in Belém and the Torre de Belém have survived.

Lisbon's and Portugal's fortunes waned thereafter, but the discovery of gold and diamonds in Brazil in 1705 fueled another wave of lavish building. The churches glistened with gold leaf, a great aqueduct was built — with such engineering precision that it withstood the 1755 earthquake and stands to this day — and Lisbon emulated all the splendors of the French court. English merchants traded in the city and established a comfortable expatriate community, eventually setting up their own English church and cemetery in the Estrêla district.

Then, suddenly, at 10 AM on All Saints' Day 1755 while the devout were attending Mass, disaster struck. As an English nun wrote to her mother, there was "a noise like the rattling of coaches." It was what came to be known as the Great Earthquake.

Overturned church candles started fires that were fanned by the wind and continued to rage for six days. People ran to the Tagus for safety, but instead, they were consumed by the tidal waves that swept up the river.

The lower part of the town was destroyed, the docks were washed away and aftershocks continued for five days. After the inevitable epidemics had taken their toll, the number of dead was put as high as 40,000, nearly a quarter of Lisbon's population. In the days that followed, King José I gave extraordinarily vast-reaching emergency powers to his prime minister, the Marquês de Pombal, who ably handled the situation, restoring law and

The Alfama district's narrow shopping streets nestle far below the Castelo de São Jorge.

order, closing the port, burying the dead, and punishing looters. His measures included dealing decisively with the remnants of the Inquisition, proponents of which saw the earthquake as an opportunity to embark upon a rampage of auto-da-fé (the burning of undesirables at the stake). It was through Pombal's persuasion and planning that Lisbon remained the capital. A special tax was levied to finance the rebuilding of the city on a grid system of wide streets and large, airy squares, the sight that greets the visitor to central Lisbon to this day.

tion. The army entered amid scenes of jubilation, and truckloads of carnations, the symbol of the revolution, were brought into the city. The rapid decolonization that followed brought an influx of 700,000 refugees primarily from Angola and Mozambique, many of whom chose to settle in Lisbon, making it delightfully cosmopolitan.

GENERAL INFORMATION

The best source of information in Lisbon, as elsewhere in Portugal, is the tourist infor-

During World War II, Lisbon again became a focus of international attention and regained a little of its lost glamour. Under Salazar, Portugal remained neutral, leading thousands of Jewish refugees to converge upon Lisbon while they awaited exit to other safe countries. It also became a refuge for exiled European royalty and heads of state, with people of all nationalities mingling in the hotels and bars. During this period, Lisbon justly earned its reputation as a city swarming with spies.

The most recent drama in Lisbon's history came on April 25, 1974, when Salazar's successor, Caetano, was overthrown in the virtually bloodless military coup that has come to be known as the Carnation Revolu-

mation offices or *Turismos* operated by the ICEP (Investimentos, Comércio e Turismo de Portugal). In the city proper, the *Turismo* ((21) 346-6307 FAX (21) 346-8772 is at the Palácio Foz, Praça dos Restauradores, just north of the Rossio. Another office is in the Lisbon Airport ((21) 849-4323 or 849-3689 FAX (21) 848-5974.

For information on the whole of Portugal contact the **Associação de Turismo de Lisboa** ((21) 361-0350 FAX (21) 361-0359 E-MAIL turismo@mail.cm-lisboa.pt WEB SITE www.cm-lisboa.pt/turismo, Apartado 3326, 1200 Lisbon, or the **Direcção-Geral do Turismo** ((21) 357-5086 FAX (21) 357-5220, at Avenida António Augusto de Aguiar No. 86.

For specific travel inquiries, the following telephone numbers may prove helpful: **Aeroporto de Lisboa** ((21) 841-3700; **General rail information** ((21) 888-4025 WEB SITE www.cp.pt; **Rodoviária Nacional de Expressos** (intercity bus travel) ((21) 354-5439 (timetables) or (21) 357-7915 (ticket office), Avenida João Crisóstomo. The main office of **TAP Air Portugal** ((21) 841-6990 FAX (21) 841-6540 is at Praça Marquês de Pombal No. 3A. For details of ferry services contact **Alcântara Maritime Passenger Station** ((21) 392-2025, at the main docks.

Arbitral do Metropolitan de Lisboa ((21) 355-8457 FAX (21) 357-4908, Avenida Barbosa do Bocage No. 5.

A fun way of getting around is the old tram system, which dates from the late nineteenth century and negotiates some of the very steep hills you may not want to climb. The bus system and the trams are easy to use as any given route is outlined at stops along the way.

Carris is the company in charge of Lisbon's buses, trams, funiculars, and elevators. Single tickets bought aboard cost 160$,

For driving information, contact the **Automóvel Clube de Portugal** ((21) 356-3931 FAX (21) 357-7930, at Rua Rosa Araújo No. 24, 1200 Lisbon.

GETTING AROUND

Lisbon has a subway system, the *Metropolitano*, which connects the Baixa and the newer areas of Lisbon. Though not extensive, it is straightforward, inexpensive, and efficient. A single trip costs 100$ (about 55¢), and the ticket is valid for one hour after being stamped. A one-day unlimited ticket costs 250$. Seven-day and 30-day passes are also available. If you should have any complaints about the system, contact the Provedor

however, at Carris and some newspaper kiosks, a roundtrip ticket will cost you the same. You can also buy a one-day pass for 430$, a three-day pass for 1,000$, and a seven-day pass for 2,320$. These are sold at many of the major metro stations, as well as at any Carris kiosk. There is also a bus service from the Lisbon airport that runs every twenty minutes from 7 AM to 9 PM and makes several stops, including a few along Avenida da Liberdade and at the Cais do Sodré station.

In addition to the usual modes of public transportation, there's a special sightsee-

The seven hills ABOVE of Lisbon rise up from the Tagus estuary while imperious arches LEFT are reminders of the nation's great seafaring age.

ing tram that tours the major monuments. It leaves the Praça do Comércio three times a day, and tickets for it cannot be booked in advance. Carris also runs open-air double-decker tour buses along two routes. A day ticket allows you to hop on and off, and is also valid for use on the public network. Prerecorded commentaries are given in Portuguese, English, French, German, and Spanish, as needed. Both tours begin and end at Praça do Comércio, and tickets are bought on board from the driver. For further information, call ((21) 363-2021.

Taxis are plentiful except during the lunch hour, and are either beige or green and black. Fares are relatively inexpensive and a taxi can be cheaper than taking a bus if there are a few of you sharing. The initial charge is 250$, and thereafter, the fare is metered. An additional charge of 300$ is added for baggage placed in the trunk or roof rack. This does not include the transport of baby strollers or wheelchairs, which by law must be carried free of charge. Phoning for a taxi will add 150$ to the fare. Fares are not metered outside the city limits, in which case check the fare before leaving. To report problems, contact ANTRAL (Associação Nacional dos Transportadores Rodoviários em Automóveis Ligeiros)((21) 357-3908.

The popular Lisboa Card has been reintroduced, and it can prove a great savings depending upon how you intend to tour Lisbon. It offers unlimited travel on the metro, buses, trams, funiculars, and elevators, as well as free entrance or discounts to 26 museums and up to 50% off entry to the others. The card also enables you to benefit from a 5% to 10% discount in certain touristic shops. Prices for adults are 1,900$, 2,800$, and 3,100$ for one-, two-, and three-day cards respectively. Prices for children from five to eleven years old are 750$, 1,110$, and 1,550$ respectively. The Lisboa Card can be purchased at the Associação Turismo de Lisboa, which is across the Praça dos Restauradores from the *Turismo* on Rua Jardim do Regedor No. 50, as well as at various points throughout the city. Ask at your hotel or at the tourist office, or contact the Associação Turismo directly by phone ((21) 343-3672/3.

WHAT TO SEE AND DO

Designated Europe's City of Culture for 1994, Lisbon is rich in attractions and, with the exception of the slightly out-of-center Belém district, the sights are within walking distance of one another. The best way of enjoying its atmosphere, shaded squares and magnificent views is on foot, making it possible to spend time at places of special interest without worrying about parking or traffic (both of which are horrendous, at best), as well as to stop when the spirit moves at an old *pastelaria* or café.

In the center are three main areas of interest: the western hilltop neighborhood of the Bairro Alto, the medieval Alfama district huddling below the castle on the opposite hillside, and the valley running between them from the Pombal statue at the top of Avenida da Liberdade, across the busy Rossio Square and down to the Praça do Comércio by the Tagus River. The fact that Lisbon is built on a number of hills — seven of them, so it is said — need not impede your visit. The city is replete with trams, buses, inexpensive taxis, funiculars, a metro system, and even elevators to spare your feet if you don't feel up to longer walks. However, a comfortable pair of walking shoes is essential. Aside from the wear and tear endured from touring, the gorgeous mosaic pavements are hard on the feet and extremely slippery when wet.

The Baixa

The Baixa, or Lower City, was rebuilt after the 1755 earthquake; the Marquês de Pombal's majestic reconstruction of the commercial and business heart of the city was rational and is sometimes referred to as Pombaline Lisbon, characterized by wide, straight streets lined with uniform neoclassical buildings. Its austerity imparts a touch of Pombal's own ruthlessness, but the overall effect is softened by the decorative black and white mosaic pavements.

Once the gateway to the city, the **Praça do Comércio** is unimaginable when first coming upon it from the streets of the Baixa. Although the arch of the praça can be seen all the way from Praça Rossio, and it is clear that the broad Tagus River lies just beyond,

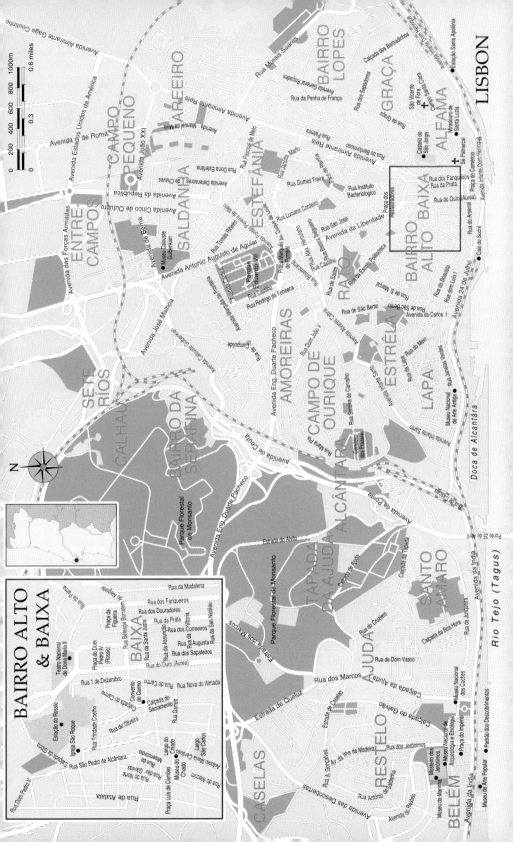

its vastness — 192 m (630 ft) long by 177 m (581 ft) wide — and its (yes, faded) majestic air comes as a shock. Situated in the center of the port, one side opens on to the river, with marble steps leading down to a landing stage. The other three sides are lined with uniform buildings with arcaded lower stories.

The endemic Lisbon sense of contradiction and assimilation again emerges. This is the square where King Carlos I and his son the Crown Prince Luís Filipe were assassinated in 1908 as they passed in an open carriage, an event that triggered the end of the monarchy. Despite its official name, and despite that the surrounding buildings house the offices of an unquestionably and fervently democratic government, people nonetheless continue to refer to the square as *Terreiro do Praça* (the Palace Grounds), as this was once the site of the royal palace. The equestrian statue in the center is of King José I, a forebear of Carlos I.

The magnificent **Arco Monumental da Rua Augusta**, the triumphal arch at the northern end, presents one of the most striking views of Pombaline Lisbon. It is crowned with statuary and straight through it runs Rua Augusta, one of the three parallel streets that, along with Rua do Ouro and Rua da Prata, form part of a geometric street grid leading to Rossio Square. They were assigned by Pombal to various enterprises and named accordingly: Rua do Ouro (now also called Aurea) means Street of Gold and Rua da Prata, Street of Silver, to this day prime areas for jewelry shops and banks, while the neighboring Rua dos Fanqueiros, Clothiers' Street, still has a number of clothing shops.

The **Praça do Dom Pedro IV**, better known as the **Rossio**, is the heart of the Baixa and the hub of Lisbon. The square was once the site of the Inquisition's autos-da-fé but is now rather mundane with its newspaper kiosks, souvenir shops, flower sellers, and lottery-ticket vendors clustered around the fountains. It is still not particularly cheerful, in fact it is somewhat seedy and aggressive with a lot of noise and traffic. But the ever-popular **Café Nicola**, dating from the late eighteenth century, and the **Pastelaria Suiça**, where they bake their own pastries, bookend the square and their outdoor tables pro-

vide ideal vantage points to observe the complexity of Lisbon. Café Nicola also serves meals, and its lunchtime fare and clientele somewhat resemble that of a Paris bistro.

The north end of the praça is occupied by the **Teatro Nacional de Dona Maria II**. Constructed in 1840 on the site of the Palace of the Inquisition, and in front of which stands the statue of the sixteenth-century Portuguese playwright Gil Vicente, it remains a vital component of Lisbon's theater life. The **Estação do Rossio**, a nineteenth-century neo-Manueline structure that is undergoing massive late-twentieth century restorations, stands on the northwestern side. As with all contemporary train stations serving major cities, the Rossio is home to its share of characters.

Just east of the Rossio is the quieter **Praça da Figueira** with its relaxed cafés. North and west of the Rossio at the **Praça dos Restauradores** an obelisk commemorates the overthrow of Spanish rule and the restoration of Portuguese independence in 1640. Tourists of all nationalities gravitate here because the *Turismo* is housed within the **Palácio Foz** on the west side of the square, facing the main Post Office.

The tree-lined **Avenida da Liberdade**, running north of the Praça dos Restauradores, is a wide boulevard dotted with statues and fountains and some of Lisbon's top hotels. It stretches for a stately 1,500 m (about a mile), and sloping uphill, culminates at the **Praça Marquês de Pombal**, a circular intersection with a statue of the marquis. To its rear is the **Parque Eduardo VII**, a charming mixture of formal and informal gardens, well worth a visit not only for the sweeping view it commands over the city, but also for its *estufas*, or greenhouses. The **Estufa Fria** and the **Estufa Quente (** (21)385-0408 ("cool" and "hot" respectively) serve as unexpected refuges of exotic tropical and subtropical plants.

The Castelo de São Jorge and the Alfama
Overlooking all is the imposing Castelo de São Jorge, its battlements crowning the steep hill east of the Baixa. (If you don't feel up to the arduous walk, take a taxi or bus up to the castle, and then explore the environs at an

The Castelo de São Jorge, with its landscaped terraces and fountains, overlooks Lisbon and the Tagus.

Lisbon and Environs

easier downhill pace.) This is the historical heart of Lisbon, the hilltop having first been colonized by the Phoenicians, and then later fortified by the succession of Romans, Visigoths, Moors, and Portuguese kings, and around which the city expanded.

The castle and ramparts have been heavily restored, and the medieval quarter of **Santa Cruz** huddles within its outer walls. The grounds have been landscaped and the castle ruins are surrounded and interspersed with lawns, fountains and pools, the domain of peacocks, swans, and other fowl. *Lisboêtas*

and tourists alike come here to sit on the terraces and feast on magnificent views over the city and the Tagus River.

After the castle, wander through the Alfama. Much of this quarter, a maze of narrow, winding lanes and alleys clinging to the hillside survived the earthquake. Once an area of rich mansions, it is now a poor quarter where small squares and churches crowd the steep slopes, and wrought-iron balconies are adorned with flowers, laundry, and caged canaries. The area is a hive of activity in the mornings when the *varinhas* (fisherwomen)

come here to sell the freshly caught fish, and in the evening, and really on into the late night, this is where the authentic *fado* music fills the *adegas*.

Stop for a while at the **Miradouro de Santa Luzia**, a small square close to the church of Santa Luzia where a terrace has been constructed on the Moorish fortifications, and enjoy the views across the terracotta-tiled rooftops to the Tagus and port below. There's a map on the street wall to help you find your way down through the maze of streets and passageways.

Around Alfama

Just west of the Alfama district, is the **Sé Patriarcal ℂ** (21) 886-6752, the imposing twelfth-century Romanesque cathedral that was Lisbon's first church. Having suffered extensive damage during the earthquakes of 1344 and 1755, it has undergone extensive reconstruction, the result of which is a patchwork of architectural styles, making the interior a little disappointing. The cloister contains pieces of Roman masonry unearthed during the work but for many, the fourteenth-century tombs of Lopo Fernandes Pacheco and his wife are the highlight. Both depict a gentle domesticity — a husband, a wife, and the family dogs. There is a chapel with a baroque nativity scene by one of Portugal's most famous sculptors, Machado de Castro. The cloisters are open from 9 AM to noon and from 2 PM to 6 PM; closed on holidays.

East of the Castelo de São Jorge lies **São Vicente de Fora ℂ** (21) 886-2544, a sixteenth-century domed Renaissance church and former monastery commissioned by Portugal's Spanish king Philip II. The cloisters are tiled with hundreds of thousands of *azulejos* depicting scenes from La Fontaine's fables, and the chapel is home to not quite as many tombs of the extensive House of Braganças. The crypt of King Carol II of Rumania, who lived in exile at nearby Estoril, is also here. Open from 9 AM to noon and 3 PM to 6 PM; closed on Mondays.

Further east of the Alfama in the Xabregas district and closer to the Tagus is the **Igreja da Madre de Deus** (Church of the Mother of God) with its **Museu Nacional do Azulejo** (National Azulejo Museum) ℂ (21) 814-7747, Rua Madre de Deus No. 4, both well worth

Ride the ornate iron elevator up to Largo do Carmo ABOVE to see the world at your feet, or simply stroll Lisbon's streets to admire the beautiful *azulejo* tile paintings OPPOSITE.

a visit. *Azulejos* are the distinctive glazed tiles, which were a feature of Islamic architectural embellishment and which the Portuguese encountered during their conquest of Ceuta on the Mediterranean coast of Morocco. They then adapted the designs and manufactured them to their own taste. Early styles often included blue and yellow glazes, but eventually the blue and white of the imported Delftware superseded this. The tiles either form descriptive murals, such as one in the church that depicts the biography of Saint Francis, or are purely decorative bands and

panels. The museum presents a cogent display of the stylistic evolution of *azulejos* from the fourteenth century to the present day. Of special interest are those portraying Lisbon in its pre-earthquake splendor. Open from 10 AM to 6 PM Wednesdays to Sundays, 2 PM to 6 PM Tuesdays, closed on Mondays and holidays. Admission is free on Sundays until 2 PM.

Bairro Alto

West of the Baixa and looking across to the Alfama is the Bairro Alto (Upper City) district. To get there you can walk uphill through the Chiado shopping area, or take the funicular tram either from Calçada da Gloria by the Praça dos Restauradores up to Rua São Pedro d'Alcântara, or from the Calçada do Combro to the Rua do Boavista. A quicker option is to ride up to the Largo do Carmo in the **Elevador de Santa Justa** that is just off the Rua do Ouro (7 AM to 11 PM),

The Manueline architecture of the Mosteiro dos Jerónimos bursts with the exuberance of Portugal's great Age of Discovery.

an elaborate and very comfortable wrought-iron elevator that was built by a student of Gustave Eiffel.

The Bairro Alto, with its Bohemian reputation and cafés, attracts both tourists and the local chic and remains Lisbon's most appealing district. In the early sixteenth century, aristocratic families settled up here, but although many buildings survived the 1755 earthquake, the district's fortunes declined and it became a venue for writers and artists. In spite of the hilly terrain, the streets are straight and narrow and lined with wine shops, cafés, bars, *fado* clubs, restaurants, art galleries, and bookshops. It is the center of Lisbon nightlife and stays awake until the early hours of tomorrow.

On a steep hill at the top exit of the Elevador de Santa Justa is the rather dour shell of the fourteenth-century **Convento do Carmo**, founded by a military leader in honor of a vow he made at the Battle of Aljubarrota. During the earthquake the roof caved in on the congregation, leaving standing only some walls, some arches, and the flying buttresses. Today, this ruin, with the sight of its startling exposed sky, houses the small **Museu Arqueológico** ((21) 346-0473. Summers, open 10 AM to 6 PM; the rest of the year, 10 AM to 1 PM and 2 PM to 5 PM.

From here it is a short walk to the Rua São Pedro d'Alcântara and the **Igreja de São Roque**, a late sixteenth-century church founded by the once-powerful Jesuits and designed by Felipe Terzi (also the architect of the Igreja de São Vicente). Despite sustaining damage to its façade, it survived the earthquake, and behind the somewhat clumsily restored exterior lies surprising opulence including painted Italianate ceilings, fine *azulejos*, and a series of side chapels. But what draws visitors here is the **Capela de São João Baptista** (fourth to the left of the altar), legendary for its phenomenal cost to construct. In 1742, King João V commissioned the chapel to be built by Luigi Vanvitelli in Rome, and upon completion, it was consecrated by the Pope, dismantled, and then transported to Lisbon. An extravagant creation with columns of lapis lazuli, angels of white Carrara marble and ivory, walls and floors covered in mosaics, ceilings and capitals of gold and silver, the chapel's equally

extravagant treasures are displayed in the **Museu de São Roque** ((21) 323-5000, adjoining the church. Opening hours are from 10 AM to 5 PM; it is closed on Mondays and holidays.

After visiting São Roque you can stroll around the **antique shops** of Rua São Pedro d'Alcântara, or partake in the refined pleasures of the **Solar do Vinho do Porto** (Port Institute) ((21) 342-3307 at Rua São Pedro de Alcântara No. 45, open from 10 AM to midnight, Monday through Saturday. Here you can relax in easy chairs in the grandeur of an eighteenth-century mansion and order a glass of port from an exhaustive list of varieties.

Between the Rossio and the Praça Luís de Camões is the **Chiado**, Lisbon's most chic shopping area. It lies on the Rua do Carmo, and extends from the Rossio, centering on the Rua Garrett to the Largo do Chiado, encompassing boutiques, bookstores, *pastelarias*, and Lisbon's few department stores. In 1988 a fire that started in the Rua do Carmo devastated the area, destroying a large number of beautiful old shops including Grandela, one of Europe's oldest department stores. Be sure to visit **A Brasileira** ((21) 346-9541, Rua Garrett No. 120, an art nouveau café that has become a Lisbon institution. It was once the meeting place of the literati; today, its clientele is an amalgam of students, artists, locals, and tourists. The great twentieth-century Portuguese poet, Fernando Pessoa, sits among sidewalk tables in the form of a bronze statue.

Belém

The riverside district of Belém (meaning Bethlehem) is about six kilometers (four miles) from the center of Lisbon. To get there take a tram or bus from the Praça do Comércio or an inexpensive taxi-ride. There are several museums here and two major sights not to be missed: the Torre de Belém and the Mosteiro dos Jerónimos, both exceptional examples of the uniquely Portuguese Manueline style.

The majestic **Mosteiro dos Jerónimos** (Hieronymite Monastery) ((21) 362-0034 was built in jubilant thanksgiving for Vasco

The Torre de Belém was built in the early sixteenth century to defend the delta.

da Gama's discovery of the Spice Route to India. It was worked on by a succession of architects, initially the Frenchman Boytac who began the work in 1502, followed by the Spanish-descended João de Castilho. The result is one of Portugal's greatest and most original architectural achievements: a subtle fusion of Gothic and Renaissance styles stamped with Manueline ornamentation, rich in seafaring motifs and other images evocative of the Voyages of Discovery.

In the southern façade stands a grand doorway surrounded by a mass of elaborately carved stonework featuring the figure of Henry the Navigator; its church of **Santa Maria** has an interior of somber magnificence. Slender, delicately-sculpted columns support a fan-vaulted ceiling that rises to a height of 75 m (246 ft) over the three aisles. The lower chancel contains the tomb of the national hero Vasco da Gama and a monument to the poet of the Portuguese epic *Os Lusíadas*, Luís Vaz de Camões. Camões' body is not interred here: in good artistic tradition he died in poverty and was likely buried in an unmarked pauper's grave. The cloisters are magnificent, each column differently carved with coils of rope, sea monsters, coral, and the like. Opening hours are from 10 AM to 1 PM and from 2:30 PM to 5 PM (until 6:30 PM in the summer months). There are other museums in and around the monastery, but my advice is to proceed first to the Monument to the Discoveries and the Torre, and if afterward, you still have energy, drop in before returning to Lisbon.

Across the road from the monastery and overlooking the Tagus is the **Padrão dos Descobrimentos** (Monument to the Discoveries). Shaped like a ship's prow, the figures of those who played a major role in the Voyages of Discovery are sculpted on it. Prince Henry the Navigator heads the procession, and alongside him stands Vasco da Gama brandishing his book. The ground before it is inlaid with a huge mosaic compass and a map of the world in colored marble with the dates of the Discoveries. Inside the monument is a museum and an elevator that goes to the top, for some extraordinary vistas of the Tagus and Belém. The elevator and

museum ((21) 301-6228 are open from 9 AM to 6 PM (until 7 PM in the summer), but closed on Monday.

From here, if you walk westward to the **Torre de Belém**, you will come across the oddly situated **Museu de Arte Popular** (Museum of Folk Art) ((21) 301-1282, a good place to study traditional handicrafts, or if you are considering some quality souvenirs of Portugal. Beyond it, the magnificent Torre appears before you like a mirage. The Torre is five stories high with loggias at the third level. In front of it projects an artillery platform, producing a slightly nautical effect. It was built in 1515 in Gothic style with delicate Moorish embellishments. In fact, when the tower was constructed, it stood in the river, but because of land reclamation it is

now on dry land. This was the send-off point for many of the discovery voyages, and for the sailors, it became a symbol of the beloved homeland that they longed for. The tower ((21) 362-0034 is open from 10 AM to 5 PM (to 6:30 PM in the summer), and closed on Mondays. Admission is free on Sundays until 2 PM.

The **Museu da Marinha** (Maritime Museum) ((21) 362-0010 is housed in the west wing of the monastery (an incongruous nineteenth-century addition) displaying every imaginable kind of vessel, from warships to fishing boats as well as beautiful scale models of ships, old sea charts (some of them reproductions), and the royal barges. The twentieth century is also on display in exhibits such as that of the first seaplane

The Tagus

For a different perspective of the city, take a ferry trip across the Tagus. It runs from Cais do Sodré or the Praça do Comércio to **Cacilhas** on the south bank, where a view of Lisbon and lunch can be combined in one of the many fish restaurants. The journey takes approximately 10 minutes each way. If you prefer a longer and more leisurely journey, TransTejo ((21) 887-5058 can take you on a two-hour scenic trip or a romantic evening cruise. Boats leave from the Praça do Comércio.

The **Ponte 25 de Abril** suspension bridge spans the Tagus and at 2,278 m (one and a half miles), it is longer than San Francisco's Golden Gate Bridge and has the longest central span of any bridge in Europe. It offers some spectacular views of Lisbon, especially if you're not driving, and brings you within a couple of miles of the monument of **Cristo-Rei**, a scaled-down version of the statue of Christ in Rio de Janeiro. The bridge has an elevator that will take you to the top.

Elsewhere in Lisbon

The **Museu Calouste Gulbenkian** ((21) 795-0236, Avenida de Berna No. 45, has been heralded as one of Europe's finest private art collections now on public display. Located in the Saldanha district, it is within walking distance of the Pombal monument. Calouste Gulbenkian was an eccentric Armenian oil tycoon who lived in Portugal from 1942 until his death in 1955 and bequeathed his fortune and superb art collection to the Portuguese nation. The Gulbenkian Foundation has been a major supporter of the arts and has concert and exhibition halls within the foundation building, a symphony orchestra, ballet and choral companies, and libraries. It also funds artistic endeavors throughout Portugal.

Housed in a cool, modern building set in gardens, the museum's original art collection consisted of approximately 3,000 works, many of which were bought in the 1920s from the Hermitage in St. Petersburg when the former Soviet Union was particularly in need of foreign currency. More works have been added since Gulbenkian's death. There are

to make a crossing of the South Atlantic. Opening hours are from 10 AM to 5 PM, closed Mondays.

An annex to the monastery houses the **Museu Nacional de Arqueologia e Etnologia** (Archaeological and Ethnological Museum) ((21) 362-0000, with its collection of artifacts dating from prehistoric to Roman times. Open Wednesdays to Sundays from 10 AM to 6 PM; Tuesdays from 2 PM to 6 PM; closed Mondays.

Close by is the **Museu Nacional dos Coches** (National Coach Museum) ((21) 361-0850, appropriately housed in what was once the Royal Riding School. The collection is generally considered the world's largest and best. Hours are 10 AM to 6 PM; closed on Mondays. Admission is free on Sunday.

Contemporary monuments and structures along the Tagus serve as constant reminders of Portugal's relation to the sea.

collections of ancient art dating from 2700 BC, oriental art, Islamic works, and a stunning collection of Hellenic coins. An eclectic array of European paintings spans the medieval period to the nineteenth century, and includes Flemish and Dutch pictures by Van der Weyden, Rembrandt, Rubens, as well as works by English artists Gainsborough and Turner. The French are represented by Manet, Degas, Renoir, and Rodin. One room is devoted to the French art nouveau decorative artist Lalique, who was a personal friend of Gulbenkian. The museum is open from 10 AM to 5 PM but closed on Mondays; admission is free on Sundays.

In the grounds of the foundation is the **Centro de Arte Moderna** (Center of Modern Art) ((21) 795-0241, Rua Dr. Nicolau Bettencourt, with its modern Portuguese works by Edouard Viana, Amadeo de Souza Cardoso, Paula Rego, Maria Helena Vieira da Silva, Almada Negreiros, and others. The center is open Tuesdays through Sundays 10 AM to 5 PM, and Saturdays 10 AM to 7 PM; closed on Mondays. The foundation, incidentally, has a very good but busy self-service restaurant.

A little further north, the **Museu Nacional do Traje** (National Costume Museum) ((21) 759-0318 is housed in a seventeenth-century palace in Largo Julio de Castilho, in the Lumiar district. There are excellent displays of eighteenth-century gowns, wedding dresses, accessories, traditional costumes, and very old fabrics. Opening hours are from 10 AM to 6 PM; closed on Mondays.

Moving south to the Lapa district, a seventeenth-century palace has been converted and extended to house the **Museu Nacional de Arte Antiga** (Museum of Ancient Art) ((21) 396-4151, Rua das Janelas Verdes No. 9. The third floor is devoted to Portuguese art of the fifteenth and sixteenth centuries, dominated by the polyptych by Nuno Gonçalves dating from around 1470. It depicts the Adoration of Saint Vincent, patron saint of Lisbon; famous people of the time also appear in the painting, including the artist himself. On the first floor of the museum are works by foreign painters including Bosch, Holbein, Dürer, Piero della Francesca, and Zurbarán. There are also collections of ceramics, carpets, porcelain, and gold and silverware. Open Wednesdays to Sundays from 10 AM

to 6 PM and Tuesdays from 2 PM to 6 PM, but closed on Mondays. Admission is free on Sunday mornings.

If you are intrigued by the contemporary art life of Lisbon, visit the recently opened **Museu do Chiado** ((21) 343-2148, Rua Serpa Pinto No. 4, where not only are Portuguese artists dating from 1850 to 1960, and stretching the scope from Romanticism to the Abstract exhibited, but there are also frequently changing shows of current artists. The museum is open Wednesdays through Sundays from 10 AM to 6 PM, and Tuesdays from 2 PM to 6 PM. Closed Mondays and holidays.

Expo '98 has come and gone, and although the general consensus is that it was a financial disaster, it has left in its wake some positive changes. The most dynamic, of course, is the site itself. The **Parque dos Nações** ((21) 891-9333 E-MAIL info@parquedasnaccoes.pt WEB SITE www.parquedasnacoes.pt is a vast urban park that stretches along Lisbon's northeastern riverside, and in addition to the countless restaurants and "food stalls," there are art galleries, music halls (Bob Dylan chose this for his most recent Lisbon stop), virtual-reality pavilions, theaters for dance and drama, playgrounds, and a circus center. Many other events are held here, whether they be stamp collecting or a boating/yacht fair. The Lisbon tourist office distributes a monthly calendar of events.

SPORTS

Soccer enthusiasts may dare to venture attending a match of one of Lisbon's two primary teams. Benfica is the best known, and its home matches are held at the huge Estádio da Luz ((21) 726-0321, Avenida General Norton Matos. Sporting Clube de Portugal makes its home at Estádio do José Alvalade ((21) 751-4068. Soccer season runs from September through May, and the *A Bola* newspaper for upcoming matches. As many fans hold season tickets, it may be difficult to by a single one. Try the ticket kiosk in the Praça dos Restauradores, or as a final resort, the ticket offices at the stadiums.

Wandering Lisbon's neighborhoods is a continual journey through the centuries. The sleek modern scene can give way to Old World charm in a matter of steps.

Horse racing is another popular spectator sport here, and if interested you should go along to the Campo Grande Hippodrome, near the city university.

Tennis enthusiasts will find courts in Monsanto Park and near the Campo Grande. For details regarding the Centro de Ténis de Monasanto, phone ((21) 363-8073. The Campo Grande facility is open from 9 AM to 8 PM and must be visited for information.

There are several municipal **swimming** pools in Lisbon, all of which are open regular hours, seven days a week. Try the Piscina

celain are all particularly good buys. The Portuguese are wonderful jewelers, and both their solid and filigree work have taken off in new directions, with some younger craftspeople creating beautiful modern pieces. Of course, works in the more traditional mode are still being made, and are still of the same high quality. The industry is highly regulated by the government, which requires that gold contain a minimum of 19¼ karats.

One of the two main shopping areas in central Lisbon is the **Chiado** area west of the Rossio and centering around the Rua do

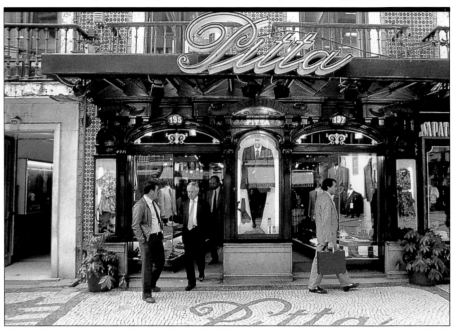

de Penha de França ((21) 812-5000, Calçada do Poço dos Mouros No. 2, or if you are near the Praça dos Restauradores, the Piscina do Ateneu ((21) 342-1365, Rua Portas de Santo Antão No. 102. There is also the Piscina do Areeiro ((21) 848-6794 on the Avenida de Roma.

SHOPPING

Lisbon's shops are stocked with an extensive range of the country's craftwork, but if you intend to travel beyond Lisbon and don't mind lugging around your purchases, goods bought in the region where they are made are about 20% cheaper. As elsewhere in Portugal, leather goods, embroidery, and por-

Carmo and the Rua Garrett. Following the devastating fire of 1988, the area was rebuilt and many of Lisbon's most fashionable shops returned, as did a few department stores. Rua Garrett has excellent bookshops, some of which stock foreign-language books. The other main shopping district is in the **Baixa** along the Rua Augusta (now a pedestrian mall) and the neighboring streets that form the geometric grid north of the Praça do Comércio. These roads, particularly the Rua Aurea and the Rua da Prata, are known for their jewelry shops, but for something really special go along to Rua Nova da Almada No. 9, where the **Casa Batalha**, one of the oldest jewelers in town, sells some fabulous costume jewelry.

The **Bairro Alto** is a good area for antique shopping, particularly Rua do Alecrim, Rua da Misericórdia, Rua São Pedro d'Alcântara, and Rua Dom Pedro V. The **Alfama** district holds its twice-a-week **flea market** on Tuesdays and Saturdays in the Campo Santa Clara behind the Church of São Vicente de Fora. Make what you will of its name: Feira da Ladra or Thief's Market.

Azulejos can make the ideal souvenir as well as a beautiful adornment for your home: two factories in Lisbon make these tiles in accordance with designs dating as far

make sure to visit **Vamtour** ((21) 342-4301/2, Avenida da Liberdade No. 13A, where you will find quite a selection of vintages from all the wine-producing regions of Portugal.

Most stores are open from 9 AM to 1 PM and from 3 PM to 7 PM on weekdays, from 9 AM to 1 PM on Saturdays, and are closed all day Sunday. There are exceptions and if you want late-night shopping there's a **mall** at the Rossio railway station that stays open until midnight seven days a week. Outside the city center, there's the huge **Amoreiras Center** ((21) 383-2558 on Avenida Duarte

back as medieval times. One, the **Fábrica Sant'Anna** ((21) 342-2537, has its store on Rua do Alecrim No. 95, and the other, **Fábrica Viúvia Lamego** ((21) 885-2408, is at Largo do Intendete No. 25. For some genuine antique *azulejos*, comb the shops on Rua Dom Pedro V, however be prepared for extreme fluctuation in prices.

Finding a good wine seller in Lisbon is astonishingly difficult. Small grocery shops off the main streets always have a few bottles, and although they are not usually of great quality, finds can be found. Pastry shops usually sell a limited selection of ports and Madeiras. Surprisingly, supermarket chains often provide the best selection and the best relative prices. But if you are an aficionado,

Pacheco, an ungainly post-Modernist lump of a building. This commercial center, with over 300 shops, as well as restaurants and cinemas, stays open until midnight every night.

If you are a citizen of a non-European Union country, you are entitled to a complete refund of the **VAT** (value-added tax) for any purchase over 11,700$ (US$62). So hold on to the receipts; at your point of departure they will be stamped by a customs official, and you will receive a reimbursement *on the spot* by a member of the Global Refund staff.

Lisbon's chic shopping OPPOSITE ranges from designer labels to jewelry, while bartering takes place among street venders ABOVE in the Alfama district.

ENTERTAINMENT AND NIGHTLIFE

The Portuguese daily *Diário de Notícias* has a useful listing of what's on, as does the weekly *Sete*, which comes out on Wednesday afternoons. The *Turismo* is always a good source of information, and it publishes a monthly English-language entertainment guide called *What's On in Lisbon.*

The **Teatro Nacional de Dona Maria II** ((21) 342-2210, at Praça Dom Pedro IV (the Rossio), has a season of Portuguese and foreign plays that usually runs between autumn and spring, but performances are in Portuguese. The opera and ballet season tends to run between December and June at the **Teatro Nacional de São Carlos** ((21) 346-5914, Largo São Carlos, and at the **Teatro Municipal de São Luís** ((21) 342-1279, Rua António Maria Cardoso No. 40. These stately old theaters attract top international companies. The **Fundação Calouste Gulbenkian** ((21) 793-5131, Avenida de Berna No. 45, has its own ballet company and symphony orchestra and also hosts performances by other companies and performers. Check local listings.

An elaborate **cultural center** was opened recently in Belém with two auditoriums, one seating 1,800 and the other 400. The **Centro Cultural de Belém** ((21) 361-2400 FAX (21) 361-2500 E-MAIL ccb@ccb.pt WEB SITE www .ccb.pt, Praça do Império, is Lisbon's most recent cultural addition, and a quite welcomed one at that. Almost daily it explodes with performances of dance, classical and jazz music, theater pieces, and all that is not definable. There are also art and photography exhibitions. The center's monthly calendar is available at the *Turismo.*

Lisbon has a large number of cinemas that screen foreign films in their original versions, with Portuguese subtitles. Tickets are inexpensive, seats are assigned, and there are intermissions allowing time for a drink at the bar. Eating and drinking are not allowed in the theater itself, a welcome change.

Lisbon has a booming nightlife; as is customary all over the Iberian Peninsula, people don't even consider going out before 10 PM, and the action continues on until the wee hours. The **Bairro Alto**, the hilltop district that rises to the west of the Rossio is, with-

out question, Lisbon's late night center. (Nowhere else would you find a Rua do Vinho — "Wine Street.") The best way to experience, and more, enjoy this neighborhood is to meander through its streets and drop into whatever bar(s) and restaurant(s) catch your eye, ear, and heart. On first glance, the overall image might appear quite young, but one of the most attractive aspects of the area is its extensive and natural integration. There is an unpretentious mingling of generations, races, and gender preferences.

No visit to Lisbon would be complete without an evening at a *fado* club. During dinner hours, these clubs or *adegas* usually function as restaurants where singers perform more of an "accompanying" *fado.* Then at about 10:30 PM the scene changes. Tables are cleared, and the music and drinking starts for real. Although these *adegas* are scattered throughout the older neighborhoods such as the Alfama and Lapa, most are to be found in the Bairro Alto. **Machado** ((21) 322-4640, at Rua do Norte No. 91, is popular with both tourists and *Lisboêtas*; at **Lisboa à Noite** ((21) 346-8557, Rua das Gáveas No. 69, the owner is herself a respected *fadista* who occasionally gives performances at the club; and **A Severa** ((21) 342-8314, at Rua das Gáveas No. 51, is a well-known and popular spot. One of the foremost (some say it's the best) is **Senhor Vinho** ((21) 397-2681 in the Lapa district at Rua do Meio à Lapa No. 18, while over in the Alfama close to the docks there is the somewhat less touristic **Parreirinha de Alfama** ((21) 886-8209, Beco do Espírito Santo No. 1, and the more upscale **João da Praça** ((21) 888-2694, Rua João da Praça Nos. 92/94.

Regardless of the hour, much time is passed in Lisbon cafés, where you will get as much of a sense of local rhythms as you will in any club. Neighborhood haunts are everywhere (and venturing in is highly suggested), but some cafés deserve special mention. At the almost-century-old **Café A Brasileira** ((21) 346-9541, Rua Garrett No. 120, you can enjoy a melange of students, tourists, and aging devotees, which in fact is the ambience of the Bairro Alto itself. **Bachus** ((21) 342-2828, at Largo da Trindade No. 9, is a very chic but friendly spot that serves food at the bar under the shimmer of candlelight. At the **Pavilhão Chinês** ((21) 342-4729,

Rua Dom Pedro V No. 89, you can enjoy a drink surrounded by chinoiserie and shoot pool. Facing the Praça Rossio is one of Lisbon's most renowned institutions. **Café Nicola** ((21) 346-0579, Rua 1 de Dezembro No. 20, was born in 1929 (as they like to say), and although its sidewalk tables offer a view of the congestion, inside is far better for people-watching. Lunchtimes it almost has the feel of a Paris *bistro*, both in terms of cuisine and clientele. The **Pastelaria Suiça** ((21) 321-4090, Praça Dom Pedro IV No. 96, does not have the historical lineage of Nicola, but

For music and dancing, again the Bairro Alto has several places to offer. Music from Cape Verde plays live at **Lontra** ((21) 369-1083 at Rua São Bento No. 155, and **Café Be Bop** ((21) 342-1626, Rua Luz Soriano No. 18, plays jazz with an afro-Latin bent and serves a cuisine to match. The lively **Gaffiera** ((21) 342-5953, on Calçada de Tijolo No. 8, has live Brazilian music, and down near Cais do Sodré, **The Jamaica** ((21) 342-1859, Rua Nova do Carvalho No. 6, plays recorded rock and reggae music. Moving upmarket but staying dockside is **Banana Power** ((21) 363-1815

just walking by will assure you that they bake their pastries on the premises.

For cool sophistication, have a drink at the **Sheraton Hotel's rooftop Panorama Bar**, Rua Latino Coelho No. 1. But for sheer elegance, sip a cognac in the one of the grand salons of the turn-of-the-century **Hotel Avenida Palace** ((21) 346-0151, Rua 1 de Dezembro No. 123.

Returning to the future, you might want to stop in at **Cyber.bica** ((21) 342-1707, Rua António Maria Cardoso E-MAIL cyberbica @cyberbica.com WEB SITE www.cyberbica .com is more than a cybercafé. Along with a few computers, it serves good inexpensive pizzas and has one of the more extensive beer menus in town. English is well spoken.

at Rua de Cascais No. 51 in the Alcântara district, an exclusive spot with a restaurant.

For the latest in African-influenced discos, go to **Leza** ((21) 396-4331, Largo do Conde Barão No. 51A. Doors don't open until 11:30 PM and don't close until 5 AM.

The Lisbon docks is absolutely the *in* area, and the plethora of bars and clubs certainly serves as supporting evidence. Avenida 24 de Julho is lined with discos and clubs. The clientele is young, and gay, straight or mixed. A brief stroll will enlighten.

But the two trendiest places at the moment remain **Fragil** ((21) 346-9578, at Rua

Lisbon's nightlife stays alive until the early hours with *fado* singing mainly in the Bairro Alto district and in nightclubs around the Alfama.

da Atalaia No. 126, where a mixed gay and straight crowd dance until they spill out on to the street, and **FrágiLUX (** (21) 888-0135, Avenida Infante Dom Henrique, which is across from the Santa Apolónia train station. Naturally, these are the type of places that come and go quickly.

WHERE TO STAY

Luxury

For grandeur, splendor, luxury and extravagance, there is nothing that remotely compares with the **Hotel Avenida Palace (** (21) 346-0151 FAX (21) 342-2884, Rua 1 de Dezembro No. 123, 1200 Lisboa, centrally located in the Praça dos Restauradores. During World War II the Palace was a hotbed of espionage, and there once was even a secret exit to the Rossio Station. More recently, it has been elegantly refurbished and upgraded to a five-star hotel replete with modern conveniences, without losing any of its magic and charm.

Some may disagree and insist that there are no greater accommodations to be had than in the **Lapa Palace (** (21) 395-0005 FAX (21) 395-0665, Rua da Bandeira No. 4, 1249 Lisboa. Formerly a nineteenth-century private palace situated on what would be sprawling grounds even if they weren't within a capital city, the hotel recently underwent major renovations. Perhaps the best suggestion is to "bookend" your trip to Portugal with a stay at both the Palace and Lapa.

The Four Seasons **Hotel Ritz (** (21) 383-2020 FAX (21) 383-1783 E-MAIL lisha@fourseasons.com WEBSITE www.fourseasons.com, Rua Rodrigo da Fonseca No. 88, 1099 Lisboa, is a large, modern five-star hotel built in the 1960s. The heavily-marbled interior is tastefully decorated with tapestries, sculptures, and a vast array of other works of art. Some of the airy guest rooms have terraces overlooking the Eduardo VII Park, and the suites are exceptional.

Next door is **Le Meridien Park Atlantic Lisboa (** (21) 381-8700 or (21) 382-0900 FAX (21) 389-0500, Rua Castilho No. 149, 1099 Lisboa. Facing the Eduardo VII Park with excellent views of the river and city, and

outstanding luxury service, this new building contains restaurants, a health club, a business center, and shops.

On Lisbon's main street, the **Hotel Tivoli Lisboa (** (21) 319-8900 FAX (21) 319-8950, Avenida da Liberdade No. 185, 1269 Lisboa, has an impressive range of facilities, including a health club, tennis court, and a swimming pool set in a garden.

The **Tivoli Jardim (** (21) 353-9971 FAX (21) 355-6566, Rua Júlio César Machado, 1250 Lisboa, around the corner and behind the Tivoli Lisboa, is managed by the same company. One star less than its five-star cousin, it is also considerably less expensive, but offers comfort, good facilities, and the rooms at the back overlook the garden.

Mid-range

Close to the Museu de Arte Antiga, a flight of steps leads up to a seventeenth-century convent now called **York House (** (21) 396-2435 FAX (21) 397-2793, Rua das Janelas Verdes No. 32, 1200 Lisboa. This provides some of the most charming accommodation in Lisbon. Overlooking a delightful courtyard, it has 37 rooms, all exceptionally well decorated and in keeping with the period of the building. Antique furnishings, marble tiles, and polished wooden floors set a traditional, peaceful, and friendly scene. The nearby **York House Residência**, Rua das Janelas Verdes No. 47, 1200 Lisboa, is under the same management. This eighteenth-century mansion was once the home of the novelist Eça de Queiroz and has 17 rooms. Prices are slightly lower than at York House.

Hotel Veneza ((21) 352-2618 FAX (21) 352-6678, Avenida da Liberdade No. 189, 1250 Lisboa, is an old building with grand public areas and a bar. All 38 rooms have soundproofing, air-conditioning, and minibar. The advertised satellite television is not. Two well-situated hotels run by the same management and that offer impeccable modern amenities are the **Hotel Presidente (** (21) 353-9501 FAX (21) 352-0272, Rua Alexandre Herculano No. 13, 1250 Lisboa, and the **Hotel Dom Carlos (** (21) 353-9071 FAX (21) 352-0728, Avenida Duque de Loulé, 1250 Lisboa. Both three-star hotels, their accommodations are far superior than many of the same category, however, their rates are comparable.

Flower sellers, fountains, and unpretentious old cafés give busy Rossio Square a unique charm.

Two rather unusual choices each offer a completely different feel, and are highly recommended. The **Hotel Lisboa Tejo** ((21) 886-6182 FAX (21) 886-5163, Poço do Borratém No. 4, 1100 Lisboa, is both modern and quaint, and in the center of it all. Adjoining is the restaurant Casa da Mó, as well as an antique wine shop. (This is not a case of a misplaced modifier.) Also moderately priced but designated as a *residencial* rather than a hotel is **Casa de São Mamede** ((21) 396-3166 FAX (21) 395-1896, Rua da Escola Politécnica No. 159. Housed in an eighteenth-century

1951 FAX (21) 342-6617, Rua Garrett No. 108, 1200 Lisboa, has an old-fashioned feel about it despite modernization. There are around 100 rooms, some with bathrooms, and prices vary between inexpensive and mid-range. Also very central is the **Hotel Internacional** ((21) 346-6401 FAX (21) 347-8635, Rua da Betesga No. 3, 1100 Lisboa, just off the Rossio where the rooms all have bathrooms, telephones, and television. It's busy, popular for its central location, and good value.

At the top exit of the Gloria elevator in the Bairro Alto there's the **Pensão Londres**

residence, the furnishings of the guest rooms and public areas adhere to the past and present creating an unexpected respite.

The **Quinta Nova da Conceição** (/FAX (21) 778-0091, Rua Ciudade de Rabat No. 5, 1500 Lisboa, at São Domingos de Benfica, presents an interesting option—it's a guesthouse operating under the TURIHAB scheme (see under ACCOMMODATION, page 279 in TRAVELERS' TIPS). This eighteenth-century house set in a large garden offers just three rooms, and thus advanced booking is essential.

Inexpensive

In the Bairro Alto, right next to the famous Café A Brasileira, the **Hotel Borges** ((21) 346-

((21) 346-2203 FAX (21) 346-5682, Rua Dom Pedro V No. 53, 1200 Lisboa, a large, high-ceilinged townhouse with airy rooms, good views, and friendly staff.

Close to the Castelo de São Jorge, the aptly named **Pensão Ninho das Águias** (Eagle's Nest) ((21) 886-7008, Costa do Castelo No. 74, 1100 Lisboa, is a strange little place with some wonderful views over Lisbon and plenty of character. Rooms are simple but clean, and some have baths. More centrally located is the **Residência Florescente** ((21) 342-6609, Rua das Portas de Santo Antão No. 99, 1100 Lisboa, which is near the Restauradores Square. Across from the Eduardo VII Park is the brand new **Residência Avenida Parque** ((21) 353-2181 FAX (21) 353-2185

E-MAIL avenidapark.com.pt, Avenida Sidónio Pais No. 6. Some rooms have views of the park; all have private bath, television, and direct-dial telephone, and with breakfast included, this becomes a great bargain.

WHERE TO EAT

Dining in Lisbon, as in other Portuguese cities, can be an unexpected pleasure. Ingredients are superbly fresh, and although simply grilled fish and meats are generally on the menu, so are dishes of subtle com-

Also in the Bairro Alto is **Tágide** ((21) 342-0720, Largo da Academia Nacional de Belas Artes Nos. 18-20, an old townhouse with an elegant upstairs dining room with views over the Tagus and across to the Castelo. The menu is extensive, and although you will find these two classic Portuguese dishes throughout your travels, this still might be the time to order the marinated grilled kid or the pork with clams that hails from the Alentejo region. The presentation is also top-class. It is closed on Saturdays and Sundays.

plexity, the spices and sauces reflecting centuries of refinement following the Spice Trade. Reservations are advisable at all better restaurants, and essential at the top ones.

Expensive

The Bairro Alto presents an excellent range of restaurants, among them **Tavares** ((21) 342-1112, Rua da Misericórdia No. 37, is Lisbon's oldest and perhaps best-known dining spot. Although the cuisine is fine, in particular some of the seafood creations, the kitchen has been usurped in recent years by several establishments. However, nowhere else in Lisbon could you possibly dine in such eighteenth-century grandeur, having first sipped an apéritif in the small salon.

Behind the Rossio's National Theater is another of Lisbon's top restaurants, **Gambrinus** ((21) 342-1466, at Rua das Portas de Santo Antão No. 25. The menu is varied, but specializes in seafood. The kitchen is extremely good, and depending on what you order, extremely expensive. Close by is **António Clara** ((21) 796-6380, Avenida da República No. 38. Located in an art nouveau house that was once the home of a famous local architect, it is decorated with antique furniture, gilt mirrors, and frescoed ceilings. Dining is elegant and delicious. Closed on Sundays.

LEFT: Men sit chatting, usually about soccer, outside the Graça district's Nossa Senhora da Graça church. ABOVE: Kids with something else to talk about at the Festa de Santo Antonio in Lisbon.

Moderate

In keeping with its location in a residential section, **Conventual** ((21) 390-9196, Praça das Flores No. 45, is frequented primarily by Lisbon's people in the know who prefer fine cuisine to opulent surroundings. The coriander soup is vibrant green and creamy, yet extraordinarily subtle, as is the stuffed pheasant marinated in port.

Near the university just off Rua da Escola Politécnica is **Terr'à Terra** ((21) 343-0201, Rua Monte Olivete No. 32A. This is one of those restaurants you fall in love with as soon as

and Saturday lunchtime. In the neighboring Graça district near the Santa Apolónia train station, the **Restaurante O Faz Figura** ((21) 886-8981, Rua do Paraíso No. 15B, is a traditional, friendly place serving local and international fare, with a dining room overlooking the river. Closed on Sundays.

On the hillside facing the Bairro Alto, **Bachus** ((21) 342-2828, Largo da Trindade No. 9, serves continental cuisine in a congenial ambience and stays open from noon until 2 AM. Inside a converted bakery, **Pap'Açorda** ((21) 346-4811, Rua da Atalaia No. 57, is

you walk in. After the small bar area (where the waiter collects portable phones and summons guests when they receive calls), there are two adjoining dining rooms followed by an outdoor garden with a few tables. Despite the lovely blue crystal glassware, dining is informal. The house specialty is a beef filet in one of a number of sauces, however numerous seafood dishes are also delicately prepared.

Within the walls of the Castelo de São Jorge, **Michel** ((21) 886-4338, Largo de Santa Cruz do Castelo No. 5, serves excellent French food in a bistro atmosphere. The restaurant occupies three old buildings — one of which was formerly a blacksmith, as the decor suggests. Closed on Sundays

popular, with a well-patronized bar at the front of the restaurant. *Açorda* is a traditional dish that combines a bread pudding of sorts with shellfish and spices, and quite surprisingly, has a vast share of devotees. **Sua Excelência** ((21) 390-3614, Rua do Conde Nos. 40-42, offers good service and the menu includes some delicious and unusual African creations, reflecting the owner's Angolan origins. Closed during September.

Inexpensive

In the Bairro Alto, **Bota Alta** ((21) 342-7959, Travessa da Queimada Nos. 35-37, is a bistro serving regional cuisine. It's open from Monday to Saturday, and you may have to wait for a table. **O Funil** ((21) 796-6007,

Avenida Elias Garcia No. 82A, is also very popular, and justly so. During your visit to Lisbon you should try, at least once, to go to the cavernous **Cervejaria da Trindade (** (21) 342-3506, Rua Nova de Trindade No. 20C. It's an institution that has been around since the nineteenth century, and as the name suggests, a lot of beer gets tapped here. Various steak dishes are the general fare, but don't miss out on the seafood, some of which comes from their private fish farms. As it gets extremely busy, try to drop in during the off-hours. Open daily from 9 AM to 2 AM.

is offered from noon until midnight. Try the curried crawfish. More intimate is the Cape Verdian **São Cristóvão (** (21) 388-5578, Rua de São Cristóvão No. 28-30. Back down behind the theater at the north end of the Rossio, the Travessa de Santo Antão has a good selection of restaurants. One of the most popular is **Bonjardim (** (21) 342-7424, which serves local fare in slightly rustic surroundings. The roast chicken is said to be the best in town, and the smells are irresistible. This is the perfect place if you are traveling with children. There are two dining

Numerous sources say the best (and/or most inexpensive) *bacalhau* is to be had at **João do Grão (** (21) 342-4757, Rua dos Coreeiros No. 222. Portuguese waters sport infinitely better fish and this restaurant, centrally located in the Baixa, is a good place to sample inexpensive renditions.

An ideal choice for lunch if you happen to be in the area of the Sé at that hour is **Estrêla da Sé (** (21) 887-0455, Largo de Santo António da Sé No. 4. Despite its location along the tram line No. 28, this 150-year-old restaurant is not remotely touristic. Traditional fare is served in private wooden-framed booths.

The best-known African restaurant is **Velha-Goa (** (21) 390-0446, Rua Tomás de Anunciação No. 41B, where Goanese cuisine

rooms and a bar for aperitifs. Open every day from noon to 11 PM.

HOW TO GET THERE

For details of air and rail services to Lisbon see GETTING TO PORTUGAL, page 271, and GETTING AROUND, page 275 in TRAVELERS' TIPS. The **Aero-Bus shuttle** leaves the airport at 20-minute intervals from 7 AM to 9 PM, and makes several stops before it reaches the Praça do Comércio. The route is clearly demarcated at the airport stop, but to ease your

White and black cobblestones as in Lisbon's shopping district OPPOSITE are a feature of many Portuguese towns. ABOVE: The Castelo de São Jorge looms over the Alfama district.

orientation, you might want first to pick up a map at the airport's *Turismo* desk. By taxi, the airport is a 20-minute drive from the center and the fare costs approximately 2,000$ (US$10).

Several bus companies operate express services linking Lisbon with major towns and cities throughout the country. The national bus company, Rodoviária Nacional, has its main station in the Avenida Casal Ribeiro near the Saldanha metro station.

Lisbon is connected by highway to Porto, 314 km (195 miles) to the north, and to Faro, 300 km (186 miles) to the south.

AROUND LISBON

QUELUZ

Just 15 km (nine and a half miles) northwest of Lisbon, the town of Queluz is graced by the **Palácio Nacional de Queluz** (Queluz Palace) ((21) 435-0039, a pink rococo affair built in the spirit of Versailles. On the orders of the Infante Dom Pedro, the younger son of João V, work began on the palace in 1747 and was completed in 1760. It became the home of Dom Pedro's wife and niece, Queen Maria I whose reign was cut short by insanity. During the brief period of French occupation, General Junot set up headquarters here. And in the reign of King João VI, his Spanish wife Carlota Joaquina, who was also less than sound, led a life of extraordinary dissipation here while conspiring with her son and anybody else who was interested to overthrow her husband. The palace was badly damaged by fire in 1934, but has since been carefully restored.

The Queluz palace is relatively intimate in scale, and despite its surprisingly dilapidated exterior, it is still used to accommodate visiting royalty and heads of state. The highly elaborate rooms have daintily painted walls and ceilings, gilt, chandeliers, chinoiserie and eighteenth-century furnishings, although many original pieces were removed, either by the royal family as they fled to Brazil or by the French who occupied it soon afterwards. The **Throne Room**, with its mirrored walls and chandeliers, is reminiscent of the palace at Versailles and is occasionally used for banquets. A good way of savoring the

atmosphere is to attend one of the summer concerts held in the ornate **Music Room**.

The carefully tended formal gardens are an elegant composition of topiary, clipped box hedges, trees, and flowerbeds interspersed with fountains, pools, and statuary. Cages that once held wild animals for royal amusement now stand empty, but the **Grand Canal** lined with eighteenth-century *azulejos* remains.

If you wish to extend your visit and partake of regal opulence, spend a night at the **Pousada Dona Maria I** ((21) 435-6158 FAX (21) 435-6181, Largo do Palácio. The house dates from the seventeenth century, and the gourmet restaurant is considered one of Portugal's superior kitchens. Aptly named **Cozinha Velha** (old kitchen) ((21) 435-6158, it serves both Portuguese and international fare and is open daily for lunch, dinner, and tea. The palace is open from 10 AM to 1 PM and from 2 PM to 5 PM except on Tuesdays; entrance is free on Sunday mornings.

How to Get There

From Lisbon take a train from the Rossio station or ask at your hotel or the *Turismo* about bus tours. If you are driving from Lisbon, regardless of where you enter the city belt system, follow signs to Sintra, which eventually will get you on the IC19 highway that goes directly to Queluz. The route to the palace is thereafter well indicated.

SINTRA AND ENVIRONS

Lo! Cintra's glorious Eden intervenes, in variegated maze of mount and glen.
                              Childe Harold's Pilgrimage
                                          — Lord Byron

The beauty of Sintra has moved a succession of poets and writers to sing praises of its every facet. Nestled in the **Serra de Sintra**, it stands on a remote ridge rising north of the Tagus estuary, washed with Atlantic rain and covered in lush and varied vegetation. The hills are often shrouded in damp mists that seem to drift into the town, keeping it cool and verdant even at the height of summer. And even when hidden in fog, the place is magical.

The eighteenth-century Palácio de Seteais outside of Sintra is now a luxury hotel.

For centuries, Sintra has been a preferred summer retreat, as is evidenced by its palaces and grand manor houses. Even Lord Byron, who notoriously loathed the Portuguese, thought it might be one of the most beautiful villages in the world. "It contains beauties of every description, natural and artificial. Palaces and gardens rising in the midst of rocks, cataracts and precipices; convents on stupendous heights—a distant view of the sea and the Tagus."

Background

Prehistoric peoples and the Lusitani tribe lived in the area long before the Romans arrived and fell in love with it. The Romans called it the *Serra Mons Lunae* — Hills of the Moon, where they worshipped Artemis (Diana), the goddess of the moon. The Moors in turn expanded the town and rebuilt it upon the Roman foundations, leaving visible reminders of their presence. In the early fifteenth century, King João I brought Philippa of Lancaster and the court to the Palácio da Vila, which remained the favored summer residence of the royal families until the nineteenth century when Queen Maria II's consort, Dom Ferdinand, built the neighboring Pena Palace.

General Information

There is a *Turismo* ((21) 923-1157 FAX (21) 923-5176 in the center of Sintra, near the Palácio Nacional in the Praça da República. Another office is in the train station ((21) 924-1623.

What to See and Do

Sintra is really three villages, all on the north side of the Serra: the **Vila Velha** (Old Town), the modern **Estefânia**, and **São Pedro**, which is furthest up the escarpment. At the center of the Vila Velha is the **Palácio Real** ((21) 923-0085, a bulky, irregular building that despite its slightly gloomy exterior is well worth a visit. Built on the site of a Moorish palace, it has been added to throughout the centuries. The first major building was carried out at the behest of King João I in the late fourteenth century and was strongly influenced by Moorish taste. The interior is decorated with some exceptional polychrome *azulejos*, particularly in the **Arab Room**, as well as in the several Moorish-style courtyards. Of note are

the **Armory**, which has a domed ceiling adorned with sixteenth-century coats of arms; the **Mermaids' Room**, with its delightful pictures of sirens and ships; and the particularly grand **Swan Room**, which has a paneled ceiling painted with white swans, each with a golden crown around its neck.

Most memorable of all must be the **Magpie Room**, where the pictures have a tale to tell. João I and his English wife Philippa had set new standards of morality for the court: João himself broke with the kingly tradition of begetting bastards after his marriage. However, he was caught kissing a lady-in-waiting, and that inevitably set the court gossiping. In retaliation he had the ceiling of this room painted with magpies, one, it is said, for every lady-in-waiting, each with a

rose and the motto *por bem* ("in honor") clasped in its beak. Whether or not the king was guilty of less noble intention, the ceiling has remained a rather touching testimony both to his affection for Philippa and to his indignation. The palace operates guided tours and is open from 10 AM to 1 PM and from 2 PM to 5 PM, but is closed on Wednesdays. Admission is free on Sundays.

This attractive village has a number of antique and handicraft shops, restaurants, and cafés. The nearby **São Pedro de Sintra** holds a **Country Fair** on the second and fourth Sunday of each month, selling local produce, craftwork, antiques, and pottery. Similar but on a larger scale is the annual **Feira Grande de São Pedro** held at the end of June.

From the town center you can taxi, drive, take a calèche (at a price), or, if you are so inclined, hike up to the **Castelo dos Mouros** (Moors' Castle). If you're driving, take the Estrada da Pena, which twists and rises southward from town. Drive past the **Estalagem dos Cavaleiros**, where Byron wrote part of *Childe Harold's Pilgrimage*, and turn left at the crossroads, which will bring you to a parking lot. From here, you can walk up to the ruins of this Moorish fortress. Built between the eighth and ninth centuries, its crenellated walls and towers have been partially restored. You can climb a staircase to the top of the

The Palácio Real at Sintra was a favorite retreat for Portuguese royalty from the fourteenth century, with successive monarchs adding their own architectural flourishes.

main tower for some sweeping views over Sintra and its *quintas*, or country houses, which oversee the coast and beyond. Admission is free and the opening hours are from 9 AM to 5 PM (6 PM in the summer).

Back at the parking lot, an iron gateway leads to the lovely **Pena Park**. You can drive through it, though a walk is more rewarding. Above stands the much photographed **Palácio da Pena** (Pena Palace), an architectural nightmare constructed in a melange of Bavarian, Moorish, Russian, Renaissance, Gothic, and Manueline styles, with superb panoramic views of the countryside and coastline. It was the brainchild of King Ferdinand of Saxe-Coburg-Gotha, Queen Maria II's German consort, who engaged one of his countrymen, Baron von Eschwege, to begin work on it in 1840. A sixteenth-century Hieronymite monastery once occupied the site but was destroyed by the 1755 earthquake, although some ruined cloisters and a chapel still stand in the palace grounds. The chapel contains an alabaster and marble altar by Nicolas Chanterene, whose work you may already have admired at Lisbon's Mosteiro dos Jerónimos.

Inside the palace things have been left as they were when the last Portuguese royal family fled the country. Little everyday items are scattered through the rooms, giving an intimate picture of the royal lifestyle. Visits of King Ferdinand's private chamber, decorated with paintings of nude women, all of whom are said to have been acquaintances of his, are now possible. The palace ((21) 923-0227 is open from 10 AM to 1 PM and from 2 PM to 5 PM, but is closed on Mondays.

Just outside Sintra, along the road that leads to Colares, is the **Palácio de Seteais**, now a luxury hotel. The name means Palace of Seven Sighs referring either to the beauty of the surroundings, or possibly to the despair of the Portuguese when French and English generals signed the Convention of Sintra here in 1809, granting the French safe passage out of Portugal with their loot. The palace, built in 1787 for a Dutch merchant, is decorated with frescoed walls and ceilings.

About four kilometers (two and a half miles) along the road from Sintra to Colares is the **Quinta da Monserrate**, a fanciful pseudo-Moorish villa built by the English-

man Sir Francis Cook in the mid-nineteenth century. It stands on the site of a house once occupied by another English eccentric, the millionaire writer William Beckford, who imported a flock of sheep from England to remind him of his home in Fonthill. The **botanical garden** ((21) 923-0137 and its adjoining greenhouse are paradisiacal. Open from 9 AM to 5:30 PM April to November and until 4:45 PM the rest of the year.

Continuing along the road, **Colares** lies nine kilometers (five and a half miles) from Sintra. This charming old hillside village with its winding lanes has Moorish arches, a square, and vineyards of particular interest to wine enthusiasts. In the latter half of the nineteenth century, the root-eating phylloxera beetle that destroyed most European vines, necessitating replanting with vines grafted on to tougher American rootstock, was however impotent in sandy Colares. Thus, the vines here are still wholly European. The output is small and Colares wines are difficult to find, but visitors are welcome to visit the **Wine Lodge** on weekdays. From Colares it is only another six kilometers (four miles) to the southwesternmost point of Europe, the wild and windswept headland called **Cabo da Roca**.

Where to Stay

Top of the list has to be the **Hotel Palácio de Seteais** ((21) 923-3200 FAX (21) 923-4277, Avenida Barbosa do Bocage No. 8, Seteais, 2710 Sintra, an eighteenth-century palace that has been converted into a five-star hotel under the management of the Tivoli Hotels Company. Surrounded by gardens, it has an exquisite interior, tennis courts, and an outdoor swimming pool. Horseback riding tours can be arranged. Reservations are obligatory, and prices are high in the luxury bracket.

There are three particularly lovely houses in the area that offer guesthouse accommodation under the TURIHAB scheme. Close to the Quinta da Monserrate Palace there's the **Quinta de São Thiago** ((21) 923-2923, Estrada de Monserrate, 2710 Sintra, a former sixteenth-century convent that has nine rooms, one suite, a music room, and a library. The **Quinta da Capela** ((21) 929-0170, Estrada de Monserrate, 2710 Sintra, is a farmhouse-like collection of buildings offering seven airy rooms with views over the countryside, some self-catering accommodation, and a small outdoor swimming pool. In the old town itself, there's the **Vila das Rosas (** (21) 923-4216 FAX (21) 923-4216, Rua António Cunha No. 4, 2710 Sintra, a nineteenth-century villa surrounded by a garden with a tennis court, and offering four rooms. Prices are moderate.

More moderately priced is the **Hotel Central (** (21) 923-0963, Largo Rainha Dona Amélia, 2710 Sintra, in the main square across from the Palácio Nacional. It is a rambling

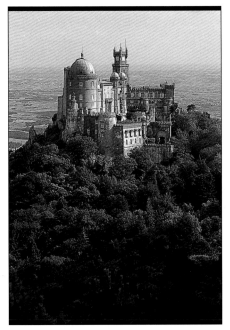

old tiled building that forms a large part of the square; the rooms, not all with baths, have simple, old-fashioned furniture. Also inexpensively priced is the **Pensão da Raposa (** (21) 923-0465 FAX (21) 923-5757, Rua Dr. Alfredo Costa No. 3, a homely old place with nine rooms. Cheapest of all is the **Pensão Nova Sintra (** (21) 923-0220, Largo Afonso de Albuquerque No. 25, a building dating from the early 1900s in the Vila Estefânia.

In Colares there's the **Pensão do Conde (** (21) 929-1652, Quinta do Conde, 2710 Sintra, an early eighteenth-century farmhouse that has been extended. Set on the slopes north of the village and surrounded by orchards, this has views of the sea and mountains. Run by an English couple, it consists of a cottage

and 10 guestrooms. The prices here are inexpensive to moderate.

Where to Eat

The setting itself would be reason enough to dine at the **Hotel Palácio de Seteais** (described above). The quality of the cuisine is also a good reason to dine here.

In the old town the best place to dine is the excellent **Tacho Real (** (21) 923-5277, Rua da Ferraria No. 4, an elegant restaurant with vaulted ceilings, tiled floors, and an extensive wine list. Both regional and international dishes are served and the prices are moderate. For inexpensive dining there are a few restaurant-bars scattered around; in Sintra itself the **Adega das Caves (** (21) 923-0848, Rua da Pendoa No. 2A, Largo da Vila Velha de Sintra, is cozy and unpretentious, as is the **Tulhas Bar (** (21) 923-2378 at Rua Gil Vicente No. 4. Right on the main square you'll see the busy **Café Paris** with its canopied pavement terrace, a good spot to sit and watch the world go by.

São Pedro has quite a few restaurants and cafés, one of the most unusual being the **Galeria Real (** (21) 923-1661, Rua Tude de Sousa. A mixture of restaurant and antique gallery, its eighteenth-century setting offers some good regional cuisine. Its prices are moderate to expensive. Also in São Pedro is the moderately-priced **Restaurante Solar de São Pedro (** (21) 923-1860, Largo da Feira No. 12, which specializes in French food, but also offers a selection of local and Italian dishes.

How to Get There

Sintra is 32 km (20 miles) northwest of Lisbon, approximately 45 minutes by train from Rossio Station. Bus service travels along the coast numerous times a day, but as train service is so extensive, buses are not recommended. The Rodoviária Nacional Gray Line service conducts sightseeing tours that take in Sintra, and from Sintra itself a Gray Line tour departs from the *Turismo* for a tour of the Mosteiro Capuchos, the Pena Palace, Colares, Cabo da Roca, and the coastline.

If you are driving from Lisbon, once you enter the city belt highway system, follow signs to Sintra. The route is clearly indicated.

Palácio da Pena rises as in a fairy tale, from Sintra's dense, green forests.

ESTORIL

Estoril is Portugal's answer to Cannes, a seaside resort with palm-lined streets bounded by flowerbeds, where spa waters and sandy beaches have attracted wealthy Europeans and Portuguese since the turn of the century. During the World War II it gained a certain cachet from exiled European royalty, heads of state, and aristocrats who resided there. Although most of the royals have left and the older villas and hotels have been overshadowed by large new complexes, Estoril remains one of the most fashionable resorts in Europe.

General Information

You'll find the *Turismo* ((21) 466-3813 across from the train station at the edge of the public park, at Arcadas do Parque.

What to See and Do

The real attractions here are the recreational facilities. The Casino ((21) 468-4521, a classy white building surrounded by carefully tended gardens in the center of the town. It has gambling machines, bingo, a cinema, restaurant, theater, night club, and of course the gaming room. The cabarets are glitzy extravaganzas that attract many big name entertainers. The casino is open from 3 PM to 3 AM; photo ID and proof that you are over 18 years old are required.

The Clube de Golf do Estoril ((21) 468-0176, Avenida da República, has what is said to be one of the most beautiful golf courses in Europe. Its nine- and 18-hole courses are used for international championships. Golfers can also go to the nine-hole Estoril-Sol Golf Course ((21) 923-2461 at Linhó, off the road to Sintra. Tennis enthusiasts frequent the Clube de Ténis do Estoril ((21) 466-2770, Avenida Amaral, Estoril, or one of the other numerous courts in town. Horseback riding is quite a serious sport in this region and the Centro Hípico da Costa do Estoril ((21) 487-2064, Charneca, is one of the more renowned outfits. For water sports, there's the International Windsurfing School ((21) 268-1665, but beware of swimming: this part of the coast has suffered badly from pollution, so check the posted signs before rushing in for a dip.

Estoril is the venue for the Portuguese Formula One Grand Prix motor race at the Autodromo and draws big crowds, as does the annual Rallye de Portugal do Vinho de Porto (Port Rally) that also begins and ends at the Autodromo.

Where to Stay

You would expect Estoril to have plenty of hotels, and most are large, modern establishments with three- or four-star ratings. Surprisingly, though, the only five-star hotel is the show-stealing Hotel Palácio ((21) 468-0400 FAX (21) 468-4867 E-MAIL palacioestorial @mail.telepac.pt, Parque do Estoril, 2765 Estoril. Built in the 1930s in the grand European manner, it offers an elegance that has pleased many royal guests. Along with a swimming pool set in manicured gardens, the hotel offers guests reduced green fees at both its 18-hole and nine-hole courses. The prices are in the luxury category.

Golfing is the theme at the luxury Amazónia Lennox ((21) 468-0424 FAX (21) 467-0859, Rua Eng. Álvaro Pedro de Sousa No. 5, 2765 Estoril, which is set on a hillside close to Estoril beach. The best accommodation is inside the main building, while other rooms are in newer structures within the grounds. The hotel can arrange golfing vacation packages and offers free transportation to the Quinta da Marinha where there are riding stables and a golf course, thus adding a country club service to its friendly ambience.

Hotel Inglaterra ((21) 468-4461 FAX (21) 468-2108 E-MAIL hotelinglaterra@mail .telepac.pt, Rua do Porto No. 1, 2765 Estoril, is built around its center piece—a nineteenth-century mansion — and is a popular choice for families because it is situated only a few minutes' walk from the beach. Prices are around the higher end of mid-range. The mid-range Hotel Lido ((21) 468-4098 FAX (21) 468-3665, Rua Alentejo No. 12, 2765 Estoril, is a good value. The hillside location of this modern three-star hotel is a quiet residential area, a little way from the Casino, with simple rooms that are nonetheless equipped with telephone, satellite television, and air conditioning; a large swimming pool lies within the grounds.

At the inexpensive end of the range there is the modern Hotel Alvorada ((21) 468-0070

FAX (21) 468-7250, Rua de Lisboa No. 3, 2765 Estoril, opposite the Casino, and the older **Pensão Continental** ((21) 468-0050, Rua Joaquim Santos No. 2, 2765 Estoril.

Where to Eat

Probably the best restaurant in Estoril, and certainly the most expensive, is the **Four Seasons Grill** ((21) 468-0400, in the Hotel Palácio, Parque do Estoril No. 4. It serves a refined international cuisine, with menu changes that are in keeping with the season. As always, seafood and fish dishes are highly

Estoril. Despite its name, it serves good Portuguese and international dishes, seafood being a specialty. **Pak Yun** ((21) 467-0692, near the Casino at Centro Comércial, Estoril Parque No. 5, serves some of the best Chinese food in the area, and for Japanese cuisine, try **Furusato** ((21) 468-4430, Praia do Tamariz. Both are moderately priced. For inexpensive eating, there are plenty of pleasant cafés and snack bars scattered around the town.

How to Get There

Estoril is only 24 km (15 miles) away from

recommended, but the chef is more than adept at meat dishes. If you want to plunge into the spirit of Estoril, dine at the **Grand Salon Restaurant** in the Casino, which serves a classy cuisine in an appropriately classy setting. Expensive.

Down on the beach, almost equidistant from the Estoril and the Monte Estoril train stations (park at either if you are not trekking along the beach) is **Jonas Bar** ((21) 467-6946. The house specialty is a seafood and chicken kabob, but they also serve an array of salads and fire-grilled hamburgers. It is also one of the few places where you will here authentic jazz. Also moderately priced and in the same area is the **English Bar** ((21) 468-1254 on the Estrada Marginal in Monte

Lisbon: fast electric trains leave at frequent intervals from Lisbon's Cais do Sodré Station, stopping at Oeiras, Estoril, and sometimes continuing on to Monte Estoril, and Cascais.

If you are traveling from Lisbon by car, by far the most preferable route to this entire region is the N6. This is the road that hugs the coast along the entire peninsula. An easy spot to enter is either near the Santa Apolónia train station, or the Praça do Comércio. Alternatively, you can enter the tangle of highways that knot around Lisbon, and follow signs first to Sintra, and then turn off on to and stay on the A5 as soon as it is indicated.

Ritzy Estoril was a hotbed of espionage during World War II. Later, the resort was a repository for deposed crowned heads.

From either Lisbon or Sintra, a taxi to Estoril is not particularly expensive.

CASCAIS

Further along the coast about six and a half kilometers (four miles) west of Estoril and 29 km (18 miles) from Lisbon, Cascais is both a fishing village and a major vacation resort: such is the charm of Cascais that its popularity has begun to rival that of Estoril.

In 1879 King Luís I and his royal entourage descended on the village and spent summer in its seventeenth-century citadel, still in use as a residence for the Head of State. In the 1930s Cascais was discovered by artists and writers who delighted in its ambience.

General Information
The Turismo ((21) 486-8204 is at Rua Visconde da Luz.

What to See and Do
One of the few buildings here that did survive the great earthquake is the **Igreja de Nossa Senhora da Assunção** at the western edge of town. It particularly merits a visit for its paintings by Josefa de Óbidos, a seventeenth-century Portuguese artist. Along the road to Guincho, the **Museu de Castro Guimarães** is housed in a nineteenth-century building set in parkland, in which are displayed various antiquities well worth seeing.

But the real attraction here is the fishing port itself, where you can watch them bringing in the catch, taking it to the **Fish Market** near the Praia da Ribeira and selling it by Dutch Auction. In this the auctioneer starts off at an excessive price, dropping it until he gets an acceptance. He who offers first gets the fish.

The beaches in Cascais can be unfit for swimming because of periodic pollution: swim here only if it has been declared safe to do so. However, many of the hotels have their own pools and there are plenty of other interesting distractions. Horseback riding is on offer at the **Quinta da Marinha** ((21) 486-

9282 FAX (21) 486-9032, along the road to Guincho. Quinta da Marinha also has an 18-hole golf course that a golfing friend has assured me is one of his preferred in the world, not just for its beauty, but for the extra challenge presented by the winds. There are also tennis courts, a swimming pool, and a bar/restaurant. If scaling rocks that seem to shoot out perfectly perpendicular from the sea (or drop off into it, depending upon your perspective) tempts you, contact the **Escola de Escalada da Guia** ((21) 847-5716.

One of the best unpolluted beaches on the coast is at **Guincho**, eight kilometers (five miles) west of Cascais, sandy, beautiful and with rough sea, but popular with windsurfers. There is a windsurfing school here and several hotels, but without the big crowds you will find in Estoril and Cascais.

Where to Stay
There are plenty of accommodation in Cascais, but as in Estoril, bargains are few and far between. Because of its popularity, reservations are a good idea, if not essential.

The classiest spot in town is the well-known and ideally situated **Hotel Albatroz** ((21) 483-2821 FAX (21) 484-4827, Rua Frederico Arouca No. 100, 2750 Cascais. Situated on a rocky promontory overlooking the sea, this hotel incorporates a magnificent nineteenth-century house built for the Portuguese royal family; since operating as a hotel it has been favored by royalty and celebrities. The modern wing contains a series of balconied rooms, a swimming pool, and sun terrace. The restaurant, with its panoramic views, is the most exclusive in town (see WHERE TO EAT, below). Definitely in the luxury class.

Estalagem Senhora da Guia ((21) 486-9239 FAX (21) 486-9227 E-MAIL senhoradaguia @mail.telepac.pt, Estrada do Guincho, 2750 Cascais, is three kilometers (one mile) outside Cascais and four kilometers (two and a half miles) from Estoril, near the Quinta da Marinha with its tennis courts, riding center, and golf course. Built in traditional style this beautifully furnished house has a large saltwater pool and terrace. Prices vary between expensive and luxury. The **Estalagem Senhora das Preces** ((21) 484-0087 FAX (21) 483-1942, Rua Visconde da Gandarinha

The pretty fishing port of Cascais has become a popular tourist resort, as well as a getaway for wealthy *Lisboêtas*.

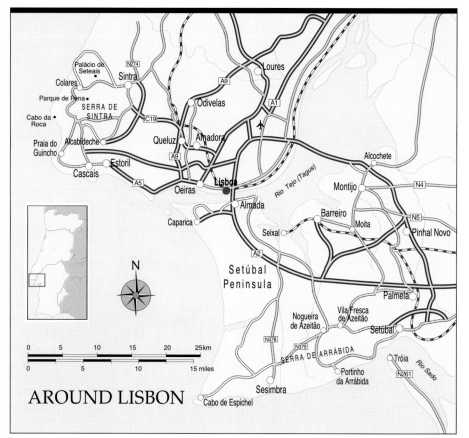

AROUND LISBON

No. 43, is close to the beach and golf courses of Cascais and combines the atmosphere of an old manor house with modern comforts. Mid-range.

An utterly unexpected delight, even once you know it's there, is the centrally-placed **Casa da Pérgola (** (21) 484-0040 FAX (21) 483-4791, Avenida Valbom No. 13. Set deep back from the street by lush gardens, what once was a private home is now one of Portugal's most charming places to stay. Guest rooms are furnished in antiques and some have wonderfully amusing tiled bathrooms. Operating under the TURIHAB scheme, there are only 10 rooms, so in almost any season, reservations are highly recommended. Mid-range prices; no parking. The **Pensão Dom Carlos (** (21) 486-8463, Rua Latino Coelho No. 8, is a restored sixteenth-century mansion with eight rooms, simply furnished and inexpensive, while the similarly priced **Albergaria Valbom (** (21) 486-5801 FAX (21) 486-5805, Avenida Valbom No. 14, is a rather

faceless modern building, but offers comfortable rooms with private bath, balcony, and telephone, and the invaluable luxury of free garage parking.

For those who prefer a more isolated setting or are mad about windsurfing, the **Hotel do Guincho (** (21) 487-0491 FAX (21) 487-0431, Praia do Guincho, 2750 Cascais, is in a seventeenth-century fort on a cliff near Cabo da Roca. The rooms are individually decorated and overlook the sea. Prices vary from mid-range to luxury.

Where to Eat

Cascais has a wide choice of good restaurants. Considering the town's popularity as a vacation resort and the reasonable prices, you are well-advised to make reservations. The best restaurant of all, and arguably of the whole Costa do Estoril, is the elegant **Restaurant Albatroz (** (21) 483-2821, Rua Frederico Arouca No. 100. Its dining room overlooks Cascais' stretch of sand, and

128

sitting on the outdoor terrace bar is almost like being on the bow of a boat. Expensive, and reservations are essential. Close to the fish market the **O Pescador** ((21) 483-2054, Rua das Flores No. 10B, is considered the best fish restaurant in town. It has a relaxed atmosphere and is expensive; reservations are essential.

Baluarte ((21) 486-5471, Avenida Dom Carlos I, is a trendy establishment that serves international dishes as well as some very good seafood at moderate prices.

For local cuisine and particularly good seafood, try **Restaurante O Batel** ((21) 483-0215, Travessa das Flores No. 4. If you like being where the action is, **Aláude** ((21) 483-0287, Largo Luís de Camões No. 8, opens on to a very busy square and offers inexpensive international cuisine in a lively atmosphere.

How to Get There

From Lisbon's Cais do Sodré station the train takes approximately half an hour to reach Cascais.

Cascais is just three kilometers (two miles) along the coastal road from Estoril, (see ESTORIL, page 124 for directions) and from Sintra is a straightforward drive along the N9. As stated above, the best route to reach any of the towns along the Costa Azul is the scenic and calm N9.

THE SETÚBAL PENINSULA

For a peaceful alternative to the busy resorts of the Estoril coast, try the Setúbal Peninsula to the south of the Tagus. The opening of the Ponte 25 de Abril has brought this region within easy reach of the city, and its clear waters with long sandy beaches have made it a popular getaway for *Lisboêtas* who refer to it as the *Outra Banda*: the other shore. Although the area does get crowded in the summer, and construction has proliferated, it remains characteristically Portuguese in temperament, contrasting greatly with the Algarve.

General Information

The *Turismo* ((21) 290-0071 at Costa da Caparica is at Avenida da República No. 18; at Sesimbra ((21) 223-5743 it's at Largo da

Marinha No. 26-27. At Setúbal the regional tourist office ((265) 539120 FAX (265) 539127 is at Travessa Frei Gaspar No. 10, and the municipal office ((265) 534222 is at the Praça de Quebedo.

What to See and Do

Along the west coast of the peninsula lies the **Costa da Caparica**, an eight-kilometer (five-mile) stretch of sandy beaches where the sea is safer and cleaner than along much of the Estoril coast. Although it is far from quiet, the beaches are considerably less crowded than those of Estoril, and the hotels and restaurants more reasonably priced.

On the south side of the peninsula the **Serra da Arrábida**, a small limestone ridge, covers the 35 km (22 miles) between Cape Espichel and Palmela, rising in a series of smooth hills to a height of 550 m (1,600 ft) then sloping down into the Atlantic, where some of the most pristine beaches and coves are to be found. Now a designated nature park, the Serra is partially covered in dense vegetation more typical of Mediterranean regions, and during springtime fields erupt in wildflowers. Their colors are stunning and their misty scent yields to the heady perfume of orange blossoms a few weeks later.

Perhaps too easily accessible for its own good, the old fishing village of **Sesimbra** lies on the southern slope of the Serra da Arrábida, just 25 km (15 miles) from Setúbal. It remains a busy fishing port packed with colorful trawlers, but unchecked development around the old town has turned Sesimbra into a crowded resort, threatening its warrens of steps and whitewashed cottages.

Heading northeastward along the N379, a turnoff to the right onto the N379-1 will take you through the Serra da Arrábida. After about four kilometers (two and a half miles) a fork in the road offers you the choice between going deeper into the Serra or going along a coastal road. To get to the small village of **Portinho da Arrábida** and to one of the most beautiful beaches in the region, bear right here and keep an eye out for the narrow turnoff down to Portinho. Unfortunately the beach is also popular during the peak summer months; bear in mind that the return trip will entail backing out in reverse up a steep, narrow road. Parking is virtually nonexistent, and its best to park by the port, and then just follow the walking masses.

Surrounded by green hills the bay, with its white sand and clear blue waters, is an idyllic place to relax and swim. Among the many caves along this stretch of coastline is the **Lapa da Santa Margarida**, one that the enraptured Hans Christian Andersen described as a veritable church. Other lovely beaches such as **Praia dos Coelhos** lie further along the coast. Access is not easy, but in part this is protects them, making it worth the climb.

Back up on the N379 along the northern edge of the Serra, vineyards, olive groves and orchards thrive, and you should stop off at **Nogueira de Azeitão**, a pleasant town to wander around. Take a look at the **Tavora Palace**, a sixteenth-century Renaissance building that once belonged to the Dukes of Aveiro, and at the tiled interior of the nearby church of **São Lourenço**. The town has a more hedonistic appeal, too: near the palace, you'll find the old nineteenth-century **José Maria da Fonseca Winery (** (21) 219-1500, and, more important, the **New Fonseca Winery (** (21) 218-0002, on the edge of town where you can tour and sample some of Portugal's best red wines and the sweet muscatel for which Setúbal is famous. Open to the public from Monday to Friday.

Close to the village of **Vila Fresca de Azeitão**, off the N10, look out for the bus station opposite which the **Quinta de Bacalhoa**, as featured on one of the famous Fonseca wine labels, lies hidden behind a wall. This beautiful Renaissance villa was built in the late fifteenth century and rescued from

dilapidation by an American woman who bought it in the 1930s. The house itself is not open to the public as the family still owns and occupies it. This whole region is prime for buying *azulejos*, and conveniently near the N10 you will find **São Simão-Arte (** (21) 218-3135, Rua Almirante Reis No. 86, Vila Fresca de Azeitão, where both contemporary and classical replicas are available.

The town of **Palmela** sits, pretty and whitewashed, in the foothills of the Serra, about 43 km (20 miles) from Lisbon and eight kilometers (five miles) north of Setúbal, overlooked by the imposing **Castelo de Palmela**, which started its days as a twelfth-century fortress, sections of which have been modified over the centuries. Some of the Moorish fortifications can still be seen, and what became the fifteenth-century monastery has now been converted into a *pousada*. The remains of the only Roman road to be unearthed in Portugal, lie behind the castle. Even if you are not staying or dining at the *pousada*, the superb views over the Serra da Arrábida and the neighboring province of Alentejo make a visit worthwhile.

Setúbal is situated on the bank of the river Sado, 48 km (30 miles) from Lisbon, a large city by Portuguese standards with a population of around 100,000. It is a fishing port and industrial city — sardine canning and car production, and is also known for its production of arguably the world's finest muscatel wine.

There are two main tourist sites here, the first being the **Igreja de Jesus** (Church of Jesus) at the Praça Miguel Bombarda, built in the Manueline stylistic period by Diogo Boytac, with a vaulted ceiling supported by six columns sculpted like twisted nautical rope. Adjoining it is a **museum** with a collection of Renaissance Portuguese paintings The second is the **Castelo de São Filipe**, high on a hill overlooking the port, this sixteenth-century castle has been transformed into a *pousada*.

In addition, Setúbal is home to several excavations of Roman ruins, one of the most fascinating is the ancient fish condiment factory that now houses the regional tourist office. Ask there for information regarding the Roman ruins of the region. Also, stop in at the **Museu de Arqueologia e Etnografia**

((265) 239365, Avenida Luísa Todi No. 162. The museum is open Tuesday through Saturday 10 AM to noon and 2 PM to 5:30 PM.

But certainly, most people visit Setúbal because of its proximity to the **Peninsula de Tróia**, a spot that has been popular since the time of the Phoenicians. Car ferries make close to 40 roundtrips a day, departing from the Doca do Comércio. Along with some fine stretches of sand and unpolluted waters, Tróia has an exceptional 18-hole golf course within the **Complexo Turística de Tróia** ((265) 44151 FAX (265) 44256, Ponta de Adoxe

Where to Stay

In Sesimbra, the **Hotel do Mar** ((21) 223-3626 FAX (21) 223-3888, Rua General Humberto Delgado No. 10, is a superlative example of resorts construction. A sprawling complex, replete with extensive sports facilities, it is perched high on a hill overlooking the beach. All rooms have private terraces, the luxury suites have Jacuzzis. Prices span from mid-range to luxury. The **Pensão Espadarte** ((21) 223-3184 FAX (21) 223-3294, Avenida 25 de Abril No. 11, 2970 Sesimbra, right on the esplanade, offers

—Herdade de Tróia, 2900 Setúbal (see WHERE TO STAY, below).

Although most visitors to the region, whether Portuguese or foreign, tend to come for the pleasures of the sea, two annual arts festivals of international status occur every spring and summer. The springtime **Festival Internacional de Cinema de Tróia** ((265) 525908 or (265) 534059 FAX (265) 525681 E-MAIL festroi@mail.telepac.pt WEB SITE www.nst.pt/festroia, Avenida Luísa Todi No. 65, 2900 Setúbal, is considered highly by members of the profession. The multi-art **Festival dos Capuchos** presents some unusual site-specific music and dance events throughout the region. For information, contact the regional tourist office in Setúbal.

simple, if somewhat worn rooms at mid-range prices.

In the Vila Fresca de Azeitão, there are several guesthouses that operate under the TURIHAB scheme, two of which have outdoor swimming pools. Both the **Quinta do César** ((265) 218-0387, Vila Fresca de Azeitão, 2925 Azeitão, and the **Quinta da Piedade** ((265) 218-9381, Casal da Portela No. 1, Piedade, 2925 Azeitão, are in the heart of the Arrábida Natural Park, and each only have four double rooms. Advance reservations are essential. Prices are mid-range.

Robust, complex Portuguese red wines OPPOSITE make for a great aged discovery. ABOVE: Barrels of port still make the journey the old-fashioned way.

On a hilltop just outside Setúbal is the **Pousada de São Filipe** ((265) 523844 FAX (265) 532538, 2900 Setúbal, which has preserved its original character without compromising comfort. Some rooms are split-level with the bedroom on the lower floor and a sitting room above. Luxury.

In the city itself is the new **Aranguês Hotel** ((265) 525171 FAX (265) 526877, Rua José Pedro da Silva No. 15, which offers services far more extensive than its three stars would indicate. Along with tastefully decorated guest rooms, there is a full spa with an indoor swimming pool, Jacuzzi, sauna, and massage rooms. Prices are mid-range. Also fine in its category is the **Residencial Setubalense** ((265) 525790 FAX (265) 525789, Rua Major Afonso Pala No. 17. Inexpensive.

Nearby the *pousada*, the **Quinta do Patrício** ((265) 338817, Ecosta de São Filipe, 2900 Setúbal, an eighteenth-century house with views over Setúbal and the Sado also participates in the TURIHAB scheme; three mid-range rooms, two in the house and one in an adjacent windmill.

On the Tróia peninsula itself you will find the sports-lovers' paradise **Complexo Turística de Tróia** ((265) 44151 FAX (265) 44256, Ponta de Adoxe — Herdade de Tróia, 2900 Setúbal. Aside from its world-renowned golf course, its sporting facilities include several saltwater swimming pools, endless water sports and tennis facilities, play areas for children, and horseback riding. Apartments are available for longer stays. Prices vary from mid-range to expensive.

In Palmela the only place to stay is the **Pousada do Castelo de Palmela** ((21) 235-1226 FAX (21) 235-1395, 2950 Palmela, built as a monastery in 1482 inside the castle walls. Skillful conversion and clever use of glass have combined to retain the feeling of cloisters while creating a comfortable environment. What used to be the monks' cells now make comfortable, large guest rooms with magnificent views. Luxury.

Where to Eat

Near the beach in Sesimbra the **Restaurante Ribamar** ((21) 223-4853, Avenida dos Náufragos, specializes in seafood and is moderately priced. In Portinho da Arrábida there are a number of beach restaurants, and at

Azeitão the **Quinta das Torres** ((265) 208-0001, Estrada Nacional 5, offers simple local cuisine in the large old dining room. In Palmela you can dine or lunch at the **Pousada do Castelo de Palmela** ((21) 235-1226, in what was once a monks' refectory. Moderate.

In Setúbal, the **Pousada de São Filipe** ((265) 532538 is a little outside of town but, worth the trip to eat in sixteenth-century surroundings. The setting of the **Restaurante Amadeus** ((265) 525912 on the shores of a lake in the middle of the Parque Bonfim is only one of the reasons to dine there. The cuisine is fine, and the service impeccable. Another very good and also moderately priced restaurant in yet another stunning setting is **Luísa Todi** ((265) 572549, Rua Nossa Senhora do Carmo. This on is high on a hill affording extraordinary views of the town. There is a plethora of inexpensive restaurants in town and **O Beco** ((265) 524617 FAX (265) 525610, Rua da Misericórdia No. 24, despite being mentioned in many guides, remains a place for quite enjoyable country cooking.

How to Get There

A ferry from the Praça do Comércio in Lisbon will take you to the Barreiro station across the river (the cost is included in the rail ticket) and from there a regular train service operates to Palmela and Setúbal. To reach the Caparica Coast, you can pick up a bus from the ferry-landing in Cacilhas on the south bank of the Tagus in Lisbon; during summer there's a narrow-gauge train to take you along the various beaches. Quicker, but not so much fun, is the bus from Lisbon's Praça de Espanha to Setúbal and Sesimbra, and there's also a service to Costa da Caparica. Local buses run between Sesimbra and Setúbal.

Driving to Setúbal from Lisbon is straightforward: after you cross the bridge, keep going on the A2-IP1. To reach the Costa da Caparica turn off at the first junction after the bridge, which will join with a coastal road. To go direct from Lisbon to Sesimbra, you need to come off the A2-IP1 at the second junction after the bridge, turning on to the N378 that runs southward.

Postcards on display in Lisbon.

Estre-
madura
and
Ribatejo

ESTREMADURA IS THE COASTAL PROVINCE northwest of Lisbon, edged with dramatic cliffs and sandy beaches and containing some outstanding monumental architecture. Much of Estremadura is within easy reach of Lisbon and can easily be visited in day trips. It also includes the Setúbal Peninsula, covered in AROUND LISBON, page 129.

The neighboring inland province of the Ribatejo, meaning "banks of the Tagus," lies in the valley of that river, for the most part on fertile alluvial plains planted with rice and grains. This is Portugal's prairie, synonymous with horse and bull breeding, and *campinos* (herdsmen) in their green stocking-caps, black pants, and red vests. Its attractions lie in the lovely town of Tomar, home of the Convent of Christ, and several small riverside villages of undisturbed beauty.

ESTREMADURA

MAFRA

Forty kilometers (25 miles) northwest of Lisbon, 18 km (12 miles) north of Sintra, Mafra is a small town overshadowed by the massive **Palácio Nacional de Mafra** ((261) 811888.

Like so many Portuguese monuments, Mafra was built in fulfillment of a vow. King João V pledged that he would build a monastery if the union with his Austrian wife was blessed with a child, and in 1717, six years and three children later, work began. The building was completed in 1735.

The cost was almost more than the country could bear. The brief had been to build something to rival Philip of Spain's El Escorial near Madrid, including a church, monastery and palace, to be paid for out of the newly discovered wealth of gold and diamonds in Brazil. Mafra almost ruined Portugal by draining not only its coffers but also the country's work force: as many as 50,000 men were employed to work on it at one point, many of whom were never paid.

Mafra's vital statistics include 4,500 doors and windows, a three-story, 220-m (722-ft)-long façade, and a total area of four hectares (ten acres). The Italianate **basilica** sits at the center of the façade, its porch filled with large Carrara marble statues. It is flanked by two long wings, each topped by a squat, rather truncated dome. Two belfries containing carillons rise over the basilica and between them carry over 100 bells that can be heard for miles around. These were made in Belgium, and when King João was told the immense cost of one set, he promptly replied, "I'll take two!" (Or so the story goes.)

To make the most use of the expertise of those summoned to work on the palace, in 1753 a school of sculpture was founded and continued to function through 1770. Today the building is primarily used by the army, only 10% of it being open to the public, although a tour still can run about one and a half hours. The highlight is the **Baroque Library**, a barrel-vaulted room 65 m (213 ft) long filled with over 35,000 volumes that date from the fifteenth through eighteenth centuries. Other areas open to the public include the pharmacy with a rather grisly array of medical instruments, the infirmary, the monks' cells, and the kitchens. Occupied by royalty into the twentieth century, the chambers are filled with antique furnishings and tapestries.

The only way to visit the Mafra palace is to join one of the guided tours that operate from 10 AM to 1 PM and from 2 PM to 5 PM Wednesday to Monday.

Near Mafra, the village of **Turcifal** makes a pleasant stop for coffee. Its streets are lined mainly with eighteenth-century buildings, and it has a church built from Mafra's left-over stone.

There is a *Turismo* ((261) 812023 in Mafra at Avenida 25 de Abril.

How to Get There

A bus service runs every hour between Lisbon and Mafra. The trip takes approximately a half an hour. There is also an hourly bus service from Sintra. For details of services check at the *Turismo* or the Rodoviária Nacional bus depot. The Rodoviária Nacional Gray Line operates sightseeing tours that take in Mafra, Sintra and Estoril. For details contact them in Lisbon at ((21) 352-2594 or 319-1090 FAX (21) 356-0668 or 316-0404 WEB SITE www .Cityrama.pt.

The continent crashes into the sea at Cabo Carvoeiro on Estremadura's rugged Atlantic coast.

If you are driving from Lisbon, take the Avenida da República from the city center, continue north out of the city and join onto the A8-IC1. About 33 km (20 miles) out of Lisbon, turn left onto the N116 to Mafra. From Sintra, Mafra is a 18-km (12-mile) drive along the N9.

IN AND AROUND ERICEIRA

The Estremadura coast is dotted with ancient and often picturesque fishing villages, as well as with modern hotels, making tourism an increasingly important alternative to income derived from traditional sea fishing. Fifty kilometers (32 miles) northwest of Lisbon along the N116 lies the small fishing port of Ericeira from which the last king and his family sailed off into exile in 1910. Perched on cliffs overlooking the Atlantic, it has four gently curving beaches, each separated from the other by rocky headlands. Its squares and narrow cobbled streets snake uphill from the harbor, lined with seafood restaurants and lively with visitors. Stroll over to the dazzling white **Hermitage of São Sebastião**, a seventeenth-century domed circular building of North African design with an *azulejos*-lined interior, which overlooks São Sebastião beach. Also on the cliff above the harbor is the **Chapel of Santo António**, which has tiles portraying the departure of the royal family.

Ericeira's highlight, however, is its surf, which was deemed sufficiently robust to earn the honor of holding the 1994 world championships. If you are traveling light, you can rent a board at **Ultimar (** (261) 62371, Rua de Outubro No. 37A.

One of the main amusements remains the **Largo das Ribas**, where you can watch the brightly-painted fishing boats return and unload their catch. The overcrowding may spoil the town for you, but you can still enjoy lunch at one of the seafood restaurants. Ericeira is famous for its many varied lobster recipes.

The *Turismo* **(** (261) 63122 is at Rua Eduardo Burnay No. 33A.

Where to Stay and Eat

The **Hotel Turismo da Ericeira (** (261) 860-4045 FAX (261) 365610, Rua Porto de Revez, 2655 Ericeira, has 200 rooms, an outdoor

swimming pool, and an acceptable restaurant. Prices are at the upper end of mid-range. The **Hotel Vilazul (** (261) 868-0000 FAX (261) 862927, Calçada da Baleia No. 10, offers good views, comfortable and inexpensive accommodation, bars, and a restaurant.

Ericeira's **O Poço (** (261) 862759, Calçada da Baleia No. 10, serves good seafood dishes and is quite inexpensive.

How to Get There

Express buses run from Lisbon to Ericeira via Mafra. By road, Ericeira lies 12 km (seven and a half miles) west of Mafra along the N116, 50 km (32 miles) northeast of Lisbon (see also NAZARÉ, below).

PENICHE AND THE BERLENGA ISLANDS

Moving north of Ericeira, and 92 km (60 miles) north of Lisbon, is Peniche, once an island but now connected to the mainland by a thin isthmus flanked by sandy beaches. This is a somewhat lackluster fishing and canning center, but it is where you can board a ferry to **Berlenga Grande**, the only one of the misty Berlenga Islands that can be visited, and which is now a bird sanctuary. Surrounded by cliffs, it is only about two and a half square kilometers (one square mile) in size, and camping is possible, or you can stay in the island's **seventeenth-century fortress**. Now a hostel, it sits on a small island connected to the main island by a stone staircase (see WHERE TO STAY AND EAT, below). It's a desolate place of black rocks that are continually pounded by the sea, and is overshadowed by the sprawling **sixteenth-century fortress**, once the Fortaleza Prison controlled by Salazar's secret police and used to incarcerate his opponents, it then became housing for Angolan refugees in the 1970s. It is now a **museum (** (262) 781848 devoted to local history.

The sandy beaches along the isthmus from Peniche have good water for surfing but not for swimming. Further north along the coast where the Óbidos lagoon meets the sea, **Praia da Foz do Arelho** is a quiet, sandy beach that can also offer the tranquil, though at times polluted, waters of the lagoon.

Fine white sand beaches skirt the Estramdura coast. Its rough waters attract surfers from around the world.

Fourteen kilometers (nine miles) further north, the village of **São Martinho do Porto** has a virtually landlocked bay, calm waters and an inviting sandy beach. It is best enjoyed off-season, however.

In Peniche there is a *Turismo* ((262) 789571 at Rua Alexandre Herculano, which also has information on the Berlenga Islands. At São Martinho do Porto, the *Turismo* ((262) 989110 is on Avenida 25 de Abril.

Where to Stay and Eat

In Peniche the only hotel of interest is **Hotel Atlântico Golf** ((262) 757700, Praia da Consolação, which is more a luxury complex than a hotel, offering all sports facilities. On Berlenga Grande the seventeenth-century fortress has been converted into a hostel, **Casa Abrigo São João Baptista** ((262) 782550, where you need to take your own food and bedding, and in the summer there's also the **Pensão Mar e Sol** ((262) 750331, which offers a handful of rooms and a reasonable restaurant. Both are inexpensive.

In São Martinho do Porto, the **Hotel do Parque** ((262) 989506, Avenida Marechal Carmona No. 3, 2465 São Martinho do Porto, is set in private grounds with a tennis court. The rooms are clean and homey, all with bathrooms, but there is no restaurant on the premises. It is open only from March to October. Prices mid-range to inexpensive.

In Peniche the **Restaurante Nau Dos Corvos** ((262) 789004, Cabo Carvoeiro, with glass walls overlooking the rocks of Cabo do Carvoeiro, naturally offers seafood on its moderately priced menu. Otherwise, stroll along the Avenida da Mar and choose your restaurant by its tantalizing outdoor grill.

How to Get There

São Martinho is served by rail. It lies on the line from Lisbon to Leiria on which the train also stops at Óbidos, Caldas da Rainha, and Valado. A bus connects Caldas da Rainha and São Martinho do Porto with Peniche, another connects Nazaré with Leiria. There's a service between Nazaré and Valado, just four kilometers (two and a half miles) away. Express buses run from Lisbon to Peniche.

The A8 from Lisbon goes only as far as Torres Vedras, where you continue north on

the IC1. Take this until its junction with N114, which goes directly to Peniche.

NAZARÉ

Thirteen kilometers (nine miles) further along the coast is the pretty but overcrowded fishing village of Nazaré. Here the locals sometimes wear their distinctive traditional dress: fishermen's capes, plaid shirts and stocking caps; while the young women wear seven petticoats beneath wide skirts. More color is added by the brightly decorated narrow boats, particularly the *meia-lua* (half-moon) type, on whose graceful crescent-shaped prows are painted eyes, stars, or other symbols.

The town is on two levels. The lower is a mass of narrow lanes and cottages, and

109 m (360 ft) above it is the **Sítio**, the site of the original town before the sea receded. A funicular takes you up to where you can see the **Ermida da Memória** (Chapel of Memory), a tiny white chapel with blue borders built to commemorate the miracle that saved the life of Fuas Roupinho, the companion-in-arms of Afonso Henriques, in 1182. While in pursuit of a white deer (said to be the devil in disguise), the mist caused Roupinho to lose his way. Our Lady appeared and halted his horse just in time to prevent it and Roupinho from falling over the cliff, where a hoofprint is still embedded in the edge. If you do decide to stay in Nazaré, this is where you have a view of the harbor below; down on the beach you'll find yourself hassled constantly by souvenir sellers or by locals trying to persuade you to take a room.

The *Turismo* ((262) 561194 is on Avenida da República.

Where to Stay and Eat

Nazaré has several modern hotels, the nicest of which is **Hotel Praia** ((262) 561423 FAX (262) 561436, Avenida Vieira Guimarães No. 39, 2450 Nazaré, where the moderately priced rooms are acceptable. The most pleasant accommodation, however, is the inexpensive **Pensão Restaurante Ribamar** ((262) 551158 FAX (262) 562224, Rua Gomes Freire No. 9, 2450 Nazaré, an old inn on the waterfront. Some of their rooms have balconies

The fishermen of Nazaré dry splayed sardines and jackfish over wooden racks on the beach.

Estremadura and Ribatejo

overlooking the fishing beach, and all have traditional furnishings. Alternatively, stay at the **Quinta do Campo** ((262) 577135 FAX (262) 577155, Valado dos Frades, 2450 Nazaré, a 600-year-old restored farmhouse now offering seven independent apartments. An swimming pool is set in one of the beautiful garden areas.

The **Pensão Restaurante Ribamar** serves traditional dishes under oak beams, and the **Restaurante Mar Bravo** ((262) 551180, Praça Sousa Oliveira, is on a square overlooking the sea. Both are inexpensively priced. **Beira-**

yellow crenellated castle walls. Within is a jumble of alleyways and small squares leading off a main street, where whitewashed houses have brightly-colored terracotta roofs, and vivid flowers seem to sprout from every corner and balcony. Óbidos is an easy day-trip from Lisbon, but if you are on the way north this is a good spot to spend the night.

Background

In its early days, Óbidos faced right on to the sea with boats moored alongside the lower wall, but centuries of land reclamation have

Mar ((262) 561358, Avenida da República No. 40, is in the port in the Barrio dos Pescadores, and as you might imagine, serves exquisitely fresh fish. Inexpensive.

How to Get There

From Lisbon, take the A8 to Torres Vedras, the IC1 to Alcobaça, and the N8-4 to Nazaré.

ÓBIDOS

The medieval town of Óbidos, 95 km (59 miles) north of Lisbon and 16 km (26 miles) from the coast east of Peniche, sits on a hill surrounded by a fertile and cultivated plain, crowned by a castle — now an excellent *pousada* — and surrounded by

left the town miles from the coast. The saintly Queen Isabella was so charmed by it that in 1282 her husband King Dinis made her a gift of Óbidos, after which it became a tradition for the town to be presented to the queens of Portugal, earning the title *Casa das Rainhas* (House of the Queens). It was to Óbidos that the wife of João II, Queen Leonor, came to mourn the death of her only son, Prince Afonso, who met his end in a riding accident. His body was borne back in a fisherman's net, which Queen Leonor took as her emblem: you can see it carved on the town's pillory.

Another famous resident was Josefa de Óbidos (1634–1684), one of the few known women in the seventeenth century. Her religious paintings and more popular studies of still life are scattered around the country, and several of them can be seen here.

General Information

The *Turismo* ((262) 959231 FAX (262) 955014 is on the main street, Rua Direita.

What to See and Do

If you're driving here, leave your car in the parking lot because the narrow streets of the town are difficult to negotiate. One of the first obstacles is the **Porta de Vila**, a

a side chapel. Open from 9:30 AM to 12:30 PM and from 2:30 PM to 7 PM.

Also in the square is the **Museu Municipal** (Municipal Museum) ((262) 959263, established with the help of the Gulbenkian Foundation, which has some works from the fifteenth century onwards, including paintings by Josefa de Óbidos. Opening hours are from 9 AM to 1 PM and from 2 PM to 6 PM.

The pillory bearing the coat of arms of Queen Leonor stands in this square. The pillory or *pelourinho* was a place of punish-

double gateway through which you have to zigzag; inside is a Renaissance balcony brightened with eighteenth-century *azulejos*, contrasting with the ancient yellowing stone walls. The gateway opens on to the narrow main street, lined with shops and old houses where you can sometimes see weavers making the town's famous cotton carpets.

Moving along the Rua Direita, just past the *Turismo*, in the square to the right stands the handsome **Igreja de Santa Maria** (Saint Mary's Church) ((262) 959231, where blue and white seventeenth-century tiles painted with African-inspired designs cover the walls all the way to the ceiling. Paintings by Josefa de Óbidos of the life of Saint Catherine adorn

ment in Portugal, and a symbol of authority. Often elaborately carved, you will find one in the main square of virtually every town.

Close by the museum stands the **Igreja da Misericórdia** built by Queen Leonor in 1498, and the fourteenth-century **Chapel of São Martinho**. One of the other churches in town, the **Church of São Pedro**, contains the tomb of Josefa de Óbidos. At the end of the Rua Direita is the **Castelo**, part of the twelfth-century fortifications turned into a royal palace in the sixteenth century and into an excellent *pousada* in the twentieth.

OPPOSITE: A woman balances a fish-drying rack on her head. ABOVE: Óbidos, tightly clustered within its formidable town wall, has inspired generations of poets and lovers.

Where to Stay

The place where everyone wants to stay in Óbidos is the **Pousada do Castelo (** (262) 959105 FAX (262) 959148, 2510 Óbidos, built into a restored section of the Manueline-ornamented sixteenth-century castle. It retains the atmosphere of a castle with antique furniture and medieval weaponry on the walls. Only six rooms and three suites are available, all with views over the surrounding countryside. Prices are expensive, but drop into mid-range off season. The second choice for accommodation must be the **Estalagem do Convento (** (262) 959214/7 FAX (262) 959159, Rua Dr. João d'Ornelas, a converted eighteenth-century convent just below the walls. The furnishings are old but comfortable and all rooms have bathrooms and minibars. Mid-range prices apply.

There are six places in town that operate under the TURIHAB scheme; two particularly picturesque ones are: the **Casa do Relógio (** (262) 959282, Rua da Graça, comprising a medieval building and eighteenth-century mansion with six rooms, and the **Casa do Poço (** (262) 959358, Travessa da Rua Nova, a building of Moorish origin with four rooms and a bar, where there is *fado* singing on Fridays and Saturdays. Both are mid-range.

Where to Eat

The **Pousada do Castelo (** (262) 959105, has an excellent restaurant furnished in provincial style that serves regional and continental food at moderate prices. The restaurant at the **Estalagem do Convento (** (262) 959214/7 offers moderately priced continental cuisine in an old-fashioned dining room or *al fresco* in warmer weather. **Restaurante Alcaide (** (262) 959220, Rua Direita, serves regional dishes and is open for tea or drinks in the afternoons. If you arrive early, you may get a balcony table. Prices are moderate.

How to Get There

Trains run frequently from Lisbon's Rossio station to Óbidos with a journey time of about two hours. By bus you will need to take the service to Caldas da Rainha and change there for Óbidos. For bus information, call **(** (262) 831067.

If you are driving, take the A8 from Lisbon and continue on the IC1 to Óbidos.

Three important centers of religious life mark the drive to Tomar and merit a visit: Batalha, Alcobaça, and Fátima.

The **Monastery of Santa Maria da Vitória** towers over a collection of small houses and shops at the side of the busy N1 highway. Nevertheless, the monastery, a magnificent Gothic extravaganza with Manueline flourishes, is surprisingly divorced from its surroundings. It was built by King João I in thanksgiving for the Portuguese victory over strong Spanish forces at the Battle of Aljubarrota in 1385, a honey-colored construction of limestone spires, flying buttresses, balustrades, and pinnacles, edged with delicate filigree stonework. The soaring interior is no less impressive.

The construction spanned from 1388 to 1533, and thus depicts a great evolution of the Manueline style. At the southern end is the **Capela do Fundador** (Founder's Chapel), an octagonal domed lantern within a square structure, with a cupola in the shape of a star. It contains the tombs of João I and Philippa of Lancaster, as well as those of their sons. In the **Claustro Real** (Royal Cloister) the delicate Gothic tracery is embellished with Manueline plants and flowers of the newly discovered lands, as well as more common seafaring motifs.

An opening off the cloister leads to the **Sala do Capítulo** (Chapter House) where a soldier guards the **Tomb of the Unknown Soldiers**, two Portuguese casualties of World War I. The single-span vault was a very daring construction in its time, rising as it does to a height of 20 m (60 ft) without intermediary supports, and only condemned criminals were used to build it.

Outside the monastery there is access to the **Capelas Imperfeitas** (Unfinished Chapels) through a vast Gothic doorway covered with extravagant sixteenth-century carving. Band upon band of delicate lace work bare the words of Dom Duarte's motto, *tam yasary* ("I shall be loyal"), repeated in the tracery. This octagonal structure with seven chapels was commissioned by Dom Duarte as a mausoleum in 1435, only three years before his death. But work was abandoned and its pillars and arches end in midair all at the same height forever exposed to the elements. The monastery is open from 9 AM to 5 PM (until 6 PM in the summer months) but is closed on Mondays.

In Batalha the *Turismo* ((044) 96180 is on Praça Mouzinho de Alburquerque.

Where to Stay and Eat
The **Pousada do Mestre Afonso Domingues** ((244) 96260/1 FAX (244) 96247, Largo Mestre Afonso Domingues, 2440 Batalha, is right next to the monastery, a modern but tradi-

There are several restaurants and cafés, the best of which is the **Pousada do Mestre Afonso Domingues** ((244) 96260/1 in Largo Mestre Afonso Domingues, which has a good, if somewhat standard restaurant with moderate prices.

How to Get There
The nearest rail link to Batalha is at Leiria (11 km or seven miles to the north). Trains arrive from Lisbon's Rossio station and from Coimbra. There is a bus service to Batalha from Leiria.

tionally-styled establishment with 20 rooms and one suite. Some have splendid views of the monastery. Mid-range prices apply here: modern *pousadas* often cost less than those housed within historic buildings.

The **Residencial Batalha** ((244) 767500, Largo da Igreja FAX (244) 767467, is a spanking new hotel linked to a shopping center, its 22 rooms including bathroom, telephone, satellite television, and sound insulation. Prices are mid-range.

Under the TURIHAB scheme there is the **Quinta do Fidalgo** ((244) 96114 FAX (244) 767401, a seventeenth-century house facing the abbey and surrounded by gardens and trees. There are five rooms and the prices vary between inexpensive and mid-range.

Estremadura and Ribatejo

To drive from Lisbon, travel north on the A1-IP1 highway. The Fátima-Batalha N356 turnoff is some 125 km (78 miles) from Lisbon. Driving from Alcobaça, continue on IC1 to Batalha.

ALCOBAÇA

Twenty kilometers (12 miles) south of Batalha, the **Mosteiro de Santa Maria** (Santa Maria Monastery) at Alcobaça is the largest church in Portugal. Before the battle of Santarém Portugal's first King, Afonso I, vowed to build a monastery there if he won. He duly captured Santarém from the Moors in 1147

The awe-inspiring Batalha monastery was built in thanksgiving for victory over the Spanish.

and handed over the domain of Alcobaça to the Cistercians.

Work began on the monastery in 1178; it is believed once to have housed 999 monks. The façade is a mixture of Gothic and baroque, altered by seventeenth-and eighteenth-century work that left only the doorway and rose window of the original façade. It was ransacked during the Peninsular Wars and the monks finally left under the 1834 ban on religious orders.

The interior of the church is impressive but simple: three aisles stretch out amid a

forest of graceful columns, and the original serenity achieved through the use of space has been returned by stripping out the later additions. The tombs of King Pedro and his beloved mistress stand in the north and south transept, a testimony to one of Portugal's great love stories and the rage and vengeance of the grief-stricken king.

Afonso IV's son Pedro was betrothed to Constanza, a princess of Navarre, but instead fell in love with her lady-in-waiting, a Castilian noblewoman named Inês de Castro. Inês was exiled from the court by Afonso, but returned upon the death of Constanza

The tomb of the lovers Pedro and Inês at Alcobaça. Legend says they will arise and face each other on judgment day.

to settle in Coimbra where she raised her royal children; she claimed that she had been secretly married to Pedro. Fearful of the harm that this union and Inês' ambitious family could cause, Afonso had her murdered. Two years later in 1357 Pedro came to power and exacted terrible revenge: he traced two of the assassins and had their hearts torn out. The story goes that he had Inês body disinterred, set upon the throne, robed and crowned, and had the entire court kiss her decayed hand in homage. Pedro became obsessed with the dispensation of justice and was often harsh, acquiring the sobriquet "The Cruel."

Their two white tombs were placed foot to foot so that on the Day of Judgment their first sight would be of one another. Inês' effigy, now without its nose, which disappeared during the Peninsular Wars, lies supported by six angels. The panel at the head of her tomb depicts the Crucifixion, and the one at her feet shows Judgment Day and the damned being cast into the jaws of hell. The tomb is supported by animals with human faces, which some believe represent her assassins. Dom Pedro's tomb is similarly guarded by angels, a faithful hound at his feet and the wheel of fortune at his head.

A Manueline doorway leads from the chancel to the sacristy, beyond which is a circular chapel lined with golden baroque carvings and busts of saints. A doorway from the nave leads into the **Claustro do Silencio** (Cloister of Silence) dating from the fourteenth century with a Manueline upper story, where there is access to the vast dormitory.

If you are at that point in your travels when one more ancient relic will make you scream, Alcobaça is a good place to indulge in shopping. The town is known for its ceramics. If you have come by car, travel down the Leiria road and approximately one kilometer east (a half mile), you will come upon the **Museu do Vinho**. Hours are daily from 8:30 AM to 12:30 PM and 2 PM to 5:30 PM.

The *Turismo* ((262) 42377 is located at Praça 25 de Abril.

Where to Stay and Eat

The **Hotel Santa Maria** ((262) 597395 FAX (262) 596715, Rua Dr. Francisco Zagalo No. 20, 2460 Alcobaça, is a modern hotel in its own gardens, across from the monastery.

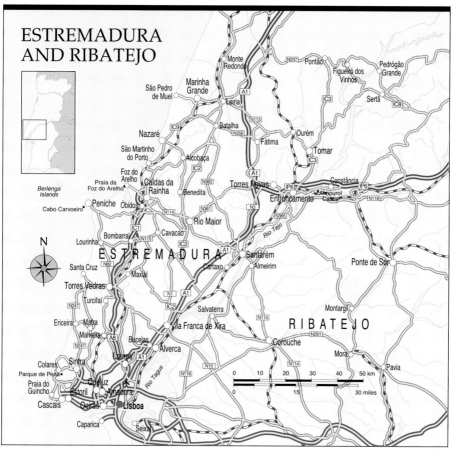

All rooms have bathrooms, telephones, and are moderately priced. The **Pensão Mosteiro** ((262) 582183, Avenida João de Deus No. 1, is an inexpensive, homey place, a little the worse for wear but very friendly. There are two guesthouses in the neighborhood that operate under the TURIHAB scheme. Conveniently located near the monastery is the century-old **Challet Fonte Nova** ((262) 598300 FAX (262) 598430, Rua da Fonte Nova, 2460 Alcobaça, which has four grand rooms, as well as an outdoor swimming pool. **Casa da Padeira** (/FAX (262) 508272, 2640 Aljubarrota, is a manor house that lies five kilometers (three miles) from Alcobaça, has eight rooms, and in the gardens, a swimming pool, miniature golf, and children's playground. Both are priced within mid-range.

The **Restaurante Trinidade** ((262) 582397, Praça Dom Afonso Henriques No. 22, serves meals and snacks. **Restaurante Frei Bernardo** ((262) 582227, Rua Dom Pedro V No. 17-19,

has its large dining room in a late nineteenth-century building and serves traditional, yet inexpensive fare, occasionally to the accompaniment of live music.

How to Get There

The nearest railway station is Valado de Frádes, only five kilometers (three miles) away from which buses connect with Alcobaça. There is also a bus service from Leiria to Alcobaça and express busses run from Lisbon.

To drive from Lisbon, follow the route to Batalha and then take the IC1 south for 20 km (12 miles). From Óbidos, continue north on the IC1 for 25 km (15 miles).

FÁTIMA

Nineteen kilometers (12 miles) east of Batalha is Fátima, revered by Catholics as a place of pilgrimage second only to Lourdes in France.

On May 13, 1917 the Virgin is said to have appeared to three children, and again on the thirteenth of every month until October that year. It was during her final appearance (she was only visible to the children) that thousands witnessed a miracle, when the sun is said to have rotated in the sky, its rays curing many of the sick. Under Salazar a vast basilica — a rather cold structure of no great architectural merit — and square were constructed there. This is not a place for casual sightseers but rather for the deeply religious; it is a place of prayer. In fact, notices at Fátima give the same advice. This is even more so on and around May 13 and October 13, when as many as 100,000 believers make their pilgrimage to honor the apparition.

The *Turismo* ((249) 531139 is at Avenida Dom José Alves da Silva.

Where to Stay and Eat

There are over 30 hotels and *pensãos* in Fátima priced from moderate to inexpensive. At the higher end, the **Hotel Cinquentenario** ((249) 533465 FAX (249) 532992 is modern and clean and near the shrine.

The **Estalagem Dom Gonçalo** ((249) 533062 FAX (249) 532088, Rua Jacinto Marto No. 100, 2495 Fátima, is a small-scale modern hotel on private grounds that is near to the shrine. Its prices are moderate and the restaurant, which is open to non-guests, is good. **Pensão Restaurante Estrêla de Fátima** ((249) 531150, Rua Cónega Formigão Periera, 2495 Fátima, is recommended for inexpensive accommodation and dining. Although there are countless places to eat in Fátima, the only restaurant of any note is **Tía Alice**, Rua do Adro ((249) 531737. The attractive setting is a centrally-located rustic house.

How to Get There

The nearest rail link to Fátima is at Leiria 20 km (12 miles) away, where trains arrive from Lisbon's Rossio station and from Coimbra. From Leiria there is a bus service to Fátima. There is also an express bus service from Lisbon.

If you are driving from Lisbon, take the airport road and continue north along the A1-IP1 highway and turn west on the Fátima-Batalha N356, some 125 km (78 miles) from Lisbon; then follow the signs.

RIBATEJO

TOMAR

Tomar, on the banks of the Nabão River at the foot of a hill, is 72 km (48 miles) west of Fátima, via Ourém, on N113, 140 km (87 miles) from Lisbon and 197 km (122 miles) from Porto. Dominated by the famous Convent of Christ — the Ribatejo's main tourist attraction — which is most definitely worth a visit.

Background

Founded by the Knights Templar in 1160, a group that was something of a religious order (participants took a vow of chastity), and something of a band of warriors, Tomar remained in their control until King Dinis disbanded the order in 1314. He reconstituted it into the Order of Christ, under the Grand Mastership of the younger sons of the Kings of Portugal. One was Prince Henry the Navigator, who used the order's wealth to finance some of the Voyages of Discovery, his sails bearing its cross. Profits from these voyages were spent transforming the monastery into a symbol of the Discoveries, as well as one of the order's power and prosperity.

General Information

The regional *Turismo* ((249) 323113 is on Rua Serpa Pinto No. 1 and has information about

The faithful find Fátima OPPOSITE a rich source of spiritual energy. Every May 13, anniversary of the Virgin's first apparition at Fátima ABOVE, more than 100,000 pilgrims gather at her shrine.

neighboring places. The municipal *Turismo* ℂ (249) 322427 is on Avenida Dr. Candida Madureira.

What to See and Do

The main attraction is the monastery, the **Convento de Cristo**, construction on which was begun in the twelfth century and not finished until the seventeenth. It is entered through the 16-sided Charola, based on Jerusalem's Holy Sepulcher; to the west an archway links it to an elaborate sixteenth-century Manueline **Chapterhouse** by Diogo de Arruda. And it is in the Claustro de Santa Bárbara that even the most jaded tourist will be taken aback by the justifiably famous **Manueline window**, with its knotted ropes, cables, coral, and seaweed, furiously entwined around the masts on either side of the window.

A passageway leads you from the chapterhouse to the top floor of the sixteenth-century **Main Cloisters** by Diogo de Torralva. Essentially an Italianate Renaissance structure, its beauty lies in its simplicity; the cloisters stand in utter contrast with the ornate chapterhouse. The spiral staircase in the east corner provides an overview of the whole structure. Open from 9:30 AM to 12:30 PM and 2 PM to 5 PM (until 6 PM in the summer months). Entry is free Sunday mornings.

Halfway down the hill is the **Capela de Nossa Senhora da Conceição** (Chapel of Our Lady of the Immaculate Conception) ℂ (249) 313481, a Renaissance building, pure in form and proportion. Opening times are the same as the monastery. The old part of town has cobbled streets lined with seventeenth- and eighteenth-century houses and is strewn with parks and gardens. In one of the streets of what in medieval times was the Jewish quarter, is a fifteenth-century **synagogue** that over the years has served a variety of secular purposes. It is now a **Luso-Hebraic Museum** ℂ (249) 322602, Rua Dr. Joaquim Jaquinto No. 73, and its hall is sometimes used for concerts. If you have a penchant for collecting things, consider a visit to the **Aquiles Lima Museu dos Fósforos** ℂ (249) 322992 in the Convento São Francisco, which boasts the greatest matchbox collection in Europe, although one has to wonder about the competition.

Where to Stay

For a taste of four-star luxury at a relatively moderate cost the **Hotel dos Templários** ℂ (249) 321730 FAX (249) 322191, Largo Cândido dos Reis No. 1, 2300 Tomar, is a good choice. With its extensive sports facilities — both indoor and outdoor swimming pools, a tennis court, a gym, and a spa — as well as a wide range of outdoor activities, it also makes a good spot for a break from the historic trail if you are traveling with children. Unfortunately, the restaurant is quite disappointing. Upper mid-range.

The **Estalagem de Santa Iria** ℂ (249) 313326 FAX (249) 321238, Parque do Mouchão, 2300 Tomar, is in the park by the river, moderately priced, with a bar and restaurant. There are several pensions in town, all of which are listed on the back of the map distributed at the *Turismo*. Highly recommended for its price/quality ratio is **Residencial União** ℂ (249) 323161 FAX (249) 321299, Rua Serpa Pinto No. 94.

Where to Eat

For a relaxing meal on a patio overlooking the river, go to **Bela Vista** ℂ (249) 312870, Fonte do Choupo No. 4, where the moderately priced cuisine equals the views. A pleasant little restaurant in the old center is **Casinha d'Avó Bia** ℂ (249) 323828, Rua Dr. Joaquim Jacinto No. 16, where the regional cuisine is appreciated by locals and tourists alike. For an inexpensive meal, try **Restaurante Tomáz** ℂ (249) 312552, Rua dos Arcos No. 31.

However, the area's three best restaurants are all somewhat outside of town. Two are down the street from one another: **Chico Elias** ℂ (249) 311067, Algarvias, is known for its unusual contemporary renditions of regional dishes, such as a rabbit stew served in a pumpkin. Prices at the upper end of moderate are appropriate for the kitchen; reservations are essential. The neighboring **Casa Velha** ℂ (249) 324277, Algarvias, serves the standard grilled meats and fish at a much higher standard. Both restaurants are reached by following the road to Torres Novas approximately one kilometer (half a mile). Elias will be on your left, Velha just a little further down the same road. The staff of the *Turismo* (and virtually anyone in town) can help with directions. A quite worthwhile eight-kilometer (five-mile) drive to the town of Portela (off the road that leads to Castelo de Bode) will take you to **Restaurante A Lúria** ((249) 312879, and place you in the artful hands of Senhor Francisco.

How to Get There

Trains from Lisbon's Santa Apolónia station and from Porto run to Entroncamento, where there is a frequent service to Tomar. An express bus service runs from Lisbon via Santarém to Tomar.

century **Igreja de São João de Alparão**, located toward the end of the Avenida 5 de Outubro and now the **Museu Arqueológico**, with its somewhat odd collection. There is a Gothic tomb bearing a long inscription, erected by the widow of Duarte de Meneses who died at the hands of the Moors while defending his King. The fight was evidently long and hard, for in a glass case in the museum is all that remained of Dom Duarte when it was over: one rotten tooth. More complete members of the Meneses family are interred in the fifteenth-century **Igreja de**

From Lisbon (140 km or 87 miles away) the most direct route to Tomar is along the A1 highway, then turn on to the IP6 going toward Entroncamento, where you will take the second IC3 exit, which comes quickly and dangerously after the first. It is indicated Tomar, but you won't have time to read the sign.

SANTARÉM

The capital of the Ribatejo is the hilltop city of Santarém, 65 km (40 miles) south of Tomar, an agricultural center with plenty of cafés, restaurants, and excellent views over the surrounding pasturelands. The real highlight of any visit here is the nearby twelfth-

Nossa Senhora da Graça. For spectacular views over the surrounding plains and a restaurant with some of the best food in town, go to **Portas do Sol**, a small public garden at the end of the Avenida 5 de Outubro.

For information on the Ribatejo as a whole contact the **Região de Turismo de Ribatejo** ((243) 333318 FAX (243) 24113 in Santarém. Santarém also has a local *Turismo* ((243) 391512 at Rua Capelo Ivêns No. 63.

How to Get There

There is a frequent train service linking Lisbon with Entroncamento via Santarém, and trains from Porto and Coimbra run to

Troubadours in traditional costume make merry at Abrantes, on the alluvial plains of the Tagus estuary.

Entroncamento. Frequent Rodoviária Nacional express buses operate between Lisbon and Santarém.

Santarém is 78 km (48 miles) from Lisbon along the A1 highway. To drive to Santarém from Tomar (a distance of approximately 60 km or 37 miles), the fastest route is to take the N113 in the direction of Leiria to the point where it intersects with the A1 highway and continue south along that route directly to Santarém. As always, the slower, more scenic routes are preferable if you have the time. It can be seen on a day-trip from Lisbon if you are basing yourself there.

ELSEWHERE IN RIBATEJO

Ourém

The fortified hilltop village of Ourém lies 20 km (12 miles) northwest of Tomar on the N113, its summit studded with olive trees and crowned with the ruins of a fifteenth-century castle. On its grounds lies a Renaissance palace, the **Paço dos Condes** (Palace of the Counts), built by Dom Afonso, the bastard son of João I. The towers have parapets supported by pointed arches. To visit the palace you enter through one of the two huge gateways, but will probably have to leave your car outside at Vila Nova de Ourém (the busy modern part of town), as driving through them would be a tight squeeze. Climb up the square tower for panoramic views of the countryside.

Below the castle, part of the old town is protected by its walls. Go into the **Colegiada** (Collegiate Church) where you can see the highly ornate limestone tomb of Count Dom Afonso.

For those who would like to stay over, Ourém has a few *pensãos*, as well as two country homes that function under the TURIHAB scheme. **Quinta da Alcaidaria-Mor** ((249) 42231, 2490 Vila Nova de Ourém, 2490 Ourém, is a splendid old house that has belonged to the same family since the seventeenth century, and has six double rooms and an outdoor swimming pool. **Quinta dos Barros** (/FAX (249) 43342, Louçãs, 2490 Ourém, offers two rooms on a small estate with its own stables. Horseback riding tours through the neighboring forests can be arranged.

Constância

Situated southeast of Tomar, the sparkling white town of Constância sits in a natural amphitheater at the confluence of the Tagus and Zêzere rivers, a cluster of stepped streets all bedecked with brightly colored flowers. Camões was exiled here between 1548 and 1550 because of his affair with a young lady-in-waiting, Catarina d'Ataide, the Natercia of his love poems. You can still see the shell of the Casa dos Arcos where he lived.

A delightful place to base yourself is the **Casa O Palácio** ((249) 99224, 2250 Constância, a lovely nineteenth-century mansion sitting on the riverbank that offers TURIHAB accommodation.

Almourol Castle

Just a few kilometers away from Constância and 22 km (14 miles) south of Tomar, Almourol Castle stands on a small craggy island in the Tagus, built in 1171 on the site of a Roman fortress (parts of the lower walls are Roman). You can be ferried across by a boatman who will wait to row you back. This fairy tale structure has never suffered attack, and has inspired countless stories of princesses and giants clinging to it. On Saint John's Eve, during the second week in June, it is said to be haunted by the ghosts of a Moorish boy, a Christian girl and an angry, heartbroken father, protagonists in a romantic and tragic legend. The outer wall is flanked by 10 round towers, dominated by the square keep, which you can climb for good views of the river.

There is a train service from Entroncamento to Almourol, from which it takes approximately 20 minutes on foot to reach the castle.

Elderly woman of Ribatejo.

Coimbra
and the
Beiras

THE BEIRAS

The three provinces of Beira Baixa, Beira Alta, and Beira Litoral (Lower, Upper, and Coastal Beira) together form a large block of land that stretches from the Atlantic coast to the Spanish border, demarcated in the north by the Alto Douro and in the south by the provinces of Ribatejo and Estremadura. This area encompasses the Dão wine growing area, the Mondego and Zêzere valleys, and coastal plains laced with lagoons and edged with long, sandy beaches.

Beira Alta and Beira Baixa make up Portugal's most mountainous region, its principal range being the Serra da Estrela. Because cultivation is difficult and the way of life hard, its population is sparse. Many settlements are encircled by solid fortifications, as this was the route into Portugal for many of its invaders.

In contrast, the Beira Litoral is a low-lying area that is well irrigated and fertile. Pine forests line the sandy coastal strip broken by the Aveiro lagoon, but this area lacks the natural grandeur of the mountain Beiras. Nonetheless, there are two important sights: the romantic, historic city of Coimbra, and the uniquely beautiful Buçaco Forest with its magnificent Palace Hotel.

IN AND AROUND CASTELO BRANCO

The prosperous capital of the Beira Baixa lies 249 km (155 miles) northeast of Lisbon at the center of the exposed Idanha plain in the south of the province. Castelo Branco makes a convenient base for seeing nearby Idanha-a-Velha, Monsanto and surrounding villages that lack accommodation for visitors, but has little else to offer. The history of Castelo Branco goes back to Roman times, but most traces of its past have been eradicated by centuries of looting and sacking. This largely modern town has an old quarter of modest proportions in the shadow of the ruined castle.

General Information

The *Turismo* ((272) 21002 FAX (272) 330324 is in the center of town at Alameda da Liber-

dade, and can supply information on Castelo Branco and the surrounding area.

What to See and Do

Take a walk around the older part of the town, and go up to the ruins of the **Templar castle** where there's a **miradouro** (viewing point) set amid pleasant gardens. Be sure to visit the eighteenth-century **Jardim do Antiga Paço Episcopal** (Gardens of the old Episcopal Palace). Small and rather quaint, its paths, stairways and pools are lined with statues of saints, apostles, Portuguese kings and the unwelcome Spanish rulers (much smaller than the others), personifications of zodiac signs, the seasons, and the Virtues. Empty plinths recall those statues looted by the French invaders.

The Episcopal Palace itself dates from the sixteenth century and now contains the **Museu de Francisco Tavares Proenca Júnior** ((272) 344277, which has a collection of prehistoric and Roman relics, Flemish tapestries, sixteenth-century and modern Portuguese art, antique furniture, and some old examples of the embroidered bedcovers or *colchas* for which Castelo Branco is famous. These are embroidered with brightly colored silks in old designs some of which incorporate motifs symbolizing love and marriage. The museum incorporates a school where the art is taught and practiced.

Other places worth visiting in the area include **São Vicente da Beira**, 30 km (19 miles) north of Castelo Branco and, a little to the northeast, **Castelo Novo**, with its granite buildings and cobbled streets. If you would like to spend a night in the area other than in Castelo Branco, try **Alpedrinha**, one of the larger villages about four kilometers (two and a half miles) north of Castelo Novo, where some grand old houses hide in the maze of streets twisting away from the main road. Thirty kilometers (19 miles) east of Alpedrinha and 43 km (27 miles) northeast of Castelo Branco along the N223, **Penamacor** sits up on a hill and harbors a medieval village within its ancient castle. Continuing northward, twelfth-century walls enclose the old quarter of

Castelo Branco is a good base for exploring the mountains and isolated villages of the Beira Baixa.

Sortelha, which overlooks the fertile valley of the Côa River.

Where to Stay

In Castelo Branco accommodations are somewhat limited. The **Hotel Colina do Castelo** ((272) 329856 FAX (272) 329759, Rua da Piscina, 6000 Castelo Branco, is a modern hotel that is now run by the Spanish Meliá chain and offers all comforts including an indoor swimming pool. Prices are mid-range. At the other end of the spectrum, the choice is between the **Pensão Arraiana** ((272) 341634

Where to Eat

Castelo Branco has several restaurants, and most of them serve traditional fare at inexpensive prices. Specialties of the region are *cabrito* (kid), as well as the locally produced goat's cheese. **Praça Velha** ((272) 328640, Largo Luís de Camões No. 17, is particularly noteworthy.

How to Get There

The rail line running through Castelo Branco links Lisbon with Guarda and makes a few daily stops at Castelo Branco and Alpedrinha.

FAX (272) 331884, Avenida 1 de Maio No. 18, 6000 Castelo Branco, where rooms are simply furnished but all have private baths, telephones, and televisions; or the **Pensão Caravela** ((272) 343939, Rua do Saibreiro No. 24, 6000 Castelo Branco, which is basic but clean, some rooms having bathrooms. Both are inexpensive.

In Alpedrinha, there is the **Estalagem São Jorge** ((275) 57154 or (275) 57354, Largo da Misericórdia No. 5, 6095 Alpedrinha, which has a good restaurant and 10 rooms, all with telephone and bath. You have another choice: the lovely **Casa de Barreiro** ((275) 57120, Largo das Escolas, a large rambling house offering accommodation under the TURIHAB scheme. Both are inexpensive.

Some trains continue to Vilar Formoso on the border where there are connections to Salamanca in Spain. If you are traveling from Coimbra you need to take the train to Guarda and change there for Castelo Branco; from Porto you change at Pampilhosa for Guarda. Express buses run to Castelo Branco from Coimbra, from Lisbon, and from Porto.

Castelo Branco lies 58 km (36 miles) west of the border town of Segura, and 249 km (155 miles) northeast of Lisbon. If you are driving from Lisbon, take the A1 from Lisbon for 103 km (64 miles) to the junction with the IP6 and continue eastward until the junction with the IP2, where you continue northward. Castelo Branco lies 103 km (64 miles) south of Guarda along the N18-IP2.

MONSANTO AND IDANHA-A-VELHA

Forty-eight kilometers (30 miles) northeast of Castelo Branco are the eerie and isolated remains of Idanha-a-Velha, once a Celtic settlement, which in 16 BC became the site of the Roman city of Egitania, rebuilt by the Visigoths in the sixth century and said to be the birthplace of King Wamba. Abandoned in the early fifteenth century because of a 100-year-long plague of ants, it remains more or less untouched and unexcavated. An ancient

and the walls begin. Climb to the castle for some wonderful views across the surrounding plain.

In May, Monsanto is the scene of a strange ritual that forms part of the **Festa do Castelo**. Its origins lie in a long siege that took place centuries ago, either during Moorish, or even possibly during Roman times. The hungry but defiant inhabitants threw the last of their food over the castle walls—a fatted calf with its stomach filled with wheat—presumably to convince the enemy that they had abundant supplies, or as a sign of determination.

basilica, partly Visigoth, contains a collection of fragments of statues found on the site and stones bearing Roman inscriptions. A small chapel contains a cache of Roman coins and pottery.

The most well-known and photogenic of the Beira Baixa's fortified villages has to be the enchanting **Monsanto**, 50 km (31 miles) northeast of Castelo Branco and just 15 km (eight miles) northeast of Idanha-a-Velha. Clinging to a steep rocky hill, it has sustained many battles and exudes an air of primitive magic. The granite houses, many of which are very basic, are built between or into the rocks. Looking down on the village from the ancient stone fortifications, it is difficult to tell where the hill ends

Either way, the ploy worked and the siege was lifted. To commemorate this act of fortitude, during the Festa women throw flowers and a calf made of roses from the walls. A scene undoubtedly worth seeing.

How to Get There

Two buses a day leave Castelo Branco for Monsanto and one leaves for Idanha-a-Velha. A problem arises because the daily Idanha-a-Velha bus returns immediately to Castelo Branco; which means that by far the best way to explore this region is by car.

"Cold, rich, strong, and ugly" Guarda OPPOSITE and ABOVE is at the heart of a high, rocky region where age-old farming methods are still practiced.

IN AND AROUND GUARDA

The town of Guarda lies 352 km (219 miles) northeast of Lisbon at the northeastern edge of the Serra da Estrela and at an altitude of 1,000 m (3,281 ft), it is Portugal's highest town, its one and only distinction. Trains run here from Spain, crossing the border at Vilar Formoso only 47 km (29 miles) away, from Lisbon, and from Coimbra. It offers a fair range of accommodation, making it a good base for touring the villages to the north as well as the lovely Serra da Estrela. The Portuguese say damningly of Guarda that it is *fria, farta, forte, e feia*: cold, rich, strong, and ugly.

General Information

The *Turismo* ((271) 222251 is near the cathedral in the Edificio da Câmara at Praça Luís de Camões. Outside Guarda, and useful if you are touring the villages, there is a *Turismo* in the border town of Vilar Formoso ((271) 572202, close to Almeida, and another at Trancoso open only during the summer.

What to See and Do

The main sight is the **Sé**, or Cathedral, a somber building at the center of the town founded in the fourteenth century, and not completed until the sixteenth. The granite exterior, with its twin octagonal towers, pinnacles and particularly threatening gargoyles gives it a fortress-like air, and although it was worked on by the sons of Mateus Fernandes (the architect of Batalha) and later by Boytac (who worked on Jerónimos), in no way does it rival either of these buildings. Inside, twisted Manueline columns mix with Gothic and Renaissance features. The gilded altarpiece in the chancel is an elaborately carved bas-relief attributed to the sixteenth-century French sculptor Jean de Rouen.

Excursions

North and northeast of Guarda the landscape is a mixture of wild countryside and fertile valleys scattered with small towns and villages, many of them set high on hillsides or outcrops of rock and fortified against Spanish invasion by the prudent King Dinis. Among these are **Castelo Mendo**, **Castelo Bom**, **Castelo Rodrigo**, **Castelo Melhor**, and

Marialva, all within easy driving distance of Guarda.

The N221 runs northeast of Guarda to the fortified town of **Pinhel**, 33 km (29 miles) from the city and close to the Spanish border. The vineyards and wine cooperative are a reminder of one of the town's main products: Pinhel wine, similar in some ways to the smooth Dão red. The old town itself is well preserved, including several noble houses decorated with coats-of-arms.

From here it is a scenic drive across a lonely plateau to **Almeida**, 29 km (18 miles) southeast of Pinhel and 40 km (25 miles) northeast of Guarda. Only 10 km (six miles) from the Spanish frontier, this quiet little town was once an important military stronghold, rendered particularly striking by its perfectly preserved 16-point fortifications in double star form, built in the eighteenth century and said to have been completed by Vauban himself. Understandably the town has attracted tourists in recent years, and a *pousada* has been built into the town walls.

Forty-seven kilometers (29 miles) northwest of Guarda the medieval town of **Trancoso** is still partly enclosed by sturdy walls and dominated by a squat **castle tower** at the northeast corner. Balconies spilling flowers overlook the arcaded lower stories of the buildings, and coats-of-arms adorn some of the nobler dwellings. Trancoso seems greatly to have appealed to King Dinis, for he married the 12-year-old Isabel of Aragón here in 1282 and gave her the town as a wedding present.

Consider continuing on to **Penedono**, 29 km (18 miles) north of Trancoso. Sitting on a craggy hilltop, the granite village lies below a triangular sixteenth-century castle whose angular crenellations on the turrets impart a fierce appearance. This is believed by some to have been the home of the legendary Alvaro Gonçalves Coutinho, otherwise known as *o Magrico*, whose chivalrous deeds were recalled by Camões in *Os Lusíadas*.

Where to Stay

Hotel Turismo da Guarda ((271) 223366 FAX (271) 223399, Praça do Município,

The sleepy, peaceful village of Almeida belies its military past as a fortified frontier town.

6300 Guarda, is Guarda's top hotel. It's a large, centrally-located, traditional building with good facilities including an outdoor swimming pool and an acceptable restaurant. Prices are mostly mid-range. Moving down-scale, the **Pensão Beira Serra (** (271) 212392, Rua Infante Dom Henrique No. 35C, is a comfortable alternative. Two stunning options are available under the TURIHAB scheme. **Solar de Alarção (** (271) 211275 or (271) 214392, Rua Dom Miguel de Alarção Nos. 25-27, 6300 Guarda, is a lovely seventeenth-century manor house in the old part of town. **Quinto do Pinheiro (**/FAX (271) 96162, Cavadoude, 6300 Guarda, is a stone seventeenth-century farmhouse on the edge of the Parque Natural da Serra. Prices at both are mid-range.

Around the villages, the choicest place to stay — indeed one of the very few — is in Almeida at the above-mentioned **Pousada da Senhora das Neves (** (271) 574283/90 FAX (271) 574320, 6350 Almeida. This relatively new building conforms to the high standards of the *pousada* system. Prices are mid-range, but rise somewhat depending on the season.

Where to Eat

Guarda has quite a few restaurants to choose from. The two best are the **Belo Horizonte (** (271) 211454, Largo São Vicente No. 1, and **O Telheiro (** (271) 211356 on the edge of the city at Estrada Nacional 16, a large restaurant with magnificent views and a good kitchen. Inexpensive.

How to Get There

Two main railway lines link Guarda with Lisbon: one via Coimbra, while the other runs through the Beira Baixa stopping at Castelo Branco, Alpedrinha, Fundão and Covilhã, where you may have to change. People traveling from Porto need to change at Pampilhosa for Guarda. Guarda's railway station is about three kilometers (two miles) out of town but a frequent bus service links it to the center.

Express buses run to Guarda from both Lisbon and Porto, and an international bus service linking Lisbon with Paris stops at Coimbra and Guarda. Local buses connect Guarda with Viseu and Covilhã. Places

mentioned under EXCURSIONS (page 165) are best explored by car, as buses from Guarda to the towns are infrequent and trains nonexistent.

Guarda is 352 km (219 miles) northeast of Lisbon, and if you're driving, follow the route described for Castelo Branco, continuing north on the N18. From Coimbra it is about 159 km (99 miles) along the N2-IP3 to Viseu, where you head east along the N16-IP5 to Guarda.

SERRA DA ESTRELA

The poetically named Serra da Estrela (Mountains of the Star) is Portugal's highest mountain range, with its highest point, the Torre, touching 1,991 m (6,532 ft). The lower wooded slopes are cut by deep, mostly cultivated valleys, while the granite crags above sometimes seem eerie in the forms they take. In winter snow settles on the peaks, giving rise to Portugal's newest sport, skiing, but there usually is not enough snow for top conditions. Summer, however, in the Serra offers plenty of other sporting possibilities such as climbing, walking, and trout fishing.

The town of **Covilhã** in the southeastern foothills close to the Zêzere Valley on the road to Lisbon is regarded as the major gateway to the Serra, and is a good base for excursions. A wool center with several mills and a population of around 22,000, this charming old town lies upon the steep mountainside and commands some excellent views. The *Turismo* (271) 322170 FAX (275) 313364 is at the Praça do Município. A short drive or bus journey along the N339 takes you to the winter sports resort of **Penhas da Saúde**, 11 km (seven miles) to the northwest, which also makes a good starting point for hiking or climbing. Penhas da Saúde is near the lofty **Torre** with unbeatable views of the region, although the mass of souvenir stalls at the summit slightly mars the romance of the scene.

Between Penhas da Saúde and the Torre, a turning off the N339 takes you along the Zêzere Valley to the small spa town of **Caldas de Manteigas**, and then on to the larger town of **Manteigas**, one of the prettiest in the Serra. If you do make it this far, be sure to make the short excursion to **Poço do Inferno** (Hell's

Well), a wooded gorge with a waterfall that freezes over in winter. North of Manteigas along the road to Gouveia there is a welcoming *pousada*.

Gouveia and **Seia**, both on the western side of the mountain range, are points of access to the **Parque Natural Serra da Estrela**, are served by public transportation. Gouveia has a *Turismo* ((238) 42185 at Avenida 1 de Maio, and there is another at Seia ((238) 25506 in the Largo do Mercado.

Another gateway to the park is **Celorico da Beira** at the northern tip, with an impressive castle. The medieval town of **Linhares** sits upon a rocky outcrop overlooking the Upper Mondego Valley 16 km (10 miles) southwest of Celorico. Take a walk along the town walls for some excellent views, and then wander among the old granite houses, some of which date from the fifteenth century. The two churches—the **Misericórdia church** and the **Parish church** — have fine examples of Portuguese primitive paintings, some believed to be the work of Grão Vasco.

The **Serra de Açor** is a southwestern extension of the Serra da Estrela. One of its most picturesque villages is **Piódão**, where houses built of shale improbably stand on a terraced hillside.

Northeast of Piódão is the village of **Avô**, worth visiting for its setting along the steep bank of the Alva River, spanned by a graceful arched bridge and backed by wooded hills.

Where to Stay

In Covilhã, the best place to stay is the **Hotel Turismo** ((275) 3324545 FAX (275) 324630, Acesso a Variante, Quinta da Olivosa, 6200 Covilhã, a new establishment that offers quality services at mid-range prices. There are also several *pensãos* to choose from. Among the better ones are the **Residencial Santa Eufêmia** ((275) 313308 FAX (275) 314184, Sítio da Palmatória, 6200 Covilhã, a fairly new and inexpensive place out of the center of town, and the **Pensão Restaurante A Regional** ((275) 322596, Rua das Flores No. 4, which offers good value for decent rooms (some with private bath) and has an acceptable restaurant.

In Caldas de Manteigas the inexpensive **Albergeria Berne** ((275) 981351 FAX (275)

982114, Quinta de Santo António, 6260 Manteigas, is quite a relaxing respite. In Manteigas itself there are a few *pensãos* and also the **Casa de São Roque** ((275) 981125, Rua de Santo António No. 51, 6260 Manteigas, a TURIHAB place in the center of town. About 13 km (eight miles) north of Manteigas the **Pousada de São Lourenço** ((275) 982450 FAX (275) 982453, 6260 Manteigas, is a modern building with a warm, lodge-like ambience and wonderful mountain views. Prices vary within the mid-range depending on the season.

How to Get There

Internal flights serve Covilhã from Porto and Lisbon. Trains running between Guarda and Lisbon stop at Covilhã, and a bus service connects Coimbra, Viseu, Guarda, and Castelo Branco to Covilhã. Buses also run between Celorico da Beira, Gouveia, and Linhares, and between Seia and Covilhã via a southern route. On weekends, there is a bus service between Covilhã and Penhas da Saúde.

For drivers, the best access points to the park are through Gouveia, Seia, Covilhã, and Valhelhas (southwest of Guarda) which link easily to the most scenic roads through the Serra da Estrela.

IN AND AROUND VISEU

Viseu, set in pine forested hills alongside the Pavia River, is the capital of Beira Alta, deserving of its title *Antiga et Nobilissima Cidade* (Ancient and Most Noble City). It lies about 292 km (181 miles) north of Lisbon. The medieval core is centered around a square at the city's highest point, within the scant remains of the old walls. In the sixteenth century it was the center of a school of painters led by Gaspar Vaz and Vasco Fernandes (the latter remembered as Grão Vasco: the Great Vasco), who was influenced by the Flemish school. Viseu continued to grow into an agricultural center, its wealth evidenced by its fine Renaissance and baroque buildings.

This center of viticulture is famous for the smooth and aromatic red Dão wines. It's a good base for exploring the cluster of ancient, scenic villages within a manageable radius

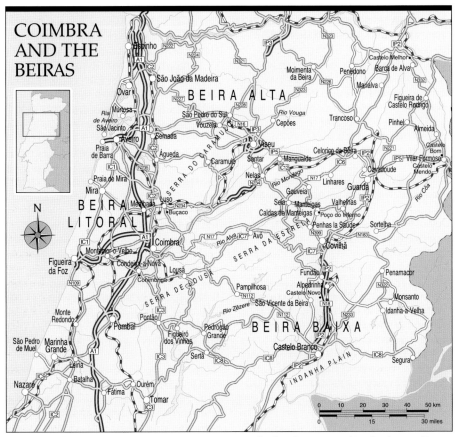

of the city, if you have your own transportation. While it is an easy car trip from Coimbra, staying overnight in Viseu affords another perspective as it is a vital modern city.

General Information

The *Turismo* ((232) 420950 FAX (232) 420957 is in the modern part of Viseu on the Avenida Gulbenkian, not far south of the Praça da República.

What to See and Do

Enter the old city through the majestic fifteenth-century gate, the **Porto do Soar** and wind your way to the **Praça da Sé** (Cathedral Square). Here you will find the somber twin towers of the **Sé** ((232) 425355, built between the thirteenth and eighteenth centuries; although predominantly Romanesque, it embodies the usual amalgam of styles. Upon entering, the golden colors come as a pleasant surprise. The most notable feature is the Manueline ribbing of the

vaulted ceiling, carved in the form of knotted ropes and supported by Gothic pillars. A gilt baroque altarpiece replaces the earlier paintings of Grão Vasco, which are now exhibited in the neighboring museum.

The ground level of the Renaissance cloisters are tiled with eighteenth-century *azulejos* and the upper floor of the old chapterhouse now houses the cathedral's treasury, which has a couple of thirteenth-century Limoges enamel caskets, a twelfth-century Bible, and some other interesting odds and ends. The **sacristy**'s ceiling is painted with satyrs, bizarre animals, birds, and flowers, and of the carving of the choir stalls in the *coro alto* celebrate the Voyages of Discovery.

Next door to the Sé is the **Museu de Grão Vasco** ((232) 422049, housed within the former episcopal palace and filled with paintings by Grão Vasco and others of the Viseu school. One room is set aside for his 14-panel work that depicts scenes from the life of Christ, and which once graced the high altar of the cathedral. Spanish works, nineteenth- and twentieth-century Portuguese paintings, and a collection of sculpture from the thirteenth to the eighteenth centuries form the museum's collection. Open from 10 AM to 1 PM and from 2 PM to 5 PM; closed on Mondays. Admission is free on Saturdays and Sundays.

While the Sé's exterior belies its more interesting interior, the reverse is true of the eighteenth-century **Igreja da Misericórdia** just across the square. Typically Portuguese baroque with whitewash and granite, elegantly twirled and scrolled, its form is pleasingly symmetrical with a tower at each end. Oddly, the interior is rather uninteresting.

Otherwise, the main attractions of Viseu are its narrow streets and alleyways of the old quarter around the cathedral square, with their mixture of sixteenth- and eighteenth-century houses that range from grand, to very humble. Streets running south are lined with restaurants and shops selling local produce and crafts.

The modern part of town centers around the **Praça da República**, commonly called the Rossio, is southwest of the Sé, where a **market** is held every Tuesday at the junction of the Rua Formoso and Rua de Luís Ferreira. From mid-August to mid-September the city sizzles each year with life as the **Feira de São Mateus** comes to town with its celebration of folk music and local food. As Viseu is not a major tourist spot, this makes for a good festival to enjoy its authenticity.

Excursions

The sleepy town of **São Pedro do Sul** lies 22 km (14 miles) northwest of Viseu along the N16, in a verdant riverside setting amid orchards and vineyards. Just four kilometers (two and a half miles) southwest, **Termas de São Pedro do Sul** is believed by some to be the oldest spa in Portugal; the ruined Roman baths near the new spa are evidence of its continuity. The setting close to the Vouga River among pine trees and although there is a fair choice of *pensãos* and hotels, they are generally filled with retirees taking the cure.

The charming **Vouzela**, three kilometers (two miles) south of Termas and west of Viseu, sits on a hillside overlooking the lush Vouga Valley. Here man-made beauties

equal natural ones: several remarkable buildings remain, manor houses amongst them. The **Igreja da Misericórdia** faced with *azulejos* stands out, as does the curved façade of the **Capela de São Frei Gil**. Beautiful in its simplicity, the thirteenth-century **Igreja Matriz** (Parish Church) fuses the Gothic with the Romanesque. It is set in peaceful gardens, its doorway and rose window screened by the bell tower that rises before it. Note the gutter supports carved with human faces. And don't leave without trying the town's specialty, *pasteis de Vouzela*, sweet egg pastries.

Caramulo lies 43 km (27 miles) southwest of Viseu, some 800 m (2,625 ft) up in wooded Serra do Caramulo where the clear air is reputedly good for respiratory problems. This is the unlikely location for an exceptional museum, the **Fundação Abel de Lacerda** ((232) 861270, with an equally unlikely combination of exhibits. The bequest of Portuguese philanthropist Abel de Lacerda, the museum houses paintings by the so-called Portuguese Primitives including work by Grão Vasco, and an exceptional collection of nineteenth- and twentieth-century work by, among others, Picasso, Dali, Dufy, Léger, and Chagall. There are exhibits of furniture, sculpture, archaeological finds, porcelain, and Tournai tapestries bearing fanciful interpretations of the arrival of the Portuguese in India. The eclecticism doesn't end there: on the lower levels is a collection of vintage motorcycles and cars.

A 40-minute walk up the road from the village brings you to the top of **Carmulinho**, the highest point in the Serra, with some dazzling vistas. If you want to stay on, there is a good *pensão* in the village and the **Pousada de São Jerónimo** on a nearby ridge.

The busy agricultural town of **Mangualde** lies 15 km (nine miles) east of Viseu. Its old quarter is a warren of narrow, twisting medieval streets. At its heart is the seventeenth-century **Palácio des Condes de Anadia** (Palace of the Counts of Anadia), pink, baroque and open to the public from roughly 10 AM to noon and from 2 PM to 6 PM.

Santar, 15 km (nine miles) south of Viseu and once known as the Court of the Beiras, is a rewarding side trip. Many of its manor houses have retained their elegance.

Regardless of which towns you choose to visit, if the weather is good, one of the pleasures of your meandering will be the winding drive through the mountain pine forests.

Where to Stay

The top-rated hotel in Viseu proper is the centrally located **Grão Vasco** ((232) 423511 FAX (232) 426444 TOLL-FREE (25) 053-4038 TOLL-FREE IN THE UNITED STATES (800) 336-3542 TOLL-FREE IN THE UNITED KINGDOM (0800) 282720 E-MAIL meliagraovasco@mail .telepac.pt WEB SITE www.solmelia.es, Rua Gaspar Barreiros, 3510 Viseu. The rooms are comfortably modern, typical of an international chain, but overlook a palm-treed garden and swimming pool. Mid-range prices. However, for practically the same price and infinitely more deluxe accommodation, stay at the ultramodern, yet not terribly glitzy **Hotel Montebello** ((232) 420000 FAX (232) 415400, Urbanização Quinta do Bosque, 3510-014 Viseu, just to the southwest of the center of the city. Set in rolling gardens, use of the health club and indoor pool are included, and for additional fees guests have access to their 18-hole golf course, sports center, horseback riding, ice skating, and discotheque. The hotel's restaurant is generally considered one of the best in town. Prices are at the upper end of mid-range.

Near the tourist office, you will find perfectly acceptable inexpensive rooms with private baths, telephone, and television at **Pensão Residencial Dom Duarte** ((232) 421980 FAX (232) 424825, Rua Alexandre Herculano No. 214. Similar accommodation can be found at the **Residencial Bela Vista** ((232) 422026, Rua Alexandre Herculano No. 510.

In Termas de São Pedro do Sul there are several inexpensive to mid-range priced hotels and *pensãos*, however, as pleasant as this town is to pass through, an overnight stay seems unlikely. In Caramulo, the **Pousada de São Jerónimo** ((232) 861291 FAX (232) 861640, 3475 Caramulo, is somewhat reminiscent of a Swiss chalet. The views it offers are spectacular, and its kitchen is superior to many other *pousadas*, the focus being more on country cooking, rather than an attempt at grand cuisine.

Where to Eat

There's no shortage of good eating in Viseu, where one or two establishments offer *fado* entertainment, and locally produced Dão wines are everywhere to be had. **O Cortiço** ((232) 423853, Rua August Hilário No. 47, is justly regarded as the best place in town, and if you are tiring of fish, order the incredibly tender marinated roast lamb. Reservations for dinner are suggested. For more a contemporary ambience, try **Casablanca** ((232) 422239, Avenida Emídio Navarro No. 70.

How to Get There

Strangely, trains no longer run to Viseu: the scenic narrow-gauge line was axed a few years ago, much to the distress of railroad enthusiasts the world over. You can travel from Lisbon or Guarda by train only as far as Nelas, where there is a bus connection for the remainder of the journey. If you are arriving from Porto or Coimbra, you will need to change at Aveiro for Sernada or at Pampilhosa for Nelas and complete the journey by bus. Bus services also run to Viseu from Lisbon, from Coimbra, and from Porto.

Viseu lies 85 km (53 miles) northeast of Coimbra, from where you drive north on the N1, turning on to the N2-IP3 to Viseu after about four kilometers (two and a half miles). From Lisbon it is 292 km (181 miles) north along the A1-IP1 to the point just north of Coimbra where you turn on to the N2-IP3.

COIMBRA

The ancient capital of Beira Litoral and one-time capital of Portugal is 196 km (122 miles) from Lisbon, 117 km (73 miles) from Porto, on a steep hillside overlooking the Mondego River. This is the seat of Portugal's first university (and one of the world's oldest) and its main center of Renaissance art. Although today the university has a smaller student body than that in Lisbon, it is still considered the country's most prestigious institution. Largely, but not solely due to its student population, Coimbra exudes a vibrant charm. There are numerous contemporary art galleries, as well as film, theater, and music festivals throughout the year. All of which becomes even more enchanting when juxtaposed with the grandeur of antiquity.

Listening to its own genre of *fado* music (which is more cerebral and romantic than Lisbon's), relaxing in its cafés and *pastelarias*, or drinking a few with some students in the bars, Coimbra easily becomes the ideal Portuguese city in which to get a feel of the counterpoint of Portugal's past and present.

It must be said that Coimbra is also a commercial center with thriving textile and handicraft industries, and over the years some less-than-attractive building has gone on. This can be ignored. Without question, however, the city suffers from horrendous traffic congestion. If you come by car, park it, and then wend your way through the old section, and the beauty and charm of the place will take hold.

BACKGROUND

To the Romans who had established a city at nearby Conimbriga it was Aeminium, but as the Roman settlement declined it acquired its new name, Coimbra — a corrupted version of Conimbriga. Moors and Christians fought over the city from the ninth century until 1064, when it finally came under Christian control. In 1143, on the accession of Portugal's first king Afonso Henriques, the capital of Portugal was moved here from Guimarães—and here it remained until 1250.

Portugal's famous university was founded in 1290 in the new capital of Lisbon; it was later moved to Coimbra, only to be moved back to Lisbon before settling finally in Coimbra once again in 1537. Jesuits and teachers from other great universities arrived in droves, and in the sixteenth century the Coimbra school of sculpture developed here under Italian-inspired French sculptors Nicolas Chanterene and Jean de Rouen, who joined forces with the Portuguese João and Diogo de Castilho.

GENERAL INFORMATION

The main tourist office for the central region is Região de Turismo do Centro ((239) 833019 FAX (239) 825576, Largo da Portages, 3000 Coimbra. There are also two municipal *Turismos*, one at Largo Dom Denis ((239) 832591 and the other at Praça da República ((239) 833202.

WHAT TO SEE AND DO

The **Velha Universidade** (Old University) crowns the hilltop on which the old city was built. To get there you must weave through a maze of steep and narrow streets. If this is too much of an effort, there are plenty of taxis around — but be sure to walk back through this most lovely part of Coimbra. Entering through the seventeenth-century **Porta Férrea** you will find yourself in the courtyard known as the **Patio das Escolas**, around which the principal old buildings are arranged. A large eighteenth-century clock known as *cabra* — the goat — stands in the courtyard, as does a statue of King João III, who was responsible for returning the university to Coimbra in the sixteenth century, and presenting this palace as a gift to it.

To the right, an elaborate staircase leads up to the **Sala dos Capelos**, a hall with a seventeenth-century painted and gilded ceiling, where portraits of Portuguese kings hang, lending suitable gravity to graduation ceremonies and other academic rites. The catwalk balcony affords a breathtaking panoramic view of the city and its snaking Mondego River, an astonishingly verdant riverbank for a city.

To the immediate left of the tower is the sixteenth-century **Capela de São Miguel**. Designed by Marques Pires, it is a supreme example of the Manueline style. Although its furnishings and paintings are worth a look, its *pièce de résistance* is clearly the grand eighteenth-century baroque pipe organ. The **Museu de Arte Sacra** adjoins the chapel.

To the left of the courtyard, a doorway heavily emblazoned with the coat-of-arms of King João V leads into Coimbra's magnificent **library**, a glittering piece of early eighteenth-century baroque that outshines that of Mafra, built by King João in 1724. Its three rooms lead one into another, at the end of which hangs a portrait of its benefactor, King João, theatrically framed by carved wooden curtains held open by cherubs.

Nearby, in what was once the archbishop's palace, is the **Museu Nacional Machado de Castro** ((239) 823727. It is worth a visit just to look around the sixteenth-century building and see the decoration in some of the upper rooms. The palace was built over subterranean vaulted passages constructed by the Romans, which now form the basement. The sculpture collection, spanning the fifteenth to the eighteenth centuries, is exhibited on the ground floor and some of the first floor.

The first floor also contains liturgical gold and silverware, jewelry, ceramics, oriental carpets, porcelain, and Portuguese and Flemish art from the same period. The museum is open Tuesdays to Sundays, 9:30 AM to 12:30 PM and 2 PM to 5 PM. Admission is free on Sundays.

The nearby **Sé Nova** (New Cathedral), dating from the seventeenth century and considered new in these environs, can be skipped in favor of the more interesting Romanesque **Sé Velha** (Old Cathedral); a fortress-like edifice built in the twelfth century. The Renaissance portal added in the sixteenth century is believed to be the work of Jean de Rouen, but is in bad condition. The cavernous interior has been returned to its original simplicity, and thus the sixteenth-century altarpiece, with its gilding carvings by Flemish artists, is that much more dominant.

The streets surrounding the cathedral have bars frequented by students where *fado* music often erupts in the evenings. Look out for the **Paço de Sub-Ripas**, on Rua Sub-Ripas, a sixteenth-century residence built in Manueline style that incorporates part of the old city walls. The doors and windows are Manueline, while the walls are covered with bas-reliefs by Jean de Rouen. As this is a private residence you will have to make do with looking at it from the outside.

Continue down through the city to the **Mosteiro de Santa Cruz**, a sixteenth-century Augustinian Monastery with numerous examples of the Coimbra school of sculpture on display. The Renaissance entrance is the work of Chanterene and Diogo de Castilho, now sadly damaged by pollution and weathering. Afonso Henriques and Sancho I, the first two kings of Portugal, lie here in richly carved tombs on either side of the high altar, and some finely gilded wood carving in the stalls of the *coro alto* incorporates images of Vasco da Gama's voyages. Open from 9 AM to noon and from 2 PM to 6 PM; Sundays 4 PM to 6 PM.

Over the bridge is one of Coimbra's strangest sights, the **Convento de Santa Clara-a-Velha**. This fourteenth-century Gothic church was abandoned in the late seventeenth century because of flooding from the Mondego. It is now a ruin partially submerged in the silt and waters of the river, yet its beautiful interior has an almost Romanesque simplicity.

The church was founded by Queen Isabel, at whose hands it was said gold turned to roses; as legend has it, her husband was less than thrilled with her great generosity. When he attempted to call her bluff during one of her charitable outings, she claimed, not quite truthfully, that her apron was full of flowers. The king insisted on seeing what it was that she was carrying, and miraculously her apron was indeed full of roses.

If you are traveling with children, a good break would be a visit to **Portugal dos Pequeninos (** (239) 441225. Next to Santa Clara-a-Velha, this is a collection of miniature famous buildings and monuments of Portugal and its former colonies. Hours are daily from 10 AM to 5 PM in the winter, and 10 AM to 7 PM in the summer.

On a nearby hill the **Santa Clara-a-Nova** (New Convent of Saint Clare) looks down on the river with some excellent views of Coimbra. Built in the seventeenth century as a replacement for the old convent, "New" of course, is somewhat relative. These days it is partly used as a barracks and houses a military museum, and despite some glittering baroque carving, it has acquired a slightly martial air. It lacks the simple beauty of its precursor, but go there to see the original fourteenth-century stone tomb of Queen Isabel, Coimbra's patron saint, removed from the old convent and stationed behind a grille. Her statue shows her in the plain garments of a Poor Clare nun, her dogs at her side. Her remains now lie in the elaborate silver tomb on the high altar, and it is said that when her body was transferred it was redolent of the perfume of flowers, showing no sign of decay although she had died some 300 years earlier. A sure sign of sainthood. Opening hours are from 9 AM to noon and from 2 PM to 5 PM.

There are many more churches and chapels to visit, and one could easily meander for a few days, but if you are tiring of sightseeing and the weather is good, take an hour **cruise** ((239) 404135 along the Mondego River. Boats leave in the afternoons from the dock at Parque Dr. Manuel Braga.

WHERE TO STAY

Luxury

If despite all efforts to remain the objective observer, *fado* has got the better of you, a stay at the **Hotel Quinta das Lágrimas** ((239) 441615 FAX (239) 826827, Santa Clara,

htcoimbramail.telepac.pt, Rua João Machado No. 4, 3000 Coimbra. It offers a full range of facilities, including a health club and an indoor swimming pool, but as it is part of a chain, the feel is somewhat antiseptic.

Mid-range

Coimbra's most charming hotel is the three-star **Hotel Astória** ((239) 822055 FAX (239) 822057, Avenida Emídio Navarro No. 21, 3000 Coimbra, a 1930s building overlooking the Mondego River and Santa Clara, edged with balconies and topped with a blue cupola.

3000 Coimbra, might be appropriate. The "House of Tears" (as its name translates) is an eighteenth-century palace built on fourteenth-century melodrama. Prince Dom Pedro fell in love with Inês de Castro, who inconveniently was his wife's lady-in-waiting. Upon orders of his father King Alfonso IV, Inês was stabbed to death on the Quinta's grounds. During the monarchy, the palace housed visiting royalty and dignitaries, and as a hotel, it has retained its demeanor. A swimming pool and an eight-hole golf course occupy the expansive gardens.

One of Coimbra's four-star hotels is the very modern **Hotel Tivoli Coimbra** ((239) 826934 FAX (239) 826827 E-MAIL

Rooms facing the river are resplendent with light and vista, yet insulated from the traffic below. The restaurant (see WHERE TO EAT, below) offers the rare opportunity to taste the famous Buçaco wines made on the premises of the Buçaco Palace Hotel in the Forest of Buçaco (see page 172). One distinct disadvantage not to be taken lightly is the hotel's lack of parking facilities. There is public parking across the street, but be prepared to return every four hours to feed the meter. If you plan on staying more than overnight, the best idea is to park your car (at no cost, with no time limit) on the other side of the

Coimbra University is one of Europe's oldest seats of learning. Its library houses more than a million tomes.

Santa Clara bridge. After crossing, immediately turn right and find a spot.

Although admittedly not quaint and without spectacular views, the new three-star **Hotel Oslo** ((239) 829071 FAX (239) 820614, Avenida Fernão de Magalhães No. 25, 3000 Coimbra, should be your choice if modern services (including parking) are your priority.

Inexpensive
Pensão Internacional ((239) 825503, Avenida Emídio Navarro No. 4, 3000 Coimbra, is close

717013, Rua Dom Manuel I, Piscinas Municipais, is a large restaurant with great views, located in a sports center. The food is again a mixture of local and continental and is considered some of the best in town. **Dom Pedro** ((239) 829108, Avenida Emídio Navarro No. 58, offers an upscale setting and a similar menu. In contrast, **O Alfredo** ((239) 441522, Avenida João das Regras No. 32, on the other side of the Santa Clara bridge, is much more low-key. It serves traditional fare, with seafood being a specialty. The stately Old World charm of the dining room at the

to the railway station with a down-at-heel grandeur. Rooms are clean but basic, and do have private bathrooms and double windows to counter street noise. Not much farther from the station, at only slightly higher prices, the **Pensão Residencial Domus** ((239) 828584 FAX (239) 838818, Rua Adelino Veiga No. 62, 3000 Coimbra, offers far superior accommodation.

WHERE TO EAT

Moderate
Trovador ((239) 825475, Praça Sé Velha, is decorated in traditional Coimbran style and serves good local and continental food to the accompaniment of *fado* music. **Piscinas** ((239)

Amphytryon in the Hotel Astória (see WHERE TO STAY, above) makes it a pleasant restaurant for classic Portuguese dishes.

Inexpensive
Zé Manel dos Ossos ((239) 823790, Beco do Forno No. 12, is a rather trendy spot with a noisy bistro atmosphere, and **Pinto d'Ouro** ((239) 441243, Avenida João das Regras No. 68, is another favorite serving regional food, with chicken the specialty.

HOW TO GET THERE

There are three train stations in Coimbra: Coimbra A ((239) 817363, Coimbra B ((239) 833525, and Coimbra Parque (used mainly for local trains to Lousã). Coimbra A is the most centrally located, but some trains stop only at Coimbra B, north of the town center, in which case you can easily pick up a connection to Coimbra A. Trains run frequently from Porto and from Lisbon's Santa Apolónia station to Coimbra B, those from Porto sometimes making a train change at Pampilhosa. Trains leave from Coimbra B for Figueira da Foz and points between.

Express buses run regularly to Coimbra from Lisbon, Porto, and also from the major towns and cities, arriving at the bus station ((239) 827081 in Avenida Fernão Magalhães. The international bus service connecting Lisbon with Paris also stops here.

Coimbra is 196 km (122 miles) north of Lisbon and 117 km (73 miles) south of Porto, just four kilometers (two-and-a-half miles) east of the Lisbon-Porto highway, the A1-IP1, which makes driving from either direction fairly straightforward.

AROUND COIMBRA

CONIMBRIGA

Conimbriga is Portugal's most extant and impressive Roman site, just 15 km (nine miles) southwest of Coimbra, where you can see the remains of a Roman city dating from between the first and fifth centuries AD. Partial excavation has uncovered houses, pools, fountains, baths, heating and cooling systems, and some exquisite mosaics. The remains of a hastily erected defensive wall cut through the city, evidence of a desperate effort by the inhabitants to fend off Suevi attack. The effort failed, and the city was taken in AD 465, its citizens either killed or enslaved. Over the years that followed, people gravitated toward the nearby settlement of Aeminium, present-day Coimbra, and Conimbriga was eventually abandoned.

The well-mounted **Museu Monográfico** ((239) 941177 houses artifacts unearthed at the site, giving a fascinating insight into how this sophisticated city actually functioned. Opening times on Tuesday to Saturday are from 9 AM to 1 PM and from 2 PM to 6 PM.

The museum has a good café, but for more substantial fare make a short detour to the town of **Condeixa a Nova**, just two kilometers

(one mile) outside Conimbriga. Worth seeing there are its eighteenth- and nineteenth-century houses, many of them emblazoned with coats-of-arms. Its finest building is the **Solar Sotto Maior**, a baroque mansion that hosted royal visitors in its time. Along with several good small restaurants, Condeixa has nine ceramics factories that sell directly to the public.

There is infrequent bus service from Coimbra to Conimbriga (the *Turismo* has updated schedules), and a more frequent one running to Condeixa a Nova, two kilo-

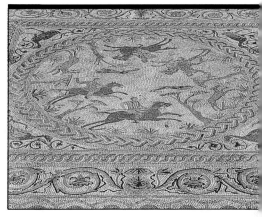

meters (one mile) away. If you take the bus to Condeixa, taxi service to the archeological site is not expensive and recommended.

LOUSÃ

The village of Lousã lies 25 km (15 miles) southeast of Coimbra, at the foothills of the wild and wooded **Serra de Lousã** by the Arouce River; with a *pensão* to stay at, it makes a good base for exploring the Serra. A scenic pathway leads up and out of the village to a ruined castle above the surrounding forests, and to the nearby **Sanctuary of Nossa Senhora de Piedade**. As befits such a romantic ruin it is shrouded in legends.

Trains run from Coimbra to Lousã, but for the trips into the Serra you will either need a car or a good pair of hiking boots.

In Condeixa, the *Turismo* ((239) 944764 FAX (239) 941474 is located in the museum. In Lousã, the *Turismo* ((239) 990370 FAX (239)

Some of the most extensive Roman remains ABOVE and OPPOSITE in Portugal, are found in Conimbriga, south of Coimbra.

990379 is found in the Câmara Municipal (city hall).

BUÇACO AND LUSO

The **Forest of Buçaco** on the northern slopes of the Serra da Buçaco is one of Portugal's most enchanting sights. At its heart lies the magnificent **Buçaco Palace**, now one of Europe's finest hotels. The forest covers 101 hectares (250 acres) and makes a delicious respite from the heat and congestion of Coimbra just 27 km (17 miles) away. If your

occupied themselves planting exotic plants from all over the world, among them maples, giant ferns, laurels, and Mexican cedars and cypresses. Under such devout preservation, the forest became famous, and papal bulls were issued threatening excommunication to anyone who damaged so much as a leaf. With an eye to the brothers' chastity, women were prohibited. (The text of the papal bulls is inscribed on the Coimbra Gate.)

The idyll was shattered when, in September 1810, an English and Portuguese army of 30,000, under the command of the Duke

trip to Portugal brings you anywhere near this part of the country, you must visit it. Ideally, stay at the Buçaco Palace Hotel, but if it is beyond your budget, try to have dinner or lunch there. The estate-bottled wines are beyond words, and although the wine list dates back to 1945, the *Tinto Reserva 1991* is sufficiently superb. Nearby Luso has plenty of more reasonably priced accommodation.

Background

The forest's religious connections began in the sixth century when Benedictine monks made a hermitage in its interior, far from worldly distractions. In the seventeenth century Carmelite monks built a surrounding wall and created a monastery. They then

of Wellington, defeated Napoleon's larger force at the Battle of Buçaco. In 1834, in accordance with the decree dissolving all religious orders in Portugal, the forest passed into the hands of laymen who continued the tradition of introducing new varieties of trees. Toward the end of the century an Italian architect, Luigi Manini, was commissioned to build a royal hunting lodge on the site of the Carmelite monastery. The neo-Manueline palace, with its ceramic depictions of Wellington in battle, was not finished until 1907, by which time the monarchy was in its death throes. When the last of the Braganças had sailed away from Portugal, the government gave permission for the royal chef to run the Buçaco Palace as a luxury hotel.

General Information

The *Turismo* ((231) 939133 is in Luso at Rua Emídio Navarro.

What to See and Do

Despite the stream of tour buses, the luxuriant forest maintains its serenity, and walking along some of its hermitage-dotted paths is a refreshingly tranquil experience. The Buçaco Palace Hotel and the *Turismo* in neighboring Luso can supply maps showing the various routes. One of the most beautiful sights is the **Fonte Fria** (Cold Fountain) where

circulatory and metabolic disorders, and skin, kidney, and urinary problems. The town's social life perks up considerably during spa season, which runs from June through October. The **Termas de Luso** ((231) 930211 FAX (213) 930168, Rua Álvaro de Castelões, 3050 Mealhada, is a fine spot to pamper yourself with the treatments — massage, physiotherapy, mud baths, etc. — all under medical supervision and reasonably priced. There are sports facilities: a jogging track near the lake, rowing, tennis courts, and swimming facilities.

a spring pours from a cave and cascades down a long stairway into a pool lined with magnolias.

The modest **Museu da Guerra Peninsular** (Peninsular War Museum) ((231) 939210 is near the Porta da Rainha, and concerns itself with the Battle of Buçaco. Little is left of the old monastery, but near the hotel the **monastery church** still stands with the cloister and cork-lined cells, one of which was used by Wellington on the eve of the battle.

Just outside the forest the spa town of Luso nestles in a valley, with a good collection of hotels. Luso is particularly popular with the Portuguese who come here to take the waters, which are said to be good for rheumatism,

Where to Stay

The **Palace Hotel do Buçaco** ((231) 930204 FAX (231) 930509, Mata Buçaco, Buçaco, 3050 Mealhada (expensive), is a magnificent confection of arcades and neo-Manueline encrustation that reaches its highest point in the lace-like filigree stonework of the restaurant terrace but maintains a human scale in the discreet entrance. The public areas are grand but not intimidating, and the overall effect relaxing. The scent of polished chestnut pervades the hallways; the service, proper yet charming, is enhanced by the obvious pride that everyone takes in the

Set in luxurious forests, sybaritic Buçaco Palace OPPOSITE and ABOVE has been described as "the shadiest hotel in Portugal."

place. The Palace retains its Edwardian atmosphere and the tranquillity of the forest around it.

There is a variety of large, airy rooms and suites with views of the palace and forest, all at luxury prices. An extensive room refurbishment project has recently been undertaken and their character is enhanced rather than diminished — a feat the Portuguese seem to have mastered.

In Luso the choice hotel is undoubtedly the **Grande Hotel das Termas do Luso** ((231) 930450 FAX (231) 930350, Rua dos Banhos, 3050 Mealhada, a very chic art deco-style place next to the spa with an Olympic-sized swimming pool, tennis courts, a spa and much more. Prices are mid-range. There are several *pensãos*, most of which are fairly good and all are inexpensive. Under the TURIHAB scheme are two country homes. On a hill overlooking the town is the **Vila Duparchy** ((231) 93120 FAX (231) 930307, Rua José Duarte Figueiredo, Luso, 3050 Mealhada. This is a late nineteenth-century house with six bedrooms, and a swimming pool set in a garden. **Vila Aurora** ((231) 930150 FAX (231) 930193, Luso, 3050 Mealhada, is a nineteenth-century rendition of a medieval castle.

Where to Eat

The dining room at the **Palace Hotel do Buçaco** is open for lunch and dinner to non-guests, though it is best to make reservations. Its carved Gothic-style ceiling and Manueline terrace are spectacular, the cuisine fine, and the cellar renowned.

Most other restaurants are attached to the hotels and *pensãos*, however, the inexpensive **Restaurante O Cesteiro** ((231) 939360, Rua José Duarte Figueiredo, on the edge of town is reliable for its local cooking.

How to Get There

Buses from Coimbra to Luso make a detour through the forest to the Palace Hotel, and express buses run from Coimbra to Luso. Buses from Coimbra to Viseu also make a detour from Luso through the forest to the Palace Hotel.

If you are driving from Coimbra, go 23 km (14 miles) up the A1 highway to Mealhada then along the N234 to Luso. If you have a little more time to spare, take the longer, more

scenic route (38 km or 24 miles) on the N110 along the Mondego to Penacova, and the N235 through the Serra de Buçaco to Luso.

FIGUEIRA DA FOZ AND ENVIRONS

The fishing port of Figueira da Foz lies 46 km (29 miles) west of Coimbra, where the Mondego River meets the sea. Formerly a working town, it was transformed into a seaside resort during the nineteenth century. Although most would say that the three-kilometer (two-mile) stretch of sandy beach is the main attraction, during the summer it is terribly crowded and Figueira's main draw should be its casino, for those so drawn. There are, however, a few cultural sites including the **Museu Municipal do Dr. Santos**

Rocha ((233) 33) 424509, Rua Calouste Gulbenkian, which has particularly good archaeological displays and sections on the decorative arts, and the **Casa do Paço** ((233) 422159, Largo Prof. Victor Guerra No. 4, a stately old building with an excellent collection of Delft tiles.

To the north of Figueira is a long stretch of somewhat quieter coastline, but the beaches are very exposed, and the surf often very rough. **Praia de Mira**, some 41 km (25 miles) north is another traditional fishing place with a wide sandy beach. You can still see oxen pulling in the nets and houses built on stilts above the water.

The old town of **Montemor-o-Velho**, down in the Mondego Valley, 17 km (11 miles) east of Figueira da Foz on the Coimbra road

is worth a visit if you are in the area. Once important in the defense of Coimbra, it is overlooked by the sprawling eleventh- and fourteenth-century castle, which although in ruins remains an impressive sight.

In Figueira da Foz the *Turismo* ((233) 22610 or (233) 402827 is on the seafront at Avenida 25 de Abril.

Where to Stay and Eat

In Figueira da Foz there is a choice of large modern hotels and *pensãos*, although it does get very full in the summer. The only four-star hotel is the **Hotel Mercure Figueira Da Foz** ((233) 422146/7/8 FAX (233) 422420, Avenida 25 de Abril, 3080 Figueira da Foz,

Misty morning haze on the tranquil lagoon (*ria*), the centerpiece of the Parque Natural da Ria de Aveiro.

looking onto the beach. It has an Olympic-sized swimming pool and guests have free access to the Figueira Casino. Expensive. **Hotel Wellington (** (233) 426767 FAX (233) 427593 E-MAIL hotelwellington@mail .telepac.pt, Rua Dr. Calado Nos. 23/27, is a good choice in the mid-range category. The **Pensão Central (** (233) 422308, Rua Bernardo Lopes No. 36, is clean and bright. This is an inexpensive establishment, however prices throughout the city become significantly inflated during the summer months. Alternatively, come for the day from Coimbra.

There is a plethora of restaurants and cafés, all serving the standard fare, none meriting particular mention.

How to Get There

A frequent train service runs from Coimbra A to Figueira da Foz, and also from Lisbon via Óbidos and Leiria. A local bus service links Figueira with Praia de Mira.

The drive from Coimbra to Figueira da Foz is straightforward as Figueira lies 46 km (29 miles) west of Coimbra along the N111.

AVEIRO AND ENVIRONS

Aveiro is more a labyrinth of canals than a city, sitting at the edge of a shallow, salty lagoon. Because of its topography, gray misty skies can yield to blue in minutes. The central canal is lined with pretty buildings and colorful wooden bridges and is a good starting point for day trips on the *ria* (the lagoon) and to explore other parts of the Parque Natural da Ria de Aveiro.

Background

Once a thriving seaport and trade center, Aveiro suffered a devastating blow in 1575 when, at the height of the city's prosperity a violent storm moved the sandbanks, blocking off access to the sea and creating a huge lagoon. Business dried up, livelihoods were lost, and the town began to empty. Centuries later in 1808 another dramatic storm helped to reopen the passage to the sea, and although Aveiro's story is not quite a riches-to-rags-to-riches fairy tale, prosperity has certainly returned, as evidenced by the slew of expensive clothing and leather-goods shops. In fact, today Aveiro's main commerce is also what makes it so picturesque: elegant swan-necked boats called *moliceiros* are used to gather seaweed for fertilizer, and the striking geometric lines of salt pans glisten with white pyramids of salt.

General Information

The *Turismo* **(** (234) 423680 FAX (234) 428326 is in Rua João Mendonça No. 8.

What to See and Do

Aveiro's major sight is the fifteenth-century **Convento de Jesús (** (234) 423297 in the Rua Santa Joana Princesa, now the municipal museum. The convent chapel, also part of the museum, is filled with gilded wood carvings, and *azulejos*. In the eighteenth century, a magnificent tomb of delicate inlaid pink marble, supported by stone phoenixes and angels, and topped with cherubs that support her coat-of-arms and crown was placed in the former chancel to honor Santa Joana. The museum is open from 10 AM to 12:30 PM and from 2 PM to 5 PM; it is closed on Mondays.

There are several other churches in Aveiro, although none are as interesting as the convent. The other main attraction here is the lagoon, which presents a variety of sporting possibilities such as fishing, water skiing and boating, but pollution can be a problem.

Consult the *Turismo* regarding all sports, as well as boat tours.

Aveiro itself doesn't have a beach, but there are several within easy reach. **Praia de Barra** at the mouth of the Vougais is the nearest, just a bus ride away, but it is usually crowded and ugly developments have spoiled the setting. Appreciation of the tall pink and white stripped lighthouse is a matter of taste. Better to travel a few kilometers further south to **Costa Nova**, a pleasant new resort that also has a penchant for bright stripes.

The hope is that promised amelioration will not destroy its personality. Mid-range.

Of the inexpensive options, the well-located **Hotel Arcada (** (234) 423001 FAX (234) 421886, Rua Viana do Castelo, 3800 Aveiro, is the choice at the higher end of the category. The interior has been updated and rooms have fine views of the Central Canal. **Pensão Palmeira (** (234) 422521, Rua da Palmeira No. 7-11, is centrally located, and in some cases, bathroom facilities are shared. **Pensão Estrêla (** (234) 423818, Rua José Estêvão No. 4, 3800 Aveiro, offers similar accommodation.

Where to Stay

Of the top-level hotels in Aveiro, only the brand new **Hotel Moliceiro (** (234) 377400 FAX (234) 377491 E-MAIL hotelmoliceiro@mail .telepac.pt, Rua Barbosa de Magalhães Nos. 15/17, 3800 Aveiro, should be considered. Sleek, but still with charm, it offers unpretentious quality accommodation at upper mid-range prices. However, the **Paloma Blanca (** (234) 381992 FAX (234) 381844, Rua Luís Gomes de Carvalho No. 23, 3800 Aveiro, is the place to stay. This Moorish villa has a loggia and a fountain in the courtyard, and a comfortable and well-equipped interior. Please note that in 2000, the hotel will be renamed **Mercure Aveiro** when it officially becomes part of the French chain.

Outside Aveiro, some of the best accommodation is to be found at the **Pousada da Ria (** (234) 838332 FAX (234) 838333, 3870 Murtosa, on the isthmus that separates Murtosa from São Jacinto, approximately 29 km (18 miles) north of Aveiro. This 1960s building is long and low, and its ample use of glass affords expansive views of the surrounding lagoon and sea, a real boon for bird lovers. Prices are mid-range.

The **Hotel Palácio de Águeda (** (234) 601977 FAX (234) 601976, Quinta da Borralha, 3750 Águeda, is close to the town of Águeda, 23 km (14 miles) southeast of Aveiro, and an

Local scenes are depicted on *azulejos* OPPOSITE at Aveiro's railway station. Three canals slice through the town ABOVE.

Coimbra and the Beiras

outstanding manor house with spacious accommodation and modern amenities. Surrounded by gardens and with plenty of sporting facilities, you probably won't want to move from it. Expensive.

Where to Eat
Seafood abounds in Aveiro, and you could easily do well just stopping in somewhere. Near the fish market are two inexpensive options where freshness is the selling point. **Telheiro** ((234) 429473, Largo da Praça do Peixe No. 20, serves local specialties; as does **O Mercantel**, Rua de António dos Santos. If they are available, try the sautéed eels. For an especially densely populated fish soup, dine at **Centenário** ((234) 422798, Largo do Mercado, where the most uncomplicated dishes are the best.

However, there is a wonderful restaurant in town that is worth getting lost to find. The unprepossessing front belies the charming wooden A-frame interior of **Salpoente** ((234) 911326, Rua Canal São Roque No. 83. Try not to get filled up with the assortment of appetizers that appear as you sit down. Naturally fish and seafood are the main fare, but grilled meats are also available. If you are an œnophile and it is still available, order a bottle of the Casa de Seima Reserva 1995 Bairrada; ichthyophiles notwithstanding.

How to Get There
Frequent train services to Aveiro run from both Coimbra and Porto, while a less frequent service operates from Lisbon, stopping at Coimbra en route. From Viseu it is necessary to take a bus as far as Sernada where you can pick up a train to Aveiro. Express buses run from Coimbra and from Porto to Águeda, 19 km (12 miles) away, where you will have to change for Aveiro, making the train journey the easiest means of public transport.

For drivers, Aveiro lies 14 km (nine miles) off the Lisbon–Porto A1 highway, an overall distance of 47 km (29 miles) from Coimbra and 69 km (43 miles) from Porto.

Swan-prowed, flat-bottomed *moliceiros* of Phoenician ancestry trawl the *ria* gathering seaweed for use as fertilizer.

Porto
and the
North

PORTO

Portugal's second city clings to the rocky slopes rising sharply from the north bank of the Douro River, 314 km (195 miles) north of Lisbon on the coast. Its heart is a fascinating and compact tumble of old buildings facing the suburb of Vila Nova de Gaia across the water, where port matures in the dark of the sundry lodges.

The broadly accepted "given" is that Lisbon is relaxed, whereas Porto is frenetic; that Lisbon parties long after Porto has tucked itself in; and that Lisbon is radical, Porto conservative. No doubt there are elements of truth here, but perhaps even due to its second-city status, Porto seems less shackled than Lisbon, and it is here that contemporary dance, music, and art thrives.

BACKGROUND

In the days of the Roman Empire the settlements of *Cale* and *Portus* (modern-day Porto) faced each other across the main crossing point of the Douro. Their names fused together and the region that lay between the Minho and Douro rivers became known as the earldom, later the kingdom, of Portucale.

The alliance between England and Portugal was sealed in the Porto cathedral with the marriage of Philippa of Lancaster to King João I in 1387. In a nearby house, also still standing, Philippa gave birth to the Infante, Henry the Navigator, who was to pioneer Portugal's golden age. This connection has remained throughout the centuries of great importance to both countries, both before and after they were empires.

In the fifteenth century Henry busied himself in Porto's thriving shipyards, overseeing the building of the ships used to carry troops to Ceuta in North Africa, where the famous battle of 1415 was fought. The citizens of Porto turned over all their cattle to provide food for the journey, leaving themselves with only the tripe, which prepared in imaginative ways remains a delicious local specialty (admittedly, an acquired taste.)

English merchants had been coming to Porto since the days of the Crusades, but in the seventeenth century, when trade relations

between France and England were strained, this city became even more attractive. The Methuen Treaty of 1703 lowered the import duty on wines to England and on wool to Portugal, effectively allowing the British to dominate the port trade. In order to break their monopoly, in 1755 the Marquês de Pombal created the world's first demarcated wine region in the Upper Douro, forming the Casa do Douro to control and administer it. Thereafter, British shippers were forced to buy brandy for fortifying port from the company, whose regulations vastly im-

proved the quality of the wine. The British, however, had assumed such a proprietorial attitude toward Porto, and had become so attached to port that despite these devastating changes many stayed on. Adaptations and circumventions proliferated. In the words of the British Captain Marryat, "...we can't get no Port Wine anywhere else."

GENERAL INFORMATION

The Porto ICEP (Investimentos, Comércio e Turismo de Portugal) has an office ((22) 205-7514 at Praça Dom João I No. 43, and one at the Aeroporto Francisco Sá Carneiro ((22) 941-2534. The municipal *Turismo* ((22) 339-3472 is at Rua Clube Fenianos No. 25.

For specific travel inquires, the following telephone numbers may prove useful: **Aeroporto Francisco Sá Carneiro** ((22) 941-3150 or (22) 941-3260; **general train information**

Porto's old town OPPOSITE has a medieval mien, while a daily market ABOVE is held on the Ribeira waterfront in the shadow of the double-decker Dom Luís I bridge.

((22) 536-4141; **Rodoviária Nacional** (intercity bus travel) ((22) 200-6954 or (22) 205-2459.

The main office of **TAP Air Portugal** ((22) 608-0239 is at Praça Mouzinho de Albuquerque No. 105.

Contact the **Automóvel Clube de Portugal** (ACP) ((22) 205-6732 FAX (22) 205-6698 at Rua Gonçalo Cristóvão Nos. 2-6, 4000 Porto, for driving information.

GETTING AROUND

Driving is just as impossible here as in Lisbon. Parking spaces are virtually nonexistent, and when one does appear, so does a street hustler demanding a tip for some ill-defined service. Thus, once again, abandon your car as soon as possible. Most of the main sights are within easy walking distance from one another, and there are plenty of buses, trams, and taxis when the hills start taking their toll.

As in Lisbon, if you intend using buses or trams frequently, it makes sense to buy blocks of tickets or to buy a tourist pass from one of the kiosks around the city. Full fares, however, are not expensive. Taxis are easy to find except during rush hours and all have meters; note that there is a fixed fare for crossing over to Vila Nova de Gaia. The Praça da Liberdade in the heart of the city is the main tram and bus terminal.

WHAT TO SEE AND DO

City Center North of São Bento

The **Estação São Bento** is a fairly central point from which to begin your explorations, and quite worth a visit in its own right. Renowned for its blue and white *azulejos* of traditional and historic scenes, the turn-of-the-century cathedral-like entrance hall opens to an iron and glass structure, beyond which, in turn, are remarkable views of the steep streets of the city. Just to the north lies the **Praça da Liberdade** which leads on to the wide **Avenida dos Aliados**, lined with grand buildings, opulent cafés, and the typical black and white mosaic pavements found throughout Portugal, here in a grand *fleur-de-lys* pattern.

To get your bearings and a remarkable overview of Porto, head westward to the

Torre dos Clérigos (Clérigos Tower), an elaborate baroque masterpiece and once the tallest structure in Portugal. It was built between 1732 and 1750 by the Italian architect Nicolau Nasoni, who also designed the stately oval church at its base. Climb the 225 steps up the 76-m (250-ft) bell tower for some splendid views. The church and tower are open daily (except Wednesdays) from 10:30 AM to noon and from 2 PM to 5 PM.

Near the tower, classy streets lined with art galleries surround the **Coardaria gardens**. At the back of the church is a network of

winding lanes where the pungent smell of *bacalhau* wafts out from little grocery shops. To the south of the tower along the **Rua das Flores** are shops that have changed little in the last 100 years. On the same street it comes as something of a surprise to stumble across another of Nasoni's grand buildings, the baroque **Igreja da Misericórdia**. Tucked away in the depths of the adjacent **Casa da Misericórdia** is one of Portugal's Renaissance jewels, an enigmatic painting from the Flemish school dating from the sixteenth century that depicts King Manuel I and his family, all in vividly colored robes, gathered around the bleeding, crucified Christ. You will need to ask at the Casa de Misericórdia to be shown the painting.

Northwest of Clérigos along the Rua Dom Manuel II, Porto's most important museum, the **Museu Nacional Soares dos Reis** ((22) 339-3770, is installed in the eighteenth-century Carrancas Palace. It was opened in the 1930s as Portugal's first national museum and was later named in honor of one of the foremost Portuguese sculptors of the last century. Some of Soares dos Reis' major works are on display here, as are early French, Italian, Flemish, and Portuguese paintings. Opening hours are from 10 AM to noon and from 2 PM to 5 PM

the quaint **Museu Romântico** ((22) 609-1131. Open from 10 AM to noon and from 2 PM to 5 PM. Closed Mondays.

A little to the east of São Bento station is the **Rua de Santa Catarina**, Porto's most expensive shopping area. Numerous well-known European names have stores here, as do a number of Portuguese mainstays such as Reis Filhos with its black art nouveau façade. Off to the west of Rua de Santa Catarina at the junction of Rua Formosa and Rua de Sã da Bandeira you will find the **Bolhão Market** where local produce and

Tuesday to Sunday. Admission is free on Sunday mornings.

In the northeastern corner of the nearby **Jardim do Palácio de Cristal** (Crystal Palace Gardens), the site of a sports pavilion, a playground and occasional exhibitions, is an attractive mansion set in gardens called the **Quinta da Maceirinha**, Rua de Entre Quintas No. 220; it contains the **Solar do Vinho** ((22) 609-4749, where you can enjoy a glass of port in an elegant, relaxed atmosphere. Open from 11 AM to 11 PM Monday to Friday and from 5 PM to 11 PM on Saturday. Another part of the *quinta* is furnished and decorated in nineteenth-century style befitting its onetime resident, King Carlos Alberto of Sardinia, who died in exile here in 1849. This comprises

flowers are on sale. It is open Monday to Friday from 8 AM to 5 PM, and from 8 AM to 1 PM on Saturdays.

Between São Bento and the River

A steep walk up the hill to the south of Estação São Bento will bring you to Porto's brooding and fortress-like **Sé** (Cathedral) set on a wide flagged square; it dates from the twelfth century and there is a dark somberness about the interior that Baroquification seems only to have accentuated rather than counteracted. The nicest part is the Chapel of the Holy Sacrament where you can see the highly prized silver retable that was sagaciously

At the mouth of the Douro, Porto looks across at Vila Nova de Gaia on the south bank.

painted over during the Peninsular Wars to escape the notice of looting soldiers. The delicate paintwork in the choir gives the impression of faded tapestry. For relief from the excesses of the high altar, turn your eye toward the south transept and the simplicity of the Romanesque arches. Climb the steps from the fine Gothic cloister for views over the battlements. Adjoining the cathedral is the former **Bishop's Palace**, an enormous example of restrained baroque designed by Nasoni. One of Porto's most prominent features, it now houses municipal offices.

One of the best reasons for visiting the cathedral is for its views. From the cathedral square overlooking the Douro and its graceful bridges you can see the port lodges across the water in Vila Nova de Gaia, with famous names emblazoned on the roofs — Croft, Dow, Sandeman—as well as Porto's extraordinary medieval district, down the hill below the cathedral in a labyrinth of steep, narrow streets hewn into the rock. This quarter is known as the **Barredo** in which both the houses and the standard of living have remained, for the most part, quite medieval. The Barredo is beginning to change, however, and plans are in the works to gentrify it. It runs south and west of the cathedral down to the **Cais do Ribeira,** a colorful dock-

side area where the smell of fish and the perfume of flowers mingle around the market. Many of the cavernous buildings have already undergone clever restoration, and tucked into their ground floors are restaurants and cafés, making this a lively nightspot. Down here you are close to another great Porto landmark, the **Ponte de Dom Luís I**. This magnificent iron bridge was built in 1886 and both vehicles and pedestrians use it. Spanning the Douro on two levels, it links both the upper and lower city with Vila Nova de Gaia. Its design complements that of the **Ponte de Maria Pia** further east, an iron railway bridge built by Gustave Eiffel in 1877.

A short walk from the riverside along the Rua do Infante Dom Henrique will take you by the **Casa do Infante**, the house where Prince Henry the Navigator is believed to have been born, now an archival museum. In the same road stands the **British Factory House,** built in 1785 by the British consul in Porto for the British merchants, and still owned by British port companies. Beautifully painted ceilings are put to the test under the weight of massive chandeliers. Although it is not open to the individual tourist, a visit can be arranged through tour operators and wine societies.

Across from the Ferreira Borges Market stands the **Palácio da Bolsa** (the Stock Exchange)—a grand nineteenth-century building. It is certainly worth visiting, and to do so, you will have to join a guided tour. But beware of elevated expectations. The assumed highlight is the Sala Árabe, which will be a disappointment, albeit a humorous one, for anyone who has seen the Alhambra upon which it was based, or any true Moorish architecture, for that matter. Concerts, both classical chamber music and jazz, are frequently held here and are open to the public. It should be noted that the ambience is superior to the acoustics.

The neighboring **Igreja de São Francisco**, however, might well be one of Portugal's most extravagant baroque creations. Originally fifteenth-century gothic, this sprawling structure overlooking the river was overhauled in the eighteenth century, and its archways are now covered with angels, birds, fruit, garlands, beasts, and flowers. It is quite credible to hear that 136 kg (300 lbs) of gold leaf was used on the interior. Opening hours are from 9 AM to 6 PM. Closed on Sundays.

The **Igreja de Santa Clara** in the Largo de 1 de Dezembro has another glittering interior: once attached to the Convent of Santa Clara, it was built in 1416 and transformed with seventeenth-century ornamentation, a refit predating that of the São Francisco. The sudden wealth that befell Portugal during this period is evident in another golden grotto. Ask and you might be allowed a close look at the finely carved choir stalls behind

Throughout the city there are many art galleries with shows of current works. Pick up the *Programa Cultural* from the *Turismo* for listings and addresses.

Vila Nova de Gaia

No visit to Porto is complete without a trip across the river to the suburb of Vila Nova de Gaia for a visit to at least one of the port cellars, and for excellent views of Porto. For the best views (unless you are acrophobic), go across the upper deck of the Ponte de Dom Luís I. **Sandeman (** (22) 370-6807 FAX (22) 370-

the grilles which have, as is often the case, some singular carvings hidden away under the seats. Open from 9:30 AM to noon and 2 PM to 6 PM; closed on Sundays.

West of the City Center and Beyond

The **Fundação de Serralves (** (22) 618-0057 or (22) 617-2694 FAX (22) 617-3862, Rua de Serralves No. 977, is a work-in-progress. Housed in a building that dates from the 1930s with interiors designed by René Lalique, it is now Porto's emerging modern art museum. The permanent collection is yet to form itself, but on offer are exhibitions of both contemporary Portuguese and international artists. The garden setting also provides respite from urban touring.

6816, Largo Miguel Bombarda No. 3, 4400 Vila Nova de Gaia, is perhaps the most internationally known port producer, but the fifteen major lodges offer similar visits, so the best way to choose is by palate. If you have a favorite port, by all means, see how they make it. All tours end with a free tasting and not too much pressure to buy. The Porto *Turismo* has a brochure that lists specifics on all the cellars, or you can contact the **Associação das Empressas de Vinho do Porto (** (22) 374-5520 FAX (22) 370-5400, Rua Barão de Forrester No. 412. General

Barcos rabelos OPPOSITE once plied the Douro from the port-growing Alto Douro region to the lodges of Vila Nova de Gaia ABOVE, where the wine ages in oak casks.

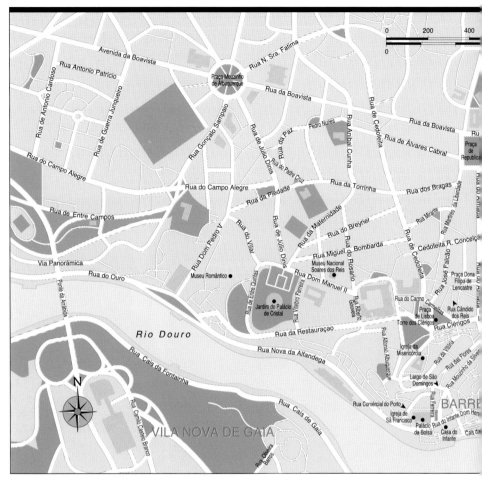

opening hours are weekdays from 9 AM or 10 AM to noon and from 2 PM to 5 PM, sometimes later. From May to October the cellars are open on Saturdays.

Afterwards, enjoy a drink (or if you have over-ported, a typically delicious black coffee) at a riverside café, and watch the flow of the *barcos rabelos*. These elegant little flat-bottomed boats, with their curved prows and square sails, were once the only means of transporting the port down the Douro to the lodges. Today the job is done by trucks, but some of the lodges keep their boats on the river for promotional purposes.

If you cross the Ponte de Dom Luís I on the upper level, it will bring you to the **Mosteiro da Serra do Pilar**, with even more stunning views of the city. The sixteenth-century convent church is unusual in its octagonal shape and its beautiful, though sadly damaged, round cloister ringed with classical columns.

BOAT TRIPS

There are several outfits that operate river cruises along the Douro that last anywhere from an hour and visit only the immediate environs of Porto and its five bridges, to those that cruise for a week and include bus trips into Spain. Prices and degrees of luxury range the gamut. For short trips, **Endouro** ((22) 3324236 FAX (22) 205-7260, leaving from the Ribeira docks, is the standard. They also run multi-day cruises. Perhaps the most luxurious cruises are offered by **Ferreira & Rayford** ((22) 339-3950 FAX (22) 208-3407, with week-long itineraries including deluxe live-aboard accommodation and airport transfers. As for other companies, contact the Porto *Turismo*

Formosa and Rua de Sã da Bandeira, the colorful **Bolhão Market** has local produce on sale every day but Sunday. Near the Clérigos Tower, in **Rua Cândido dos Reis**, the famous Vista Alegre porcelain factory has its shop, while several others in the vicinity sell pottery and earthenware. **Rua Mouzinho da Silveira** and the adjacent streets is another area worth exploring for buys on leather goods.

Porto is renowned for its gold and silverware and is one of the best places to buy Portugal's famous delicate filigree work: some of the best jewelry shops are along the **Rua das Flores**. Neves & Filha at No. 117 has fine classic pieces, but also contemporary designs at appropriate prices.

Continue down Rua das Flores and you will come upon a small *praça*, and with it, one of Porto's best wine stores. The staff at **Vinoteca (** (22) 208-2181 FAX (22) 332-5692, Largo de São Domingos No. 67, are knowledgeable and speak English.

There are several big shopping complexes in town: two of the most central are **Clérigos**, just beside the Clérigos Tower at Praça de Lisboa, and **Brasilia** on the Rotunda de Boavista. Like Lisbon, Porto is an excellent place to shop for traditional craftwork, and the **Ribeiro Craft Center** down by the riverside at Rua da Reboleira No. 37 offers a very good range.

or the closest international Portugal tourist office prior to leaving.

SHOPPING

Porto has in recent years become rather cosmopolitan when it comes to shopping. Large malls housing familiar names (and familiar prices) are becoming the norm, making shopping not a particularly worthwhile way to spend time. Locally made jewelry and leather goods, however, remain extremely well crafted.

Rua de Santa Catarina is a main shopping street with many shoe shops and some international fashion boutiques. The particularly attractive and exclusive Reis Filhos store sells expensive tableware, antique furniture, leatherwear and more. Close to the Rua de Santa Catarina on the corner of Rua

ENTERTAINMENT AND NIGHTLIFE

It is absolutely not true that Porto is a city of drudges who don't know how to enjoy themselves as their Lisbon cousins do. Quite astoundingly, the Porto *Turismo* has prepared a 20-page document that not merely lists the bars and discos, but describes them in such detail as to include what kind of music is played (live or DJ), who frequents the place (sexual preference, "fashionable people," age), and even locates them on inset maps, indicating the correct bus line to take. Of course, there are many others, as the scene is constantly evolving. There are some well-known mainstays, such as **Mal Cozinhado** (See WHERE TO EAT, below) which is a restaurant that presents *fado* music after dinner hours, and **Aniki-Bóbó (** (22) 332-4619, Rua Fonte Taurina No. 36, which occasionally offers performance-art and live jazz. But exploration of the newer ones is hardly an imposition. Just down from the Bolsa facing the river is **Ribeira de Ouro** ((91) 983-7363, Rua Nova da Alfandêga No. 7. This is a multi-level, sharp, sleek place that serves contemporary cuisine with Portuguese roots and turns into a dance hall after midnight, and with a DJ on weekends. A youthful atmosphere reigns at the **River Caffé** ((22) 617-1124, Calçada João do Carmo No. 31, where there is at times live jazz, blues, or country music. An older, more chic crowd can be

STATES (800) 528-1234 FAX (22) 205-4937, Praça Dona Filipa de Lencastre No. 62, 4050 Porto, centrally located just off the Avenida dos Aliados. Built in the 1950s, its prices range from expensive to sky-high, with services and facilities in accordance. For the category, there is no question that this should be your choice. The **Meridien Park Atlantic** ((22) 607-2500 FAX (22) 600-2031 E-MAIL reservasporto@ lemeridien.pt, Avenida da Boavista No. 1466, 4100 Porto, offers cool, modern elegance with a French accent. (But remember, it is part of a French chain.) A little way out of the cen-

found at the nearby **House Caffé** ((22) 609-7889, Rua da Boa Viagem No. 1.

For the more sedate, Porto boasts some beautiful cafés, such as the art nouveau **Café Majestic**, at Rua de Santa Catarina No. 112, with its mirrors and fading leather, as well as the **Imperial** in the Praça da Liberdade, and **A Brasileira** at Rua de Bonjardim No. 116. For a more subdued elegant atmosphere, there is the **Solar do Vinho do Porto** (see WHAT TO DO AND SEE, above).

ter, this glass and concrete highrise has a health club with gym, sauna, Turkish bath and massage, as well as a first-rate restaurant, bars, and entertainment.

Nearby the Meridien, the **Hotel Porto Palácio** ((22) 608-6600 FAX (22) 609-1467 E-MAIL sheraton@mail.telepac.pt, Avenida da Boavista No. 1269, 4100 Porto, offers similarly comprehensive facilities and luxurious rooms in a grand modern setting, it is considered by some to be Porto's choice modern hotel.

WHERE TO STAY

Luxury

Porto's top hotel is the **Hotel Infante de Sagres** ((22) 200-8101 TOLL-FREE IN THE UNITED

Mid-range

Porto's most amusing accommodation is to be found at the **Pensão Castelo de Santa Catarina** ((22) 509-5599 FAX (22) 550-6613,

Rua de Santa Catarina No. 1347, 4000 Porto. This small palace built on a terrace set back from the street is surrounded by gardens, palm trees, and a complex of smaller buildings with independent guest rooms, which are great if you are traveling with children. The entire structure is faced with tiles. In the main house, a narrow staircase leads up to the guest rooms, each equipped with bathroom, telephone and television, and individually decorated with antique furniture. For a treat, reserve the hotel's best suite, which consists of a bedroom, dressing room, and bathroom. Furnished in rococo rosewood, its walls are covered in damask and wood paneling, and chandeliers hang from a ceiling painted with rosy cherubs. In addition to somewhat kitsch charm, the free off-the-street parking makes this an exceptional choice.

The **Albergaria São João** ((22) 200-1662 FAX (22) 205-6114, Rua do Bonjardim No. 120, 4000 Porto, is also a bit unusual, on the fourth floor of a conveniently located modern building (with elevator) where the interior exudes warmth, as does the staff. Unfortunately, there is no parking. Prices are at the lower end of mid-range. The **Grande Hotel do Porto** ((22) 200-8176 FAX (22) 205-1061, Rua de Santa Catarina No. 197, 4000 Porto, is centrally located on the pedestrian section of one of Porto's main shopping streets, across from the Café Majestic. Art deco features abound in public areas, the lounge and pretty restaurant, however the bedrooms could stand refurbishing.

If you are looking to stay in the old part of the city, the **Hotel da Bolsa** ((22) 202-6768 FAX (22) 205-8888, Rua Ferreira Borges No. 101, 4050 Porto, despite being the only option, is an excellent one. A turn-of-the-century building with completely modern facilities, it is away from the hectic center, yet near many of Porto's sites and close to its nightlife. Without question, this is a highly recommended spot.

Inexpensive
Residencial Pão de Açúcar ((22) 200-2425 FAX (22) 310239, Rua do Almada No. 262, 4000 Porto, is a large, centrally located art deco building that and has rooms with private bathrooms. Reservations are essential.

The **Pensão Astória** ((22) 200-8175, Rua Arnaldo Gama No. 56, 4000 Porto, an old house in a quiet location overlooking the river, offers good value and is deservedly popular. Less homey, but certainly an extraordinary find is the **Século Residencial Hotel** ((22) 509-9120 FAX (22) 509-9128, Rua de Santa Catarina No. 1256. This inexpensive option offers rooms with satellite television, telephone, minibars, and even at the higher end, bathrooms with Jacuzzis. In addition, they quite astoundingly have a private garage. **Pensão do Norte** ((22) 200-3503, Rua Fernandes Tomás No. 579, 4000 Porto, is a likable, slightly disorganized old place where some of the rooms have bathrooms and those without are as cheap as you can get.

WHERE TO EAT

Expensive
There are two superior restaurants in Porto, and predilection has less to do with quality of cuisine than setting, as both are. **Portucale** ((22) 537-0717, Rua da Alegria No. 598, the more expensive of the two, is more contemporary in both ambience and menu. Occupying the top floor of the Albergaria Miradouro, dining here is refined cuisine in an elegance not overwhelmed by its panoramic views. One of the house specialties is the traditional *cabrito a serrana* (kid cooked in red wine), however a bit more daring is the roasted duck served with a sauce of reduced raspberries. **Escondidinho** ((22) 200-1079, Rua Passos Manuel No. 144, has much more of the Old World intimate feel, with a comparably conservative menu. The cuisine incorporates French influences into a classical Portuguese base with fine results, as evidenced by the filet of sole in Madeira sauce.

Telégrapho ((22) 332-2019, Rua Ferreira Borges, is a justly formal restaurant housed in the Bolsa serving dishes that are as elegant as the setting. Dining here before attending a concert in the Arabian Room would create an evening in the foreign that one rarely achieves.

Throughout the fishing towns of northern Portugal, craftswomen display lacework outside their homes.

Moderate

Restaurants abound in the busy riverside Ribeiro district, and among them is the very popular **Taverna do Bebobos** ((22) 205-3565, Cais da Ribeira 24-25, which has been in business for over a century, offers the standard fare, supplemented by a wonderful wine list. Reservations for dinner are essential. Also in the Ribeiro, **Mal Cozinhado** ((22) 208-1319, Rua do Outeirinho No. 13, has a traditional interior and offers *fado* music in the evenings.

For good dining in an utterly non-touristic setting, dine at **O Mordomo** ((22) 502-8815, Rua do Bonjardim No. 1143. At the top of the street just off the good garden, this is a new spot that quietly is gathering its sophisticated clientele. Refined but not pretentious describes both the place and the cuisine.

Inexpensive

For large quantities and very reasonable prices, try **Tripeiro** ((22) 200-5886, Rua Passos Manuel No. 195. For Chinese food, the place to go is **Restaurante Chinês** ((22) 200-8915, Avenida Vimara Peres No. 38, close to the Ponte de Dom Luís I (upper deck). **Casa Aleixo** ((22) 537-0462, Rua da Estação No. 216, serves regional food and is favored by the locals. **Abadio do Porto** ((22) 200-8757, Rua Comércio do Porto No. 22, is roughly behind the Bolsa and might be the place to try the *tripas à moda do Porto* (Porto-style tripe). This traditional restaurant is worth visiting just to see its walls of *azulejos*. There is a string of inexpensive restaurants at the bottom of Rua Bonjardim that are suitable for lunch. The pervasive aroma of roasting chickens will point you in the right direction.

How to Get There

The Francisco Sá Carneiro airport is 13 km (nine miles) north of Porto and, along with a plethora of taxis, there is a shuttle bus service connecting it to the Praça de Lisboa in the city center, near Clérigos. International and domestic flights arrive here. There are numerous flights from Lisbon each day and three flights a week from Faro in the Algarve.

Trains from the south, including a frequent service from Lisbon via Coimbra B, arrive at Estação de Campanha, outside the town center. From here are frequent local connections to the centrally located Station, a journey that takes just a few minutes. Trains from Viana do Castelo, Braga, other places north of Porto, as well as from the Douro Valley arrive at São Bento Station. Local trains come in at Trindade Station, north of the Avenida dos Aliados. Express buses run frequently to Porto from Lisbon and Coimbra, and other services connect Porto with most northern towns and the Galician cities of Spain.

By road, Porto lies 314 km (195 miles) directly north of Lisbon and 118 km (73 miles) north of Coimbra. Both are connected to Porto by the A1 highway. The A4 highway leads to cities to the east, notably Vila Real, and ultimately Bragança near the Spanish border.

AROUND PORTO

There are several rather well-known beach resorts both to the north and to the immediate south of Porto. I can only say that in none of them — Espinho, Vila do Conde, Póvoa de Varzim — will you find a relaxing respite from the rigors of your more historically-oriented touring. These towns, although internationally known for their sprawling white sand beaches, seem much more defined by their crowds and pretensions. The pleasures of traveling through Portugal, specifically the verdant, unbuilt landscape, the gently simmered country cuisine, and the easygoing, if somewhat distant nature of the people, are all absent. If you are looking for a seaside break from touring, either head for the **Costa Azul** which stretches south of the Tagus, or the **Costa do Estoril** near Lisbon (see page 124), or preferably, such coastal towns as Caminha and Moledo north of **Viana do Castelo** (see page 212).

Espinho

A seaside resort 19 km (12 miles) south of Porto, Espinho is popular with *Portuenses*. It has a casino, a beach and an 18-hole golf course, a vast array of water sports, and even a bullfighting arena. However, it is not strong on character, and is becoming ever more crowded. But tourists who might need a seaside break from the city, just like locals, could consider Espinho a pleasant day-trip.

For those more bent on a lucky break, the town is home to one of Portugal's splashier casinos, offering the usual gaming tables, as well as a grand, perhaps less than politically correct floor show. If you are game for this kind of entertainment, you will probably want to stay overnight. With its indoor swimming pool, health club, restaurant, disco, and central location overlooking the

sea, the best choice in town is the four-star **Hotel Praiagolfe** ((22) 731-3385 FAX (22) 731-3397 E-MAIL pgolf@mail.telepac.pt, Rua 6, 4500 Espinho. This is an extremely popular place, and if you are considering a stay during the summer months, advance reservations are crucial.

The *Turismo* ((22) 720911 FAX (22) 731-1053 is at Ángulo das Ruas No. 6.

VILA DO CONDE

If you do wish, however, to have more of an extended stay at a seaside resort in the area, you would do better to visit either Vila do Conde or Póvoa de Varzim, both of which are just to the north of Porto.

Vila do Conde, 26 km (17 miles) north of Porto, has more to enjoy than just its beach. Popular, yet still leafy and with a few serene corners, it somewhat manages to maintain its old fishing village character along with its traditional crafts, boat building, and lace making. Along with its wide beach, the shipyard at the mouth of the Ave River where craftsmen use traditional shipbuilding methods, and the noisy Friday market, there are also a few interesting historical sites.

Visit Vila do Conde around Saint John's Eve during the second week of June and you will be able to witness the **Festas de São João**, when sumptuous costumes are on parade, with singing and dancing around bonfires, and a candlelit procession down to the sea led by the lace-makers.

General Information

The *Turismo* ((252) 642700 is located at Rua 25 de Abril.

What to See and Do

Vila do Conde is dominated by the austere **Mosteiro de Santa Clara** (Convent of Santa Clara) ((252) 631016, now a reformatory for boys. Founded in 1318 and virtually rebuilt in the eighteenth century, the convent's origins are only evident today in its church, which contains the Renaissance tombs of the founders Dom Afonso Sanches (an illegitimate son of King Dinis) and his wife, Dona Teresa Martins. Church hours are 9 AM to noon and 2 PM to 5 PM.

In the town center is a sixteenth-century Manueline **Igreja Matriz**, richly carved both inside and out, the work of Basque craftsmen. Visit the **lace-making school** at Rua Joaquim Maria de Melo No. 70. The town centers around a busy and colorful fishing port worked by a very old, closed community who preserve the traditions of centuries past. The excellent **Museu Etnográfico** (Ethnographic Museum) ((252) 631491 in the Solar dos Carneiros will tell you all about its history.

Where to Stay

The best place to stay is the central **Estalagem do Brasão** ((252) 642016 FAX (252) 642028,

Traditional headdress and chains of gold adorn villagers at folk festivals in the Minho.

Avenida Dr. João Canavarro, 4480 Vila do Conde, which offers well-equipped, if not overly spacious, rooms at good value. The **Motel de Sant'Ana (** (252) 641717 FAX (252) 642693, Monte de Sant'Ana, Azurara, is a country club-style place on the Ave with one-, two- or three-person apartments and recreation facilities including an indoor swimming pool. Moderately priced, it makes an ideal choice for families.

Where to Eat

Vila do Conde has several restaurants along the seafront that offer panoramic views and quite good cuisine, particularly if you stick with the simpler dishes. At the southern end of the bay is **Pioneiro (** (252) 632912, Avenida Manuel Barros, which serves regional dishes and seafood, for the most part at moderate prices although, depending upon what you order, prices can skyrocket. At the opposite end of the beach is **Caximar (** (252) 642492, Avenida do Brasil, another large restaurant where the fresh fish and seafood dishes can be quite good. Once again, simple is better. For something more intimate, try the family-run **Restaurante Ramon (** (252) 631334, Rua 5 de Outubro, where the food is traditional and inexpensive, and in the evenings they offer outdoor dining in a cobblestone alley.

How to Get There

Trains from Porto's Trindade Station to Póvoa de Varzim stop at Vila do Conde en route. There is a regular bus service from Porto.

Drivers should take the N13 out of Porto, and continue north, then following signs that will lead you into town.

PÓVOA DE VARZIM

Póvoa, 30 km (18 miles) north of Porto, reportedly has the longest beach in the entire country, and the water is generally much cleaner than in Espinho. The town has more than its share of sports ranging from scuba diving, sailing, and windsurfing to tennis, golf, and shooting. The *Turismo* has details about each.

It is, however, the type of town I cannot wholeheartedly recommend. During the summer months, it becomes outrageously

crowded with either the self-appointed chic, or a younger version longing to be such. But if you are looking for a sizzling social life centered around the casino, the seaside discos, and the nightly outdoor concerts, Póvoa is certainly the locale for it all.

General Information

In Póvoa de Varzim the *Turismo* **(** (252) 614609 FAX (252) 617872 is at Avenida Mouzinho de Albuquerque No. 166.

Where to Stay

Póvoa de Varzim has several inexpensive *pensãos*, but its top hotel is the four-star **Hotel Vermar (** (252) 615566 FAX (252) 615115, Rua Alto de Martim Vaz, 4490 Póvoa de Varzim. It is sharp and comfortable, with sports and recreation facilities. Rooms have balconies, some with sea views, and the service is excellent. Prices vary widely within the mid-range and expensive categories depending upon season and the room. Another quite acceptable choice at much more moderate prices is **Hotel Luso Brasileiro (** (252) 690710 FAX (252) 690719, Rua dos Cafés No. 16. On a small street just steps away from the beachfront, it offers the full services of a higher grade hotel, but as it has no restaurant, it only rates two stars. Although rooms don't afford sea views, they are air conditioned and infinitely quieter.

All the same, I strongly advise staying in one of the seaside inns outside of town. **Estalagem Santo André (** (252) 615666 FAX (252) 615866, Agucadoura, Aver-o-Mar, 4490 Póvoa de Varzim, is a few kilometers north of Póvoa. This is a long, low complex right on the beach and a far cry from the bustle of Póvoa. Its 50 modern rooms are a bit uninspired, but the beach, and the outdoor pool, and the moderate prices are its main draw. Nearby, the **Estalagem São Félix (** (252) 607176 FAX (252) 607444, Monte de São Félix, Laúndos, 4490 Póvoa de Varzim, is set on a pine-clad hill overlooking the valley and sea. It has just eight rooms, a large restaurant, and also an outdoor pool. Prices at both places are mid-range.

Harvest time in the port-growing region. Grapes are carried in wicker baskets. At some *quintas*, traditional treading by foot still takes place.

Where to Eat

Inexpensive seafood restaurants are to be found on almost every small side street, and Rua Dr. Caetano de Oliveira is no exception. An utterly unpretentious place that caters to both locals and tourists is **Firmino ₵** (252) 684695, where the cuisine is robust if not too refined. Traveling north along the Estrada Nacional 13, you will find two popular and rather touristic restaurants, but with quite different ambiences. **O Marinheiro ₵** (252) 682151, which is shaped like a boat and may well be the most kitsch creation in all of

and when approaching the city, follow the signs, as new routes were in the midst of construction at the time of publication.

AMARANTE

Sixty kilometers (37 miles) east of Porto in the foothills of the Serra de Marão, Amarante is a town of comfortable and comforting proportions. It lies along the banks of the Tâmega River, which is traversed by an eighteenth-century granite bridge. Willows run the length of the riverbank, as does a narrow

Portugal, specializes, as you might suspect, in all things from the sea. Plain grilled or sautéed dishes are recommended; shellfish and crustaceans can be outrageously expensive. A little further down the road on the opposite side is **Restaurante Chelsea ₵** (252) 681522. A little down-scale, its vast dining hall is less than intimate, but the seafood is fresh and the spit-roasted chicken a pleasant change of palate.

How to Get There

Trains leave Porto's Trindade Station for Póvoa de Varzim and there is a bus service from Porto.

Póvoa de Varzim lies 30 km (19 miles) north of Porto: drivers should take the N13

beach, from where paddle boats can be rented. There is a sandy little island that is home to gaggles of geese. Cafés abound and a festive atmosphere prevails.

General Information

The regional *Turismo* ₵ (255) 432980 is close to the art gallery in the convent building at Rua Cândido dos Reis; while the municipal *Turismo* ₵ (255) 432259 is just over the bridge on the Esplanada Teixeira de Paseãoes.

What to See and Do

After relaxing on one of Amarante's café terraces that overlook the river, and after indulging in some of the sweet pastries for which the town is famous — *foguetes, lérias, brisas do Tâmega, galhofas* — and / or sipping some *vinho verde*, do visit the **Igreja de São Gonçalo** near the bridge. The church was built between 1540 and 1620 and is instantly recognizable by its red-tiled dome. To the left of its elaborate Renaissance portal, there is an arcaded loggia with niches that contain statues of the kings who reigned during the long period of construction. The hermit-saint is also represented. The interior is baroque with columns wreathed in cherubs and flowers. Even the organ is supported by golden mermen.

A small side chapel contains the tomb of Saint Gonçalo — a matchmaking saint believed to have come to Amarante from Guimarães in the thirteenth century and to have built the first bridge across the river. His effigy, which is adorned with flowers, candles, and votive offerings, is in places blackened by the kisses of women who, over the centuries, have prayed to him for a husband.

Along the river, the white and green convent buildings as well as a second cloister have been converted into the **Museu Amadeo de Souza-Cardoso**. The extensive use of plate glass around the cloisters gives the galleries a wonderfully light airiness, without diminishing their beauty. The collection is dominated by works of the

twentieth-century Portuguese artist Amadeo de Souza Cardoso (1887–1927), a local who was one of the earliest Portuguese Modernists. Opening hours are from 10 AM to 12:30 PM and from 2 PM to 5:30 PM; it is closed on Mondays.

During the annual **Romária de São Gonçalo** held in June, single women give phallus-shaped cakes to male prospects. They (the cakes) are quite delicious.

Where to Stay

In Amarante the modern **Hotel Residencial Navarras** ((255) 431036 FAX (255) 425891, Rua António Carneiro, 4600 Amarante, is convenient and acceptable, but antiseptic at best. It has an outdoor swimming pool, a bar, restaurant, and large, comfortable rooms at mid-range prices. The **Albergaria Dona Margaritta** ((255) 432110 FAX (255) 437977, Rua Cândido dos Reis No. 53, São Gonçalo, despite its name change, is still owned by the Silva family, and has infinitely more character. All rooms have private baths, direct-dial telephones, television, and some have terraces overlooking the river. Prices are mid-range, value high.

There are several country homes in the vicinity that operate under the TURIHAB scheme, and although the most talked about in the center of town does not live up to its reputation, others are far superior. **Casa da Cerca D'Além** ((255) 431449 is an eighteenth-century house overlooking the river with four guest rooms. **Casa da Obra** ((255) 446907 has seven guest rooms and a swimming pool.

Where to Eat

A great new restaurant just across from the Albergaria is **O Mulas** ((255) 433367, Rua Cândido dos Reis. The cuisine is traditional with a contemporary touch (for example, grilled salmon served with a delicate herbed butter), the setting serene and modern (not an easy feat), the prices moderate and appropriate (including the exceptional wine list). A much more modest place is the **Restaurante Lusitana** ((255) 426720, Rua 31 de Janeiro. If weather permits, take one of

OPPOSITE: The damming of the Douro for hydroelectric power has turned the river into a series of serpentine lakes. ABOVE: Port grape vines cover the mountain terraces of the Douro.

the tables on the terrace overlooking the river and order the roast kid. You will, however, want to avoid the house red wine.

While strolling through town, drop in to **Kilowatt** ((255) 433159, Rua 31 de Janeiro. There are only two tables, but hanging hams and sausages abound. Even if pork is not to your taste, the ambience is amusing and the owner welcoming. Back across the street and a little closer to the bridge is the **Confeitaria da Ponte**, with its terraced café, light food, and delicious local pastries.

(Please note: although I try not to offer negative advice, when necessary, I prefer to avoid its omission. The Casa Zé de Calçada is terribly overrated and overpriced. This is true regarding both its rooms and its restaurant.)

How to Get There

Trains run frequently from Porto to Livração, linked to Amarante by bus. Buses run hourly between Porto and Amarante. By car, Amarante is 60 km (37 miles) from Porto along the A4 highway.

ALTO DOURO

The Douro River cuts a dramatic gorge through the province of Trás-os-Montes and Alto Douro, its stony flanks ribbed with vine-growing terraces. It slices across the breadth of Portugal for 210 km (130 miles) between Porto and Barca d'Alva at the Spanish border, where it turns north and continues for another 110 km (69 miles) to form the border between the two countries.

The spectacular Douro valley has been well-served by the elements, making it an ideal region for growing vines, and now synonymous with the production of port and other superior quality red wines.

Although harvest time entails backbreaking work, particularly in this hilly terrain, it is still a magical season. The night air comes alive with the festive sounds of accordions and drums. Occasionally, after dark, workers will link arms in the time-honored fashion and tread upon the grapes throughout the night, all to a rather hypnotic rhythm.

Porto is the ideal starting point for a tour of the Douro Valley, setting off into its lower reaches of green undulating hills, where *vinho*

verde is grown. There are four ways to visit the valley: by boat, car, bus, or train. An excellent choice is to take the Douro railway from São Bento station in Porto; a daily train leaves for Pocinho at the ends of the line, while more frequent service runs as far as Peso da Régua and Tua. Initially, which is to say as for the first 40 km (25 miles) or so, the track runs north of the valley, dropping south at Livração, and the journey is not particularly scenic. Then the sweeping vistas begin.

Driving out of Porto on the N108 allows you to hug the river more closely from the outset, however you will have to keep your mind on the road, which can get rather heavily trafficked during the summer months. If you want to visit any of the *quintas*, make arrangements at Porto's *Turismo* before setting off, as otherwise you are unlikely to be given a guided tour. If the idea of spending a night in the valley appeals, there is a *pousada* near **Alijó**, north of the river along the N322 in the depths of the port-producing region, and near the village of **São João da Pesqueira** there is a particularly appealing *quinta* (see WHERE TO STAY, page 203 under VILA REAL). If a trip down the Douro is the only chance you have to explore the Alto Douro province of Trás-os-Montes, be sure to make a side trip to the famous **Palácio de Mateus**, one of Portugal's loveliest buildings: a detailed description is included in the section VILA REAL on page 202.

LAMEGO

Lamego, 108 km (67 miles) east of Porto, is surrounded by orchards and vineyards. This baroque town is overlooked by two hills, one of which is crowned by the ruins of a twelfth-century castle, the other by the Igreja de Nossa Senhora dos Remédios, a pilgrimage destination. Lamego is famous for a sparkling white wine called Raposeira, its delicious smoked hams, and the monumental double staircase that zigzags up the hill to Nossa Senhora from the lower town's main avenue.

General Information

The municipal *Turismo* ((254) 612005 is at Avenida Visconde Guedes Teixeira. The

The church atop Bom Jesús do Monte.

regional *Turismo* ((254) 612005 or (254) 625770 FAX (254) 614014 is at Rua dos Bancos.

What to See and Do

Lamego has been an episcopal town since the sixth century. Its **cathedral** is twelfth-century Romanesque in origin but the only remaining original part is a section of the tower; the rest is mainly sixteenth-century Renaissance and eighteenth-century encumbrance. Behind the cathedral square, the eighteenth-century episcopal palace houses the excellent **Museu de Lamego** ((254) 612008. The emphasis is on religious art, and it includes some complete baroque chapels rescued from the Convent of Chagas, which was demolished earlier this century, as well as five of the original 20 panels by Grão Vasco that once graced the cathedral's altar. The others were lost or destroyed during major restorations that took place in the eighteenth century. The collection also includes six stunning Flemish tapestries that date from the early sixteenth century and a room full of fine examples of sixteenth- and eighteenth-century *azulejos*. Open from 10 AM to 12:30 PM and from 2 PM to 5 PM, closed on Mondays. Admission is free on Sundays.

The elaborate **baroque staircase** at the top of the Avenida Dr. Alfredo de Sousa leads to the Sanctuary of **Nossa Senhora dos Remédios** atop the wooded hill. The eighteenth-century church itself is overwhelmed by this lavish nineteenth-century construction that resembles the older Bom Jesús stairway near Braga. The over 600 steps present quite a trial for devout pilgrims, some of whom perform the task on hands and knees. For tourists, it is accessible by car. The structure is white-wash and granite trimmed with balustrades and *azulejos*.

At the southeastern edge of town the unprepossessing seventeenth-century exterior of the **Capela do Desterro** (Chapel of the Exile) along Rua Cardoso Avelino hides a flamboyant gold interior with blue *azulejo* decoration and a fine painted ceiling. Nearby is the **Barro do Fonte**, Lamego's old and poor neighborhood on the banks of the river, a sharp contrast to the prosperous town center.

Where to Stay and Eat

A bit above town, the **Hotel de Lamego** ((254) 656171 FAX (254) 656180, Quinta da Vista Alegre, 5100 Lamego, is a modern, and only somewhat sterile, hotel replete with both indoor and outdoor swimming pools, sports facilities, and a purportedly good restaurant. It is appropriately priced at the upper end of mid-range. The **Albergaria do Cerrado** ((254) 613164 FAX (254) 615464, Lugar do Cerrado, 5100 Lamego, is closer to town on the same road as the Hotel Lamego, and although it is short on character, it is modern, clean, and comfortable. Mid-range prices apply. Up on the other hill by the church, the **Hotel do Parque** ((254) 609140 FAX (254) 615203, Parque Nossa Senhora dos Remédios, 5100 Lamego, is in tranquil surroundings and has the best views. Once a monastery attached to the church, it now provides inexpensive rooms and a large, moderately priced restaurant. The best inexpensive option in town is the **Pensão São Paulo** ((254) 613114, Avenida 5 Outubro No. 22C, 5100 Lamego. The rooms are certainly acceptable, and quite amazingly, it offers private parking.

If you are interested in staying at a country guesthouse, there are several in the area. **Villa Hostilina** ((254) 612394 FAX (254) 655194 WEB SITE www.minotel.com, Almacave, 5100 Lamego, offers nineteenth-century furnishings with twentieth-century comforts that include a swimming pool, tennis courts, and a health club. High on a hill, the panoramic views are breathtaking. A more formal and somewhat more expensive option is **Casa de Santo António de Britiande** (/FAX (254) 699346, Britiande, 5100 Lamego. It is a grand manor house with a seventeenth-century chapel, with furnishings dating from the twelfth century. It too offers tennis and swimming facilities.

In addition to the hotel restaurants, the best dining in the area is to be had at **Restaurante Turissera** ((254) 656198. It serves good regional cuisine and has spectacular views.

How to Get There

Lamego does not have a railway station. The nearest is at Peso da Régua, where there is hourly bus service to Lamego's central bus

---

The renowned baroque staircase leading up to Bom Jesús do Monte.

station. Douro line trains run to Régua from Porto's São Bento Station and along the Corgo Line from Vila Real. Lamego is well-served by intercity buses, as well as Rodoviária Nacional Express buses that run frequently from Viseu, Coimbra, and Lisbon.

By road Lamego lies 358 km (222 miles) northeast of Lisbon and 108 km (67 miles) east of Porto. Drivers from Lisbon should take the A1 to just north of Coimbra, and then turn on to the IP3-N2 to Lamego via Viseu. From Porto take either the A4 highway (becoming the N15) to just outside Vila Real,

In place of the pictured swan gliding across the pond in front of the house there is a partially-submerged statue of a nude woman, the work of contemporary sculptor João Cutileiro. Its realism sets up a marvelous contrast to the setting.

Although the tour of the house does not take you through all the rooms, the guides are charming. The most striking features of the interior are the beautifully carved chestnut wood ceilings and the library. Unfortunately, many of the furnishings are badly in need of repair, perhaps a consequence of the

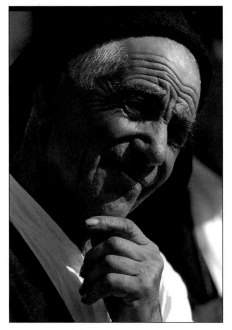

then drive along the N2 to Lamego. Far more scenic would be a slower drive along the N108 from Porto to Entre-os-Rios, crossing the Douro on the N224 to Castelo de Paiva; continue along the N222 then turn off along the N226 just north of Lamego, which leads you into the town.

VILA REAL

Vila Real is famous for the international motorcycle races held there in the summer, but its main attraction is three kilometers (two miles) away: the eighteenth-century **Palácio de Mateus**, immortalized on the label of the Mateus Rosé bottle. As you might expect, reality far outpaces the reproduction.

family having sold the reproduction rights to Sogrape in perpetuity for one lump sum.

One of Mateus' greatest charms is the garden behind the house, which is an appealing blend of formal and informal. Box hedges are neatly trimmed, and within them blossom masses of flowers with, of course, their attendant butterflies. A hearty yew hedge has been shaped to form a dark tunnel that leads to another garden, beyond which lies rolling a countryside with its vineyards.

The Serras de Marão and Alvão frame the town, which is somewhat outshone by its setting. Apart from the cafés of the Avenida Carvalho Araújo, Vila Real has few attractions for the visitor other than making a useful base from which to explore the surrounding countryside, as it is only 82 km (51 miles) east of Porto. Obviously, it is best to visit during spring and early summer, when the gardens are resplendent.

The Vila Real *Turismo* ((259) 322819 is at Avenida Carvalho Araújo No. 94.

Where to Stay

In Vila Real, the **Hotel Miracorgo** ((259) 325001 FAX (259) 325006, Avenida 1 de Maio No. 78, 5000 Vila Real, is a tall, modern building with particularly attractive common areas, a swimming pool and a health club, and outstanding views over the gorge. Prices are mid-range.

In the environs of Vila Real, traveling 44 km (27 miles) along the N322 toward Alijó is the **Pousada Barão de Forrester** ((259) 959467 FAX (259) 959304, Rua José Rufino, 5070 Alijó. This is a lovely stately house equipped with a swimming pool, where the staff arrange tours of the local wine-producing quintas, as well as cruises along the Douro. The prime reason for a stay here is its location in the heart of the Douro River valley. South of Alijó on N222 (which runs along the southern bank of the Douro and leads west to Lamego) and 18 km (10 miles) west of the village of São João da Pesqueira is the **Quinta de Ventozelo** ((254) 731181 or (22) 609-3691 FAX (254) 731180 or (22) 609-6673, Ervedosa do Douro, 5130 São João da Pesqueira. Documented reference to this stone house, once the home of wine-producing friars, dates to 1288. Guests are invited to enjoy tastings in the cellars.

Where to Eat

Regardless of the price range, you can eat well in Vila Real. So even if you choose not to stay here overnight, you might want to indulge in a leisurely lunch following a visit to the Palácio de Mateus. An ideal spot to do so would be **Espadeiro** ((259) 322302, Avenida Almeida Lucena, where in warm weather you can (and should) dine on the terrace. The cuisine and service merits its comparatively higher prices. For ham aficionados, there is the moderately priced **Museu dos Presuntos** ((259) 326017, Avenida Cidade de Orense No. 43. For very good Brazilian cuisine, try **O Mateus** ((259) 325607, Fruteira Bloco F.

How to Get There

Internal flights run from Lisbon to Vila Real six days a week, two times a day. Train travelers from Porto must take the Douro Line to Peso da Régua and change there onto the Corgo Line bound for Vila Real. The Rodonorte bus company is based in Vila Real and their buses link with Lisbon, Porto, Coimbra, Bragança, and Peso da Régua. Rodoviária Nacional buses also operate services between these cities and Vila Real. There is no central bus station, although one is in the plans.

By road Vila Real lies 82 km (51 miles) east of Porto along the A4-IP4. From Bragança it is approximately 130 km (81 miles) along the A15-IP4. The Palácio de Mateus is three kilometers (two miles) out of Vila Real along the N322.

THE MINHO

This undulating, verdant region of the country is spectacular, both in terms of its historical sites, and certainly, its physical beauty. Although much of it can be seen on day-trips from Porto, doing so would undermine the true pleasure of the visit. Without doubt, this is an area that deserves the assimilation of its tempo. Some of Portugal's most renowned country homes are found here (Casa de Sezim and Quinta da Boa Viagem are both terribly difficult to leave). There are wonderful cafés, restaurants, and towns with winding streets and not much to do. Some of Portugal's best beaches — and certainly not the most chic — are found here. And inland, there is the vast **Parque Nacional da Peneda-Gerês**, with its scenic drives, mountain lakes, and array of treks and other sports.

Bordered by Galicia in Spain to the north and the Atlantic to the west, the Minho forms a major part of the region known as the Costa Verde, the Green Coast, and high levels of rainfall together with a mild climate ensure that it lives up to the name. Even the wine is green.

Generally considered conservative by nature, the *Minhotos* have held on to tradition perhaps a bit more ardently than people of other regions. So oxen are still to be seen

Faces of the north.

pulling carts, and pretty stone walls still demarcate small land holdings. Traditional religious festivals are celebrated with a special fervor, with women dressing in colorful costumes and the family's gold heirlooms.

However, along with the folkloric that is more readily apparent to the tourist breezing through, the Minho, as all regions of Portugal, sports a contemporary life replete with cybercafés. Enjoying the juxtaposition, and more, the coalescence, is part of the trip.

BRAGA

For centuries Braga, 50 km (31 miles) north of Porto, has been the religious capital of an exceptionally religious country, and the Archbishop of Braga still wields significant power. In spite of a staggering number of churches — something in the region of 30 — the face of the city is changing. Although formerly all industry here had been related to ecclesiastical needs, today leathers, textiles, and engineering constitute major components of the city and its economy. Braga is rapidly modernizing into the largest metropolitan area north of Porto and the capital of the Minho.

General Information

The *Turismo* ((253) 262550 is located at Avenida da Liberdade No. 1.

What to See and Do

Braga's historic quarter is centered on the imposing **Sé**, built in the eleventh century on the site of an earlier church. A series of restorations and modifications has left few traces of the original Romanesque structure: only the south portal and the arch over the main entrance carry scenes from the medieval story of Reynard the Fox. The cathedral acquired an eastern extension with a fancy rooftop in the sixteenth century, and a fine granite statue of Nossa Senhora do Leite (a nursing Madonna and Child) graces the exterior of the chancel and has been attributed to Nicolas Chanterene. The interior is predominantly baroque, with the occasional Manueline embellishment. The upper choir is wonderfully carved and gilded, together with a pair of ornate organs covered in blasting trumpets and cherubs.

The vaulted **Capela dos Reis** contains the tomb of the founders, Henri of Burgundy, the father of Portugal's first king, Alfonso Henriques, and his wife Dona Teresa. It also holds the mummified remains of Archbishop Lourenço Vicente, a veteran of Aljubarrota whose body was found undecayed many years after his death and is now permanently on view. The **Treasury** is now a museum devoted to religious art with some outstanding pieces that span over five centuries. Cathedral opening times are from 8:30 AM to 1 PM and from 2 PM to 6:30 PM; it is closed on Mondays.

On Praça da República, there is the art deco **Café Viana**, while on the Avenida da Liberdade is the mildly less touristic **Café Astória**. Wander around the streets near the cathedral and browse through shops filled with devotional items, embroidery, pottery, rag quilts, and the unavoidable Barcelos cockerel, the most widely recognized symbol of Portugal.

Braga has some fine mansions, the most beautiful being the elegant eighteenth-century **Palácio do Raio**, with its flowing lines designed by architect André Soares. He is also responsible for the graceful **Câmara Municipal** (Town Hall), with its unusual **Pelican Fountain**. Close by in the Rua do Raio is the oldest of Braga's sights, the **Fonte do Idolo** (Fountain of the Idol), a small Lusitanian rock-hewn shrine that was carved in pre-Roman times.

The **Casa dos Biscaínhos**, right by the Town Hall, is a seventeenth-century aristocratic house that now serves as a small museum ((253) 217645. A passageway cutting through the façade was designed to allow horses through. Inside are collections of period furniture, pottery, glassware, silverware, textiles, jewelry, and porcelain, as well as a new section devoted to Roman artifacts recovered during recent excavations in Braga. Open from 10 AM to 12:30 PM and from 2 PM to 5:30 PM; closed on Mondays.

Religious festivals afford Braga the opportunity to air its spiritual supremacy. The city overflows during Holy Week when the most spectacular of Portugal's festivals takes place. Decorations are to be found every-

The cathedral at Braga, ecclesiastical capital of Portugal.

where, as barefoot, hooded penitents bearing torches take part in the famous **Ecce Homo** procession. The climax of the week is the great procession of **Entero do Senhor** (Burial of Our Lord), in which thousands of people participate.

Around Braga

The most unusual religious monument in the entire area lies six kilometers (four miles) east of Braga. This is the **Igreja de Bom Jesús do Monte**, or, more specifically, the stairway leading up to it. The church is atop a wooded hill, and its eighteenth-century monumental double stairway is a whitewash and granite rococo construction that predates the one at Lamego. It is, in fact, a series of three sections, built over centuries and incorporating different symbolism. Each level is ornamented with statuary, gardens, grottoes, chapels, and fountains. That on the first landing represents the wounds of Christ while others allegorize the five senses and the three virtues. Although the climb up the stairs affords great views, so does the funicular that goes to the top. You can also drive, but be forewarned, the road, like the staircase, ascends in a series of steep hairpin bends.

On a silent hilltop 12 km (seven and a half miles) east of Braga and 10 km (six miles) southeast of Bom Jesus, the ruins of an Iron Age settlement shelter behind vestiges of defensive walls. The **Citânia de Briteiros** was occupied from around 300 BC; there are the remains of roads and a water supply system, and two of its circular dwellings have been reconstructed. Many of the artifacts unearthed here are on display in Guimarães at the Museu Martins Sarmento (see GUIMARÃES, page 208).

Where to Stay

In Braga the **Hotel Turismo Braga** ((253) 612200 FAX (253) 612211, Praceta João XXI, 4700 Braga, is a large 1950s building offering air-conditioned comfort and many amenities, including an outdoor swimming pool, at mid-range prices. If you decide to stay in Braga, this should be your choice.

However, Bom Jesús offers three far superior places. The **Hotel do Elevador** ((253) 603400 FAX (253) 603409, Parque do Bom Jesús do Monte, 4700 Braga, is an elegant villa with

spectacular views of Braga, as well as a good restaurant. Rooms are airy and modern, prices are mid-range. Run by the same management and the similarly priced, the **Hotel do Parque** ((253) 676548 FAX (253) 676679, Parque do Bom Jesús do Monte, 4700 Braga, dates from early this century and has a conservatory and courtyard where drinks are served; as it has no restaurant yet, you will have to eat at the Hotel do Elevador or one of the other establishments described below. Another choice, and no doubt the best if you can get reservations, is the **Castelo do Bom**

Jesús ((253) 676566 FAX (253) 677691 E-MAIL charmhotels@mail.telepac.pt, 4700 Braga, a neo-Gothic eighteenth-century manor house designed by the Swiss architect Ernest Korrodi, it exudes a certain misplaced northern charm.

Where to Eat

Braga's top restaurant is generally held to be **Inácio** ((253) 613235, Campo das Hortas No. 4, where local cuisine can be enjoyed in what could be called a chic rustic setting. **Abade de Priscos** ((253) 276650, Praça Mouzinho de Albuquerque No. 7, is a small first-floor restaurant, family-run and with a more intimate atmosphere. Among the regional dishes served at both restaurants is *arroz de* *sarrabulho*, a stew of meats cooked with pig's blood and rice. Both restaurants are moderately priced. Another small restaurant that is less known by tourists (and highly recommended by local friends) is **Pórtico (** (253) 676672, Arco Bom Jesús. Again the cuisine is typical of the region, fish dishes the specialty, quality superior.

In the inexpensive category is the popular **Restaurant a Ceia**, Rua do Raio; a little way out of the center, the **Restaurante Moçambicana**, Rua Andrade Corvo No. 8, has African food. Remember that Braga has some delightful old cafés. At **Café Astória**, Avenida da Liberdade, you can have a snack and sometimes listen to live music; **A Brasileira**, Rua Dom Março at the top of Rua do Souto, has a street terrace, and there is also the **Café Viana** on the Praça da República.

How to Get There

There is one flight per week from Lisbon to Braga. Trains run frequently from Barcelos and Viana, but travelers coming from north of Viana will need to change at Nine. Trains run direct from Porto but a more frequent service will take you to Nine where you have to change. Rodoviária Nacional Express buses run from the main northern towns into Braga, as well as from Coimbra, Lisbon, and, less frequently, Porto.

By road Braga is 50 km (31 miles) north of Porto along the A3-IP1, and 53 km (32 miles) southeast of Viana do Castelo along the N13 and N103.

BARCELOS

The town of Barcelos lines the north bank of the Cávado River, 22 km (14 miles) to the west of Braga. Besides agriculture, this area is know for its pottery. Most typical is the brown tableware decorated with patterns of little yellow dots, but there is endless demand from collectors for locally produced ceramic figurines.

The city is also responsible for perhaps the most widely recognized symbol of Portugal, the Barcelos Cock. This story, dating back at least the thirteenth century, recounts the tribulations of a pilgrim wrongly accused of theft and sentenced to death. He was spared when, as he had predicted, the roasted chicken that was about to be the judge's dinner, resurrected itself and crowed. Today, brightly painted ceramic cockerels are mass produced and sold throughout Portugal.

Although Barcelos has a number of hotel and restaurants, neither they nor the town truly merits a prolonged stay.

General Information

The *Turismo* **(** (253) 811882 FAX (253) 822188 is at Torre de Menagem (the Keep), Largo da Porta Nova.

What to See and Do

The **Campo da República**, a huge square shaded by trees and centered on a Renaissance fountain, bursts into life on Thursday mornings when vendors bring produce, clothing, household goods, and pottery to sell. By and large, this is not an affair for tourists, but rather farmers and merchants from the surrounding area doing business. And therefore, it is still a lot of fun. To be honest, it is the highlight of the town.

On the southwestern side stands the pretty **Igreja do Nosso Senhor da Cruz**, a neat octagonal building of whitewash and granite with a balustraded roof and a tiled cupola, richly decorated with gilt, *azulejos*, and some elaborate chandeliers.

Fine buildings surround the square, but the most interesting interior belongs to the **Igreja do Terço** on the north side along the Avenida dos Combatentes da Grande Guerra. Formerly the church of a Benedictine convent, it blends into its surroundings, with nothing to suggest its sumptuous interior. Inside, eighteenth-century *azulejos* portray scenes from the life of Saint Benedict, tableaux of monastic life, trompe l'œil windows, and the occasional surprise on the dado: the cockerel with a devil's tail admiring himself in a mirror, or anxious monks trying to control a prancing half-devil. Of a quite different tenor is the gilded baroque pulpit supported and surmounted by cherubs.

Southwest of the Campo da República, close to the river and the old bridge, a group of historic buildings comprise the town's oldest quarter. The ruined building with a

The market town of Barcelos sits on the north bank of the Cávado River.

thin chimney is the remains of the fifteenth-century **Paço dos Condes**, the Palace of the Dukes of Bragança. The ruins now are the site of an open-air archaeological **museum** covered in ancient sarcophagi and tombstones. Open from 10 AM to noon and from 2 PM to 6 PM; closed Mondays.

How to Get There

Trains run frequently to Barcelos from Porto and Viana do Castelo; from Braga you must change at Nine. There are direct connections with all stations north of Barcelos. Buses run frequently from Braga and Viana, stopping at the southeastern edge of the square.

By road Barcelos lies 55 km (34 miles) north of Porto, and 22 km (14 miles) west of Braga. From Braga travel west on the IC14-N103 to Barcelos. From Porto, the most direct route is to travel north along the A3-IP1 to its conjunction with the N103, and then continue along that road to Barcelos. As always, slower more scenic routes are preferable.

GUIMARÃES

The heart of historic Guimarães, 21 km (13 miles) southeast of Braga, is a complex of medieval squares and cobbled streets, overlooked by both a brooding hilltop castle close to the town center and a solid monastery that is now one of the preferred *pousadas* in Portugal.

Background

Guimarães developed around a monastery, a castle, and a small settlement founded by the Countess Mumadona, a Galician noblewoman of the tenth century. In the eleventh century Henri of Burgundy and his wife the Princess Teresa held court in Guimarães castle, and it was here that their son, Afonso Henriques was born in 1110.

Through persistence and ruthlessness Afonso was able to declare himself the first King of Portugal in 1139, making Guimarães (often referred to as the Cradle of the Nation) the capital of the newly formed country. Its glory was short-lived, however, as in 1143 the capital was moved to Coimbra.

Guimarães was Portugal's first capital.

General Information

There are two municipal *Turismos*, one at Avenida Alameda da Resistência ((253) 412450, and the other at the Praça de Santiago ((253) 518790. The regional *Turismo* ((253) 518394 FAX (253) 515134 is at Largo Cónego José Maria Gomes, but can also be contacted by E-MAIL camaraguimaraes@mail.telepac.pt and visited at their WEB SITE www.cm-guimaraes.pt.

What to See and Do

Start your explorations at the **castle**, which stands atop a rocky hill to the north of the center. The original part was built by Countess Mumadona in the tenth century to protect the village and monastery from attacks by the Normans and Moors. Extended and strengthened by Henri of Burgundy at the end of the eleventh century, it has sustained extensive restoration work, and today its crenellated square keep, surrounded by seven smaller towers, exudes a certain medieval ferocity. A bronze **statue** of Afonso Henriques in his battle dress stands nearby, the work of the nineteenth-century sculptor Soares dos Reis.

Just below the castle is the simple and tiny twelfth-century **Igreja de São Miguel do Castelo** (Church of Saint Michael of the Castle), where it is believed that Afonso Henriques was baptized, presumably in the font that is still standing. A burial ground for crusading knights, the central area of the floor is cordoned off to prevent further wear on the carved tombstones.

A little further down the hill looms the somewhat ungainly **Paço dos Duques de Bragança** (Palace of the Dukes of Bragança) ((253) 412273 FAX (253) 517201, built for Dom Afonso, Count of Barcelos, Duke of Bragança, and illegitimate son of João I. Abandoned in the sixteenth century, the palace subsequently fell into ruin and was rebuilt at Salazar's behest in the 1930s. Today it contains artifacts from numerous periods: porcelain, furniture, tapestries, and paintings. Opening hours are daily from 9:30 AM to 5 PM, and until 7 PM during July and August. Admission is free on Sundays. A note to drivers: just behind the Paço is the perfect, legal place to abandon your car for the entire day.

To get to the old town from the palace, continue down the hill past the seventeenth-century Carmo Church and walk along the **Rua de Santa Maria**; with records citing it as far back as the twelfth century, it is one the of the oldest streets in the city. Fine houses line the way, many of them dating from the fifteenth-century, with their wrought-iron balconies, iron lanterns, and grills. The street brings you to the **Convento de Santa Clara**, a sixteenth-century building with a baroque façade.

Rua de Santa Maria meets another ancient street, the **Rua da Rainha**, at the beautiful **Largo da Oliveira**, named after the Legend of the Olive Tree. In the sixth century, a delegation of Visigoths pronounced to Wamba as he ploughed his fields that he had been chosen to be their king. Less than thrilled, Wamba stuck his staff into the ground declaring that the chances of his accepting the title were about as great as of his staff sprouting olive leaves, which of course it did. A small Gothic structure of covered arches sheltering a cross marks the spot of the legendary occurrence.

Behind this cross and dominating one side of the square is the **Igreja de Nossa Senhora da Oliveira** (Collegiate Church of Our Lady of the Olive Tree) ((253) 416144. A monastery was founded here in the tenth century, possibly on the site of a sixth-century temple commemorating the miracle, and in the fourteenth century, King João I extended it in thanks for his victory at Aljubarrota.

The cloister and convent buildings now house the **Museu Alberto Sampaio** ((253) 412465 FAX (253) 517814, a striking collection of church treasures including the robe worn by King João I during the Battle of Aljubarrota, a beautiful silver-bound Bible, and, prized above all, the delicately crafted silver-gilt triptych depicting the Visitation, Nativity and Annunciation, said to have been captured from the King of Castile's tent following his defeat at Aljubarrota. Open from 10 AM to 12:30 PM and from 2 PM to 5:30 PM; closed Mondays. Admission is free on Sunday mornings.

Guimarães has one other important museum, the **Museu de Martins Sarmento** ((253) 415969, which occupies the Gothic cloister of the São Domingos Convent along

the Rua de Paio Galvão. Named after the nineteenth-century archaeologist who devoted himself to the excavation of the Citânia de Briteiros, it contains many artifacts unearthed there and at other hilltop sites. Three items deserve mention: the ancient carved stone slab known as the Pedra Formosa which, after much debate, is now generally believed to have been used to block the entrance of a tomb; a miniature bronze votive cart pulled by men and oxen; and the mighty Colossus of Pedralva, a 3,000-year-old, three-meter (10-ft)-tall statue of a seated man with an upraised arm and pleasantly large phallus. Open from 9:30 AM to noon and 2 PM to 5 PM, closed Sundays.

Overlooking the town and high up on the slopes of the Penha is the **Santa Marinha da**

Costa, once an Augustinian monastery and now one of Portugal's most-respected *pousadas*. The monastery was founded in the twelfth century by Dona Mafalda, wife of Afonso Henriques, in fulfillment of a vow to Santa Marinha. Then, in the sixteenth century, it passed to the order of São Jerónimo. The cloister is elegant, with its rare and delicate Mozarabic archway dating from the tenth century. During recent restoration work, traces of a Visigoth church were found, while other archaeological evidence suggests that this was the site of a Roman (and possibly even pre-Roman) temple. The best way of getting to see the monastery is staying as a guest of the *pousada*, but even if you just come for a meal or a drink, you will be able to look around a bit, and get an impression of the place.

Where to Stay

Guimarães is the only city in Portugal that offers two *pousadas*, one in the center of the old town, the other about two and a half kilometers (one and a half miles) outside. The out-of-town one is the **Pousada de Santa Marinha** ((253) 514453 FAX (253) 514459, 4800 Guimarães, a carefully converted monastery with origins dating from the twelfth century, it sits on a hillside overlooking the town proper. The majestic feel is accentuated by the wood-paneled ceilings, granite fountains, and salons with immaculate *azulejo* walls. The modern extension that houses some of the guest rooms is not jarring. Prices

Largo da Oliveira in Guimarães marks the spot where a dead olive tree miraculously broke into leaf.

range between the high end of mid-range and expensive.

In the center of town, the **Pousada de Nossa Senhora da Oliveira** ((253) 514157 FAX (253) 514204, Largo da Oliveira, 4800 Guimarães, has an utterly different ambience, which is to say, one that is far more intimate. Comprised of what was once several houses in the heart of the old town, it has 16 rooms (some of which can be small), as well as a few suites, and overlooks the Largo de Oliveira. Mid-range prices apply. There are a number of modern hotels in town that offer what their stars and façades intimate.

Obviously, my heart lies elsewhere. There are several TURIHAB options, essentially all of which are fine. One, however, is extraordinary. At the **Casa de Sezim** ((253) 523000 FAX (253) 523196, Apartado 410, 4800 Guimarães, you are welcomed into a former diplomat's home that has been in his family for over 600 years. The house is filled with antiques that, differing from the usual, are not merely to be seen from afar, but are proudly used. The shared sitting rooms are furnished in pieces that often date from the sixteenth century, and their walls are papered in the original works of the French painter Züber. The corner guest room has a bed that is carved from exotic wood and, dating from the fifteenth century, sports the family crest. In addition to the pleasure of the exquisitely maintained gardens, the *casa* has an outdoor swimming pool and stables, where horseback riding tours can be arranged. The family also produces one of the finer *vinho verdes*, the vineyards being part of the grounds. Prices are mid-range.

Where to Eat

Both *pousadas* mentioned above have lovely dining rooms, each reflecting its own character — the **Pousada de Santa Marinha** with its vaulted ceilings, sophisticated *azulejo*-tiled rooms, and crystal chandeliers; the **Pousada de Santa Maria da Oliveira**, a cozy, country-style room with dried flowers, wooden beams, and gleaming copper. It must be said that, although the settings are grand and the china fine, the food does not live up to expectations at either *pousada*, however, it is universally agreed that Santa Marinha has the superior kitchen.

For the city's best dining, go to **Solar do Arco** ((253) 513072, Rua de Santa Maria. This restaurant is thoroughly deserving of reputation for superior fish dishes. Another choice is **Val de Donas** ((253) 511411, Rua de Donas No. 4, grilled foods are particularly noteworthy. For a light lunch, there are a few good cafés in and around the Largo da Oliveira and the Praça de Santiago.

Guimarães' latest addition is **Carramão** ((253) 413815, Rua de Santa Maria, which is a wonderfully conceived bar with an enclosed garden — replete with orange trees and a goldfish pond — where concerts are held during the evenings. Upstairs, along with another bar is a cybercafé with several computer stations, as well as a separate room for those seeking quiet. Light food and desserts are served.

How to Get There

One train service from Porto runs direct to Guimarães, while others involve changing at Lousádo. If you are traveling from Braga by train, it is necessary to change at both Nine and Lousádo. Buses run frequently from Braga to Guimarães, and express services run from Porto, Lisbon, and Coimbra.

By road Guimarães lies 53 km (32 miles) northeast of Porto, north along the A3-IP1 and then east on the A7 directly into the city. The city is 21 km (13 miles) southeast of Braga along the N101.

VIANA DO CASTELO

The Minho's top resort is built around a lively fishing port at the mouth of the Lima River, and quite different from the usual seaside town, the beach is a ferry ride across the river. Viana do Castelo itself is elegant, vibrant, but in no way raucous, although there are a few late-night bars and clubs. What the French would call "comfortable in its own skin," the town manages to absorb its tourists without demeaning its refined personality. A prosperous maritime history has endowed Viana with fine Manueline and Renaissance buildings, restaurants and cafés abound in its center, which is largely a pedestrians-only labyrinth. Situated within a thermocline,

Dazzlingly regional costume is worn on feast days and special occasions in Viana do Castelo.

exotic Brazilian trees flourish, time moves gently, and the beach has waves big enough for surfing, but not too rough to prevent swimming, all making Viana an unequivocal pleasure to fall upon.

General Information

The *Turismo* ((258) 822620 FAX (258) 827873 is at Rua do Hospital Velho.

What to See and Do

The heart of the city is the spacious **Praça da República** where sixteenth-century

Reis, where you will find the **Palácio dos Condes da Carreira**, first built in the sixteenth century and renovated in the eighteenth, it now serves as the Town Hall. Another houses the **Museu Municipal** ((258) 820377, Largo de São Domingos. Its collection of decorative art is biased towards ceramics, for which Viana is famous. Opening times are from 9:30 AM to noon and from 2 PM to 5 PM; closed Mondays.

The **Monte de Santa Luzia**, with its massive basilica, seems to oversee the town, and its extraordinary panoramic views can be had

buildings look onto a Renaissance fountain. Most striking is the **Misericórdia** (alms house), the upper tiers of which are supported by ominous sixteenth-century caryatids. Adjacent to the Misericórdia is the **Antigos Paço do Concelho** (Old Town Hall), its lower story an arcade of pointed arches and its façade emblazoned with Viana's coat-of-arms and a carved ship. Its setting, outdoor cafés, restaurants, and nighttime music are enchanting.

There are several fine houses in the vicinity of the *Turismo* (itself housed in a converted fifteenth-century building), which has brochures pointing out some of the more stunning mansions. The **Rua da Bandeira** brims with them, as does the **Rua Cândido dos**

either by taking a climb through the pine forest, or boarding the funicular that runs every half-hour. Built earlier this century, the **basilica** is a rather cold structure. Behind it stand the grand **Hotel Santa Luzia**, and the remains of a Celtic-Iberian settlement, similar to Briteiros.

Apart from the charms of the town itself, people come here for the beaches. The **Praia do Cabedelo** is a ferry ride from the Largo 5 de Outubro, while to the north of Viana is **Vila Praia de Ancora**, which also has a sandy stretch. Beyond lies **Moledo**, close to the Spanish border. During the summer months, there are boat trips from Viana that take in the beaches and the docks, details are available from the *Turismo*, or just go to the ferry dock. Viana is also a jumping-off point for trips to Spain, up the Lima, and into the Peneda-Gerês National Park. Again, ask at the *Turismo* for details of what is available or call in on a travel agent—several have offices in the Avenida dos Combatentes.

Where to Stay

The grandest accommodation in Viana is in fact five kilometers (three and a half miles) out of town. The **Pousada do Monte de Santa Luzia (** (258) 828889 or (258) 828890 FAX (258) 828892, Monte de Santa Luzia, 4900 Viana do Castelo, is a palatial hotel overlooking the city. This late nineteenth-century building was recently renovated in art deco style. There are tennis courts, a swimming pool, an acceptable restaurant, and over 50 rooms all within the mid-range price bracket. Down in the center of town, the **Hotel Viana Sol (** (258) 828995 FAX (258) 823401, Largo Vasco da Gama, has well-equipped rooms and there are good sports facilities.

In the inexpensive category, the **Residencial Viana Mar (** (258) 828962, Avenida dos Combatentes No. 215, is an older hotel on the main shopping street offering basic rooms that are clean and comfortable.

Once again, by far the best lodgings are to be found at the country homes, and this region is particularly rife with them. The TURIHAB office is in Ponte de Lima (see ACCOMMODATION, page 279 in TRAVELERS' TIPS), an old river town 23 km (14 miles) east of Viana that has, as one might expect, an unusual share of options. However, almost nothing could possibly compare with the **Quinta da Boa Viagem (** (258) 835835 FAX (258) 836836, Além do Rio, Areosa, 4900 Viana do Castelo. The main house dates from the eighteenth century, and a series of low-lying buildings have been transformed into separate apartments of varying sizes, all with fireplaces and equipped kitchens. The hilly grounds, with views of the ocean, are lush with terraced gardens, most are more wild than tame. One shaded expanse has a sunken swimming pool. The comfort of the respite is complemented by the warmth of the family. Reserve by fax with as much advance notice as possible, as many guests come back every year.

Where to Eat

There are several restaurants in the pedestrian-only part of town. These two are the best, as well as the most popular, and in high season require reservations. **Os 3 Potes (** (258) 829928, Beco dos Fornos No. 9, near the Praça da República was once the city bakery and is a popular restaurant. The decor is traditional, the menu basically regional with some international dishes slipped in, and traditional entertainment such as folk dancing or singing is often also on the menu. **Cozinha das Malheiras (** (258) 823680, Rua Gago

Coutinho, is housed in the Malheiras Palace; its seafood is very good. Both the restaurants are moderately priced.

For inexpensive and perfectly acceptable food, try the locally popular **Túnel (** (258) 822188, Rua dos Manjovos No. 1.

However, if you have a car, there are three restaurants that could even be considered obligatory. Each different from the other, each excellent for itself. **Sargaceiro (** (96) 374834, Praia de Moledo, is an informal place directly on the beach, where they serve the equivalent of Spanish *tapas*, mostly of fish. Don't skip the grilled squid. Full meals are also available at inexpensive prices. To reach it, travel north on the N13 and turn off at the sign indicating the *praia*. (The odd telephone number is a portable.) Between Moledo and Viana do Castelo in the town of Afife, you will find **Mariana (** (258) 981327, where the house specialty is sea bass steamed in seaweed. The creation is far more delicate than

OPPOSITE: Viana do Castelo's annual August *festa* is the largest in the Minho. The Santa Luzia basilica ABOVE perches high above the city.

it sounds. Order the soup of the day, and a huge tureen is placed on your table. Traveling all the way to Caminha, which should take only fifteen minutes, presents a chance for fine dining. The primary decoration at **Duque de Caminha** ((258) 722046, Rua Ricardo Joaquim de Sousa, are bottles of wine, all of which are available. And although the wine list might be reason enough to drop in, it is equaled, if not surpassed, by the cuisine. Daily specials such as lobster with rice should be sampled, but the house specialty is marinated lamb that is slowly baked beyond all previously known degrees of tenderness.

How to Get There

Trains run direct to Viana from Porto via Barcelos, and from stations north of Viana. Passengers from Braga need to change at Nine. Buses run frequently from Porto, Braga, and other main northern towns, and a less frequent service runs from Lisbon and Coimbra.

By road Viana is 67 km (42 miles) north of Porto along the N13-IC1; from Braga it is 52 km (32 miles) along the N103-IC14, and then the N13.

THE LIMA VALLEY

The Lima is a magical, sleepy green valley, surrounded by wooded hills and graced with noble *quintas*.

General Information

In Ponte de Lima the *Turismo* ((258) 942335 is in the Praça da República, as is the headquarters for the Minho *Turismo de Habitação* scheme (TURIHAB) ((258) 741672 FAX (258) 741444, Praça da República, 4990 Ponte de Lima, which organizes manor house and farmhouse accommodation.

Ponte de Lima

Ponte de Lima's charms lie in its setting and its buildings rather than in any specific sights. Only 21 km (13 miles) east of Viana, it demands unhurried exploration, maybe even a stay at one of the many manor houses in its environs. It is the center from which the province's TURIHAB scheme is operated, and if you drop in at the office they may be able to fix you up with some accommodation at short notice.

Two bridges cross the river here: a modern one, and the famous, much-photographed older structure, which is part Roman, part medieval. There are plenty of restaurants in the town, and leisurely lunches seem to be the tradition.

Ponte da Barca

Seventeen kilometers (11 miles) east of Ponte de Lima, at Ponte da Barca attention again focuses around a bridge, dating from the fifteenth and eighteenth centuries. There is an old belief in these parts that an expectant mother who is worried about her pregnancy should ask the first person who crosses the bridge after midnight to baptize her belly with water from the Lima in order to safeguard her unborn child. You might want to bear this in mind if you are prone to midnight strolls.

The town is not quite as charming as Ponte de Lima, but the riverbank is perhaps even more serene. Next to the appropriately named **Jardim dos Poetas** (Poets' Garden), the **Pelourinho Bar**, with its exposed granite walls, offers a cool (literally) respite during the day, and a young hangout at night. Sandwiches are available inside and out on the patio.

Soajo

About 15 km (nine miles) east of Ponte da Barca, the N203 enters the Peneda-Gerês National Park. A short deviation from the river road, just four kilometers (two and a half miles) north along the N304 will bring you to Soajo. This remote and hardy little village in the Serra do Soajo is surrounded by cultivated land punctuated by rocky granite outcrops. On one is the sight that brings cameras to Soajo: a collection of strange, coffin-like stone granaries raised on stilts. Known as *espigueiros*, these rectangular slatted boxes have pitched roofs, and their funereal appearance is enhanced by the crosses on each of them. *Espigueiros* can be seen throughout the Minho, and even in parts of Galicia, but it is rare to find such a large grouping as this, evidence that communal farming is still practiced.

Viana do Castelo's Praça da República is fun place to have drink in the sun.

Lindoso

Continuing another approximate six kilometers (three and a half miles) along the N203 past the turn off for Soajo will lead to the town of Lindoso and the border with Spain. The **Castelo de Lindoso** was founded in the beginning of the thirteenth century, and was essentially used as a military garrison continuously through the eighteenth century. It did spend two years in the hands of the Spanish during the Restoration Wars. There is a tiny museum with relics from Roman times, and even a shard thought to date from 2000 to 1500 BC.

However, the highlight of this drive along the N203 is the drive itself. The snake of the route parallels the snake of the river subsidiary, every turn presenting an even more extraordinary view.

Where to Stay

This region may lack hotels, but it more than makes up for that with its glut of TURIHAB accommodation. The head office for Minho TURIHAB in Ponte de Lima (see GENERAL INFORMATION, above) can supply you with details, or for advance booking you can obtain a brochure from the larger *Turismos* and ICEP offices. There are over 30 establishments in the Ponte de Lima district alone with prices from inexpensive to mid-range. The **Paço de Calheiros** ((258) 947164 FAX (258) 947294, Calheiros, 4990 Ponte de Lima, is a noble eighteenth-century house set in gardens with views of the Lima that lies approximately seven kilometers (four miles) outside Ponte de Lima. Another good choice in the area is the **Casa de Abbades** ((258) 948227 FAX (258) 948444, São Martinho da Gandra, 4990 Ponte de Lima. A charming family offers apartments in a manor house dating from the seventeenth century.

How to Get There

The Lima Valley is not served by rail. A bus service runs frequently from Viana do Castelo to Ponte de Lima, and four buses a day run to Ponte da Barca. They also run from Braga to Ponte da Barca and Ponte de Lima.

By road, Ponte de Lima lies 21 km (13 miles) east of Viana de Castelo. Two roads run inland from Viana along the Lima

Valley: the N202 on the north bank and the N203 on the south bank. The N202 has the best views.

PARQUE NACIONAL DA PENEDA-GERÊS

Portugal's largest reserve encompasses some 72,000 hectares (177,916 acres), including four mountain ranges — Peneda, Gerês, Soajo, and Amarela — cut by deep river valleys. The park is a crescent-shaped area taking in parts of both the Minho and Trás-os-Montes, skirting around an intruding chunk of the Spanish province of Orense. It encompasses a system of dams and reservoirs of interest to watersports enthusiasts and over a hundred villages; quiet spots can always be found, especially at the less-visited northern section. The hub of the park is the pretty spa town of **Caldas do Gerês**, where most of the accommodation is to be found. It is a sedate, rather Victorian spa, good for sipping herbal teas, taking the waters, and as a base for excursions. It tends to fill up on summer weekends.

With deep wooded valleys, rocky summits, streams, and cascades, this is ideal hiking territory, however, a map of the park is essential. Driving through the park is also a possibility, as long as both you and your vehicle can cope with large potholes and roads that disintegrate into rough tracks. Mountaineers, trout fishermen, campers, and pony trekkers will all find fulfillment in the park, which gets the highest rainfall in the country. The result is dense forests of cork oak, silver birch, pines, ferns and sycamores, together with Gerês fern and the Gerês iris, unique to the area. Wild ponies and cats, deer, and wolves roam free, while the bird population includes golden eagles and barn owls. Prehistoric dolmens, some of them 5,000 years old, have been found, while many Roman milestones recall a less-distant past, especially at **Portela do Homem** near the border where part of the Roman road that once linked Braga to what is now Spain can still be seen.

The *Turismo* in Caldas do Gerês is at Avenida Manuel Francisco da Costa ((253) 391133 FAX (253) 391282. The park's head office is in Braga at Rua de São Geraldo No. 19.

Where to Stay

Most of the accommodation in Caldas do Gerês are *pensãos* but there are a handful of hotels. The **Hotel do Parque (** (253) 391112, Avenida Manuel Francisco da Costa, 4845 Caldas do Gerês, is a charming turn-of-the-century place with an outdoor pool. Prices are inexpensive. The **Hotel das Termas (** (253) 391143, Avenida Manuel Francisco da Costa, is another old-fashioned spa hotel with similar facilities and mid-range prices.

If you are really looking to get away from it all but still have a swimming pool and tennis courts at access, the best place to stay is the **Pousada de São Bento (** (253) 647190 FAX (253) 647867, 4850 Caniçada, near Caniçada, 10 km (six miles) south of Gerês. The views and mountain hikes are spectacular. Prices are mid-range.

How to Get There

The northern section of the park can be approached from Arcos de Valdevez and from Melgaço on the Minho River. Other points of entry are the more central Caldas do Gerês and Covelães in the province of Trás-os-Montes. It is best to travel there by car, but there are six buses a day running between Braga and Caldas do Gerês.

TRÁS-OS-MONTES

Trás-os-Montes is separated from the neighboring Minho region by the Marão and Gerês mountain ranges, and is bordered by Spain to the north and west. This northeastern extremity of Portugal is not merely physically remote, but it must be said that its overriding regional consciousness is as well. That is a sweeping statement, but Trás-os-Montes does stand aloof and very much apart from the rest of Portugal. Named with customary Portuguese directness, Trás-os-Montes means Behind the Mountains. There are two faces to this land beyond the mountains, which are simply referred to as *Terra Quente* (Warm Land) and *Terra Fria* (Cold Land). *Terra Quente* is the southern area that encompasses the cultivated sections of the Tua and Corgo rivers, and the upper reaches of the Douro Valley where, along with port grapes, olive, almond, and fruit trees are

harvested. Early spring becomes a rash of blossoming trees, their mild fragrances heady with the density. *Terra Fria* lies to the north, a rugged plateau cut by deep valleys where the land is poorer, and the bitterness of winter and cruel heat of summer — nine months of winter and three months of sizzling heat — combine with poor communications to enforce the isolation and independence of many villages. Mobile phones are making inroads, as are European Union-funded road developments, but the tenor of the place has yet to change tremendously.

So it remains true that ancient traditions flourish here, as do strange dialects, and superstitions still hold sway. The local *bruxa* or witch might still be consulted on matters of health, and religious belief is ardent, although its practice may be somewhat unorthodox. Small communities exist in a state of near self-sufficiency, however in recent years, there has been a high instance of emigration out of the region. Paradoxically, magnificent sprawling houses with well-tended gardens can be seen from all the mountain roads, and it appears that city people have discovered the region, bringing with them a certain

An onion-shaped church spire, typical in the Minho, rises over the town of Ponte de Lima in the heart of the province.

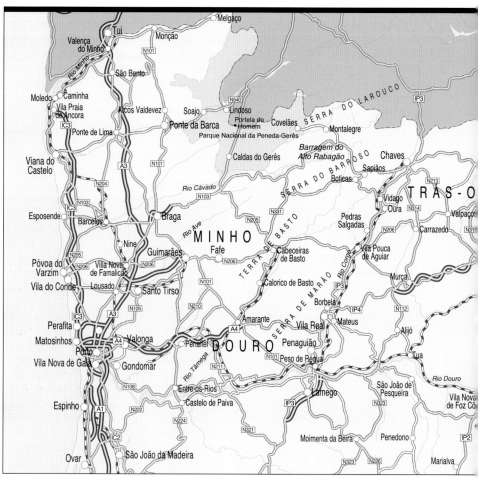

gentrification that to date seems, at least to the outside observer, largely positive.

Roads to the main cities — Bragança, Chaves, Miranda do Douro — have been greatly improved, making the province more accessible. Although intercity bus service is reliable, it is still infrequent, and the best way to appreciate the region remains traveling by car. And although you will be continually advised — by people ranging from the *Turismo* staff to gas station attendants — to loop back and catch one of the main highways, disregard their well-meaning words and persevere. As long as the weather is good, driving is not remotely as difficult as most say, the roads are newly paved, the views unequaled, and the fragrance and quality of the air unsurpassed. It may have well been the chance concurrence of good weather and virtually no traffic, but without hesitation, I

can say that by far my favorite drive is winding along the N103, having set out from the western coast town of Viana do Castelo, and ending up in the late afternoon in the spa town of Chaves, a good 200 km (120 miles) to the east.

CHAVES

Chaves lies in a wide, fertile valley, a mere 11 km (seven miles) away from the Spanish border. Once a key point of attack for invading armies (hence the name Chaves, meaning keys), these days the town is pleasant, and in addition to its spa, has a few sites worth visiting. However, restaurants, accommodation, and general ambience are lacking, and it is far better to visit during the day and then dash off to the comforts of Vidago (see below).

220

THE NORTH

seventeenth-century **Misericórdia Church** ornamented with twisted columns. In front of it stands an elegant Manueline **pillory**. Also in the square, the onetime palace of the Dukes of Bragança now houses the **Museu de Região Flaviense** (Regional Museum) **(** (276) 21965, with archaeological and ethnographic displays on the region, including a prehistoric stone relic in the form of a human. Opening times are from 9:30 AM to 12:30 PM and from 2 PM to 5 PM; closed Mondays. Admission is free on Sundays.

Behind the palace, the fourteenth-century keep contains the **Museu Militar**, which is part of the Municipal Museum, the entrance fee covering admission to both. There are displays of ancient weaponry and armor, but the museum deals most thoroughly with the Portuguese role in World War I and its twentieth-century colonial wars. The keep itself is all that remains of King Dinis' castle, a square, chunky tower affording views over the valley. Opening hours are the same as for the Municipal Museum.

Beyond the keep and below the old walls, a very ordinary modern complex houses the **spa** where you can try out the effects of the warm spring water on your hypertension, rheumatism, or gout. Better still, stop at a nearby café to try some of that wonderful ham (*presunto*) and maybe a glass or so of the local red wine with its own restorative properties.

General Information

The municipal *Turismo* **(** (276) 333029 is at Terreiro de Cavalaria. The regional office is the *Turismo do Alto Tâmega e Barroso* **(** (276) 333029 FAX (276) 21419 E-MAIL rturismoatb @mail.telepac.pt, Avenida Tenente Valadim No. 39, 5400 Chaves.

What to See and Do

The Romans were particularly fond of Chaves, or *Aquae Flaviae* as they called it, for its hot springs. Their legacy remains the bridge over the Tâmega River, which is now almost 1,900 years old and still bearing up well, although over the centuries it has lost a few arches and some masonry. Posts at the southern end bear Roman inscriptions and were once used as milestones.

The center of the old quarter is the attractive **Praça de Camões** where there is a

Around Chaves

Southwest of Chaves along the N2-IP3 are two popular spa towns, both surrounded by trees and hills. The first is **Vidago**, 17 km (10 miles) from Chaves, where there are tennis courts, a nine-hole golf course, horseback riding, and good walks. The spa itself had been housed in an art nouveau building on the grounds of the Hotel Palace, the most impressive sight in Vidago, but it no longer functions as a true spa, rather a health club for guests of the hotel. Twelve kilometers (seven and a half miles) further south along the N2-IP3, **Pedras Salgadas** has a similar character.

About 120 km (75 miles) west of Chaves a collection of villages centers around the large lake at the **Barragem do Alto Rabagão** — Sapiãos, Boticas, Vilarinho, Sendim, Seara

Velha, Pardornelos, Montalegre to name a few — sheltering in the Serra do Barroso and the foothills of the Serra do Larouco. Monsanto has a café and a *pensão* or two, and hotels and restaurants are scattered about, but it may be better to base yourself at Chaves, Vidago, or the spa town of Carvalhelos.

Where to Stay

Of the two four-star hotels in Chaves, the **Forte de São Francisco** ((276) 333700 FAX (276) 337001, 5400 Chaves, is the only acceptable choice. Perched atop the Pedis-

and decor. The hotel's modern extension is actually more expensive, but has less charm. Try the excellent restaurant and wine list. Mid-range to expensive prices, depending upon the season.

If you prefer a pension, choose the **Pensão Primavera** ((276) 907230, Avenida Conde Caria, 5425 Vidago, directly across from the palace.

Where to Eat

In Chaves, the **Hotel Trajano** (see WHERE TO STAY, above) has a cellar restaurant that serves

queira in a restored seventeenth-century convent, the hotel has deluxe accommodation that tastefully work within the ancient setting. Mid-range prices. The modern **Hotel Trajano** ((276) 332415 FAX (276) 327002, Travessa Cândido dos Reis, 5400 Chaves, has a nice terrace overlooking the old town. Inexpensive to mid-range.

Regardless of the category you choose, Vidago, with its infinitely superior accommodation, restaurants, and setting, is far preferable to Chaves as a place to stay. There are several hotels and *pensãos* in Vidago, but the best choice is the turn-of-the-century **Hotel Palace de Vidago** ((276) 907356 FAX (276) 907359, Parque, 5425 Vidago, in its stylish garden setting. Rooms vary in size

good regional food, as does the **Restaurante Carvalho** ((276) 321727, Alameda do Tabolado, with its traditional kitchen defying the modern ambience. In Vidago, go to the restaurant at the **Hotel Palace de Vidago** (see WHERE TO STAY, above).

How to Get There

For many years, Portugal's narrow-gauge railways were a source of delight for train enthusiasts, but sadly they have fallen to modernization. There are two left, however: the Tua Line that runs from Tua along the Douro to Bragança, and the Corgo Line that runs from Peso da Régua to Vila Real. They make a delightful way to see some beautiful countryside, and as the trains' continued longevity cannot be predicted, catch them while you can.

The old Tua narrow-gauge railway used to run to Chaves from Peso da Régua, but sadly has been pruned back as far as Vila Real, nowadays the nearest train station to Chaves. Passengers traveling from Porto must take the Douro Line as far as Peso da Régua, change to the Corgo Line for Vila Real, then complete their journey by bus. It should be said, however, that short as it is now, the Corgo is still one of the great train journeys of Europe. Buses run to Chaves

from Bragança and Braga, and there are express buses from Lisbon, Coimbra, Porto, and Vila Real.

By road, Chaves lies 61 km (38 miles) from Vila Real along the N2-IP3, the route that drivers from Porto will take. For drivers coming from the Atlantic coast, the fastest route is to pass through Guimarães, from where you pick up the IC5 and continue east to the conjunction with the N2-IP3, which goes directly into Chaves. However, if you have the time, far preferable is the journey east along the N103, which can be picked up at Viana do Castelo or Braga. This route winds through an extraordinary mountain countryside, with its river subsidiaries, lakes, and pine and eucalyptus trees. In good weather,

this is truly not a difficult trip. The road is newly paved and not highly trafficked.

BRAGANÇA

When you reach this hilltop citadel what you will find is truly extraordinary: a complete rustic, medieval village, dominated by its ancient castle, a symbol of Bragança's isolation.

Bragança's other persona is as the administrative capital of Trás-os-Montes, a rapidly changing city. This agricultural center with an expanding textile industry and university is keen to exploit its proximity to various Spanish cities, as well as its direct road link to Porto. New roads are eroding Bragança's image of isolation, but one suspects it may take much longer to rid the city of its deep-seated self-sufficiency and independence.

General Information

The municipal *Turismo* ((273) 381273 is at Avenida Cidade de Zamora, and the regional office ((273) 331078 FAX (273) 331913 can be found at Largo Principal. For brochures and information on the Parque Nacional de Montesinho, drop in at the park headquarters ((273) 381444 FAX (273) 381179 in Bragança, Bairro Salvador Nunes Teixeira No. 5.

What to See and Do

A cluster of public buildings and white-washed houses huddle within the hefty walls fortified by 18 towers, above which rises a tall keep. In this medieval **citadel** a community still keeps livestock and grow a few small crops. Most extraordinary of all the buildings is the **Domus Municipais** (Municipal Hall), a twelfth-century Romanesque meeting-place where respected members of the community once gathered to discuss public matters and settle disputes. Built over a cistern, which is visible through a grille in the floor, it is a pentagonal structure lit by arched windows around the entire building and topped with a pitched tiled roof. The meeting room has a simple stone bench along the

Fortified Bragança was once at a strategic crossroads crucial to the defense of Portugal. Today, the city is an important agricultural hub.

walls and a carved frieze running above the arches. If you want to look inside you may have to ask around in the village for the keyholder. (This is neither as strange nor as difficult as it might sound.)

Stone vines climb the twisted columns that flank the Manueline doorway of the sixteenth-century **Igreja da Santa Maria** next to the Domus Municipais. Facing the church, a twelfth-century **keep** rises above the castle towers to challenge Spain. It now houses a **Museu Militar**, open Friday to Wednesday, 9 AM to 12:30 PM and 2 PM to 5 PM. Below the

the chancel is magnificently inlaid with a Moorish-style geometric pattern.

Very close by along Rua Abilio Beça, the former episcopal palace houses the **Museu do Abade de Baçal**. It is named after Francisco Manuel Alves (1865–1947), Abbot of Baçal, a campaigner for religious tolerance who studied the history of Bragança in depth with particular attention to the history of its Jewish community. The museum has a fascinating collection of exhibits that include traditional costumes, furniture, coins, illuminated manuscripts, religious

castle walls near the keep, a **pillory** curiously rises out of a prehistoric sculpture of a pig, by which the unfortunate beast was skewered. There are several of these odd prehistoric stone pigs, known as *berrões* or *porcos*, throughout Trás-os-Montes, the most famous is the one that stands in the main square of the town of Murça. (It is possible that they were fertility symbols or offerings to the gods.)

Outside the walls in front of the castle, the churches of **São Bento** and **São Francisco** stand close together. The Renaissance São Bento is the most interesting church in Bragança. In the nave, there is an eighteenth-century barrel-vaulted ceiling painted with a stunning trompe l'œil, while the ceiling of

art, and paintings of Transmontano landscapes by Alberto Souza. Open from 10 AM to 12:30 PM and from 2 PM to 5 PM; closed Mondays.

When the Jews of Spain were expelled by Ferdinand and Isabella in 1492, many of them sought refuge in Portugal. However, Manuel I had them forcibly baptized in 1497, thus compelling the community to practice its religion in secret while outwardly adhering to the Christian faith. Many of these New Christians, as they became known, chose remote corners of the country in which to live in peace. Bragança's isolation was ideal for them. They have left their mark on the local culture, the specialty on sale at the *mercado* next to the city's unexceptional cathedral, are *alheiras*, cunning sausages made with chicken or turkey rather than pork and designed to fool the masters of the Inquisition.

Where to Stay

Just outside Bragança the **Pousada de São Bartolomeu (** (273) 331493 FAX (273) 323453, Rua de Turismo, 5300 Bragança, is a 1950s building on the heights of Serra da Nogueira. Its balconied rooms and pleasant terrace afford superb views of the citadel and surrounding hills. Expensive. The **Hotel São José do Nordeste (** (273) 331578, Avenida Sá Carneiro Nos. 11-15, is highly recommended in its category. Another modern building with similar views over the citadel, it is in the city proper and has comfortable rooms, some with terraces, some with picture windows, a restaurant, and a bar. Guests have free access to the movie theater in the same complex. Quite a value at mid-range prices.

In the inexpensive category, the **Pensão Poças (** (273) 331175, Rua Combatentes da Grande Guerra No. 206, offers immaculate, if somewhat characterless room and is the best of its range. The **Residencial São Roque (** (273) 381481, Zona da Estacada, Lote Nos. 26-27, has simply-furnished rooms with private bathrooms and views of the castle.

Where to Eat

Without question, the top restaurant in town is the superb **Solar Bragançano (** (273) 323875, Praça de Sé No. 34. On the second floor of an old townhouse, you can dine on fine cuisine — regional specialties such as the deliciously subtle chestnut soup and stuffed pheasant — in great charm and with attentive service. Also served are delicately prepared dishes that are a bit less exotic, along with a well-chosen, well-priced wine list. Moderate prices apply.

As always, the *pousada* (see WHERE TO STAY, above) has a reliable restaurant, here serving primarily Transmontano dishes at moderate prices. At **Plantório (** (273) 312426, Estrada Cantarias, the views are as good as the delicious regional cooking, and prices are inexpensive to moderate. **Arca de Noé (** (273) 381159, Avenida do Savor, is essentially a Bragança wine cellar serving good, inexpensive food.

How to Get There

Internal flights run on weekdays from Lisbon to Bragança. Cabanelas buses run daily on weekdays to the Spanish border town of Quintanilha, and twice daily on weekdays from Lisbon to Bragança, stopping at Coimbra and Vila Real en route. The Internorte express runs from Porto to Quintanilha and Zamora via Bragança once a day from Tuesday to Saturday.

If you are traveling by train from Porto, you will need to change at Tua to join the old Tua Line that nowadays only runs as far as Mirandela. From Mirandela there is a bus connection to Bragança.

By road, Bragança is approximately 130 km (81 miles) from Vila Real along the N15-IP4, while Porto lies a further 82 km (51 miles) from Vila Real along the same road.

MIRANDA DO DOURO

High on a hill, 160 km (99 miles) northeast of Vila Real, Miranda do Douro overlooks the Douro Gorge, which has been dammed to form a lake that borders with Spain at this point. Despite numerous attacks over the centuries, Miranda's old walled town remains relatively intact. There is a local dialect, *Mirandês*, which is similar to Low Latin, and the town is famous for its traditional dances: the Pingacho, the Geribaila, and in particular the dance of the Pauliteiros, whose origins most likely come from an ancient war dance.

General Information

There is a *Turismo* (** (273) 41122 at Largo do Menino Jesús da Cartolinha.

What to See and Do

Miranda's greatest coup was when it was made a diocese in 1545, it was the province's religious capital until the eighteenth century when the bishopric was moved to Bragança. The sober **Renaissance cathedral** overlooking the gorge has a lavish interior: its gilded altarpieces are a mass of intricate carving, and there is an elaborate organ. The most endearing feature is the Menino Jesús da

Bragança's medieval aura lives on amid the cobbled streets and the old cottages found at the foot of the austere castle keep.

Cartolinha — the Child Jesus in a Silk Hat. This porcelain statue of the child Jesus is kept in a glass case in the south transept, and his clothes are regularly changed. He has a rather substantial wardrobe of specially made costumes.

As legend has it, at a crucial point during the 1711 battle with the Spanish in Miranda, a little boy filled the Portuguese with courage and led them into attack. After they had won, he could not be found and it was naturally assumed that it was the child Jesus who had come to help them in their hour of need.

The statue commemorates the incident and is one of Miranda's most cherished possessions.

Around the cathedral are some medieval dwellings, especially on the **Rua da Castanilha** where carved windows and coats-of-arms adorn some of the grander houses. The **castle** stands in ruins, a reminder of the gunpowder store explosion during the siege of 1762. To learn more about the history of the region and of the Transmontano lifestyle, visit the **Museu Regional da Terra de Miranda**. In their collection are ancient stones with Latin inscriptions, artifacts from Moorish, Roman, and Celtic times, and an array of implements for things you never knew needed doing. The museum's hours are from 10 AM to noon and from 2 PM to 5 PM; it is closed Mondays.

Of the traditional *Mirandês* dances the most famous is the **Dance of the Pauliteiros**, performed during the **Festas da Santa Bárbara** (held in mid-August) by young men wearing strange, rather feminine costumes: white skirts, striped socks, hats festooned with flowers, embroidered shirts, and a pair of incongruously heavy boots. The banging of sticks and thudding of boots has led some to believe that the dance originated from an ancient war dance. It's quite a sight to behold, and experiencing it you really feel thrust into the depths of time.

Where to Stay and Eat

The modern **Pousada de Santa Catarina** ((273) 431005 FAX (273) 431065, Estrada da Barragem, 5210 Miranda do Douro, overlooks the gorge and dam, offering 12 rooms and one suite at mid-range prices. If you'd like to stay in the old town, then it has to be the **Pensão Santa Cruz** ((273) 41374, Rua Abade de Baçal No. 61, 5210 Miranda do Douro, the only accommodation there. It is a family-run establishment and rooms are available with or without bath. Inexpensive.

There are a few restaurants scattered about town, and both the *pousada* and the *pensão* have their own.

How to Get There

Trains run twice daily from Porto to Pocinho, the nearest train station to Miranda do Douro. From Pocinho you must continue the journey by bus. Bus services also link Bragança and Guarda with Miranda.

The Spanish border crossing to Zamora is just across the dam, but only cars can use this road. By road Miranda lies 83 km (52 miles) east of Bragança along the N218. It is 160 km (99 miles) northeast of Vila Real along the N15-IP4 and the N317, which connects with the N218 into Miranda.

Minhoto locals in traditional clothes.

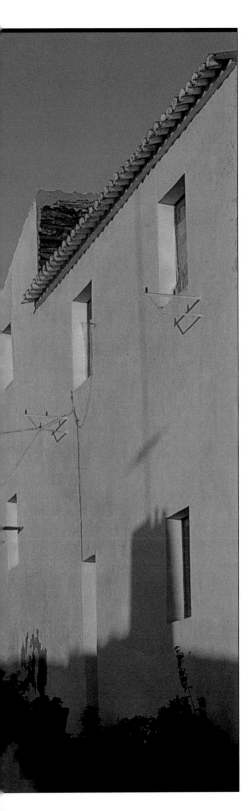

The
Alentejo

THE PROVINCES OF ALTO (UPPER) AND BAIXO (LOWER) ALENTEJO stretch from the coast to the Spanish border, and together cover roughly a third of the country. Wide, sweeping plains of wheat fields are dotted with olive trees and cork oaks, with a thin scattering of whitewashed settlements huddled around castle-topped hills. In the blistering summer heat, the wheat, the red soil, and the strangely naked-looking cork trees stripped of their bark turn the plains into a palette of reds and golds, intensified by the bright blue of the sky. Some prefer spring to explore the Alentejo, when the days are cool and wildflowers are a rash across the fields.

In sharp contrast to the small holdings of the north, in the Alentejo land is gathered into huge estates known as *latifúndias*. These were formed in Roman times and worked by the landless peasantry, a system that has continued into the twentieth century. In the early days of the 1974 revolution, locals led by communists seized the lands to form cooperatives, with ultimately less than advantageous results. For a time agrarian reform banned the holding of large estates by individuals, but lack of experience on the part of the new managers, along with political tide changes and powerful lobbying, led to the return of many estates to their previous owners, while some cooperatives simply dissolved. Despite its size and although the world's largest producer of cork, the Alentejo remains relatively poor, inhabited by only 12% of the country's population.

This is a little-visited region, with most of the heavy traffic racing along the Lisbon to Algarve road. It is still not particularly well-served by public transportation, however, as almost everywhere in Portugal, roads have been freshly paved and here are generally straight and relatively quiet. The Alentejo has much to offer its visitors, sleepy villages with old castle walls, some good wines (light and crisp and particularly suited to the warm weather), and a jewel of a city called Évora.

ÉVORA

Évora is Portugal's most thoroughly beautiful city. Easily accessible, being only 150 km (93 miles) east of Lisbon, its ancient walls embrace Moorish alleyways, Renaissance

squares, sixteenth-century *palácios*, and monuments ranging from Roman to the rococo. Such wonderfully preserved architecture has brought Évora's old town under the protection of UNESCO, through its World Heritage scheme, making the restoration and preservation of Évora an international concern. More than just a museum town, its lively squares, cafés, and university life make the town an immensely enjoyable place to visit. Stay here if you can: there are a number of tempting accommodations and much more to do than merely see the sights.

BACKGROUND

Évora flowered during the Middle Ages when, under the House of Avis, it became a center of power where the king often held court. Such patronage inevitably brought in its wake the artistic and literary elite of the time, the construction of palaces and, in 1559, the founding of a university. Things took a downward turn during the years of Spanish rule, from which time onward Lisbon was the favored royal seat. Évora's decline was furthered by the Marquês de Pombal, whose campaign to rid the country of Jesuits led to the closure of the university. During the following years, Évora redefined itself as a market center and only regained its high profile after the 1974 revolution when, as the capital of the Upper Alentejo, it became the center for sweeping agrarian reform.

GENERAL INFORMATION

The *Turismo* ℂ (266) 702671 is located in the Praça do Giraldo.

WHAT TO SEE AND DO

The **Praça do Giraldo** at the center of the town is a good place to begin a tour of the city, not least because it has a parking lot. The *Turismo* is here, and the square is a popular meeting place, particularly on Tuesdays when the market comes to town. Outdoor cafés make it an ideal spot in which to soak up some of Évora's atmosphere. The Rua 5 de Outubro

Marvão is one of the Alentejo's most medieval-feeling fortified hilltop towns.

leading off the eastern side of the square will bring you to Évora's most important cluster of monuments, where you will find the **Temple of Diana** which, dating from the second or third century, is the best-preserved Roman ruin in the country. It is raised on a stone platform, and the close proximity of buildings some 1,200 years younger emphasizes its antiquity. Corinthian columns of granite topped and based with Estremoz marble still stand on three sides, quite possibly because the temple had been bricked up and adapted for various uses over the

centuries. In its history it has served as a fortress, a store, and, somewhat ignominiously, until 1870 it was a slaughterhouse.

Facing the temple is the **Convento dos Lóios**, built in the late fifteenth century by Dom Rodrigo Afonso de Melo on the site of Évora castle. The convent buildings now house one of the country's most magnificent *pousadas* and even if you are not staying there as a guest, ask for permission to look at the Moorish-inspired Manueline cloister and some of the elegantly frescoed public rooms.

Be sure to visit the **Museu de Évora** housed in the former episcopal palace. The museum's highlights are its collection of sixteenth-century paintings and a thirteen-

paneled *Life of the Virgin* by Flemish artists, which was once on the cathedral's altar. Among its sculptural treasures is the bas-relief of a vestal virgin, the fine classical tomb carved by Nicolas Chanterene, and a collection of modern work including some strange figures by João Cutileiro, sculptor of the nude female figure in the lake of the Palácio de Mateus. Hours are 10 AM to noon and 2 PM to 5 PM; closed Mondays. Admission is free on Sundays.

Behind the museum looms the battle-mented **Sé**, a redoubtable twelfth- and thirteenth-century building that has been added to over the years. Its twin square towers are topped with sixteenth-century cones, and Apostles join with animals and strange creatures in ornamenting the elaborate Gothic doorway. The somber interior has one of the longest naves found in any cathedral in the country, measuring 70 m (230 ft). The stalls of the upper choir carry some fine sixteenth-century carvings.

Wander around the spacious fourteenth-century cloister, and certainly also the treasury, which houses some unusual works of art, most notably, the small thirteenth-century ivory of the Virgin whose abdomen opens to reveal intricately carved scenes from her life. To get your bearings, climb up to the roof and view Évora in the grand perspective it deserves. Open from 9 AM to noon and from 2 PM to 5 PM; closed Monday.

A short stroll from the Sé leads to the **Igreja de São Francisco**, a sixteenth-century Gothic church with Manueline and Moorish flourishes, and the macabre **Capela dos Ossos** (Chapel of Bones). The inscription at the entrance to the chapel reads in translation, "We bones are here awaiting yours." Inside, when closely observed (and in truth, you don't have to get too close), the pebble-like decoration around the walls will reveal themselves to be human bones stacked with impeccable neatness. Open from 8 AM to 1 PM (to 11:30 AM on Sundays).

A short walk south along the Rua da República to just outside the city walls will bring you to what looks like an old Hollywood version of a medieval castle. It is

The city of Évora, with its cultural treasures dating from several eras, has been declared a UNESCO World Heritage Site.

the **Ermita de São Brás**, an extraordinary fifteenth-century building with chunky round buttresses tipped with cones, large battlements, and gargoyles. Going back north up the Rua da República and turning right after passing São Francisco will bring you to the **Igreja de Nossa Senhora da Graça**, which like São Brás has an exterior of considerably more interest than its interior. Constructed in an Italianate Renaissance style, it has four strange giant figures sitting on its side pillars bearing flaming spheres.

WHERE TO STAY

The most sought-after accommodation in town is the **Pousada dos Lóios (** (266) 704051 FAX (266) 27248, Largo Conde de Vila Flor, 7000 Évora, installed in the old fifteenth-century monastery overlooking the Temple of Diana. High vaulted ceilings, archways, frescoes, and antique furniture create a memorable interior. Do bear in mind, however, that the guest rooms were originally monks' cells, and can be a bit cramped by

To the east of Graça and slightly south of the cathedral is the **Largo das Portas de Moura**, centered on a Renaissance fountain and in the form of a white marble orb. From here the Rua Conde da Serra da Tourega will bring you to the **Universidade de Évora**, with its elegant Renaissance courtyard lined with *azulejos*.

Throughout the old town you can trace the remains of fortifications that date from the first to the seventeenth centuries. Almost every inch of old Évora has something captivating: numerous convents, mansion houses, winding streets crossed by Moorish arches. With the major monuments illuminated and the calmly bustling late-night café life, evenings here are a delightful meld of past and present.

contemporary luxury standards. Prices rise to the luxury category in the summer and drop to mid-range out of season.

For modern luxury, the choice is the **Hotel da Cartuxa (** (266) 743030 FAX (266) 744284 E-MAIL hotelcartuxa@mail.telepac.pt, Travessa da Palmeira No. 4, 7000 Évora. Centrally located, along with all expected accoutrements, it has an outdoor swimming pool. Expensive.

If either of the above are not within your budget, you need not feel that luxury is out of reach, as instead, you can stay at the **Albergaria Solar Monfalim (** (266) 750000 FAX (266) 742367, Largo da Misericórdia No. 1. This is a lovely sixteenth-century mansion in a leafy corner of Évora, and after passing through the entrance, it comes as no surprise to find guestrooms furnished in a style that would do a *pousada* proud. There is an arcaded loggia for breakfast or drinks in the warm weather. All rooms have private bath, television, and telephone, and are moderately priced. Make reservations in advance to avoid disappointment.

Pensão Policarpo ((266) 702861, Rua da Freiria de Baixo No. 16, is an equally ancient place with a warm, friendly atmosphere, cheerful decor, and inexpensive prices. Another interesting option is to base yourself at a country home and visit the towns in the radius. There are quite a number in the region, some operating under the TURIHAB scheme, or alternatively, the Évora *Turismo* can provide information.

WHERE TO EAT

For the surroundings alone the **Pousada dos Lóios** (see WHERE TO STAY, above) is a real treat. Dining, often accompanied by a classical guitarist, is in a grand cloister with its vaulted ceiling, and glassed-in enclosure to counter the winter cold. The cuisine is both regional and international, with an emphasis on seasonal local game. The setting, however, surpasses the quality of the kitchen. Prices are generally moderate, daily specials can be expensive. **Fialho** ((266) 703079, Travessa das Mascarenhas No. 16, has a far-reaching reputation as Évora's best independent restaurant that it more than lives up to. Moderately priced. A little, and little-known, place that stays long in the memory is **Martinho** ((266) 723057, Largo Luís Vaz de Camões No. 24, where roasted lamb is the house specialty. **Cozinha de Santo Humberto** ((266) 704251, Rua da Moeda No. 39, is tucked away in a narrow street. They serve good regional food and prices are moderate. **Guião** ((266) 703071, Rua da República No. 81, offers excellent Alentejan food at inexpensive to moderate prices.

HOW TO GET THERE

Trains run to Évora station (about one kilometer southeast of the center) from Lisbon, Faro, and Beja. Travelers from Lisbon need to take the Sul Line from the Barreiro station,

and some of the trains require a change at Casa Branca. Rodoviária Nacional Express buses run from Lisbon, Beja, less frequently from Porto, and from other towns in the Alentejo (Portalegre, Elvas, Évoramonte, Estremoz, and Vila Viçosa). One bus a day runs from Faro in the Algarve.

By road Évora lies 150 km (93 miles) east of Lisbon. If you are driving, leave the city from the south along the A2-IP1 in the direction of Setúbal; then take the A6-IP7, which splits off after much advance notice, directly to Évora.

AROUND ÉVORA

ARRAIOLOS

Twenty-one kilometers (13 miles) northwest of Évora, this village of white and blue houses is shadowed by the walls around its hilltop castle and ancient parish church. Arraiolos is famous for its handmade rugs, and throughout the village, in factories, private homes, and workshops, weavers work away with brightly colored wool to produce them.

The inspiration came from Persian carpets of the Middle Ages, and in the seventeenth century the village began to produce its own out of hemp or linen embroidered with wool. Initially Persian-derived patterns were used, but then simple animal and flower designs took hold. As the work involved is extremely time-consuming, they are not inexpensive, however prices are certainly lower here than in Lisbon.

The *Turismo* in Arraiolos ((266) 499105 is in the Câmara Municipal at the Praça da República.

PAVIA

The Alentejo, particularly around Évora, is rich in **dolmens**, prehistoric structures consisting of two or more upright slabs of stone supporting a horizontal one. The *Turismos* provide details of where to find them, but the most readily visible example lies in the middle of the otherwise unremarkable village of Pavia, 20 km (12 miles) north of

The most impressive Roman ruin in Portugal is Évora's Temple of Diana. Nighttime views are even more spectacular.

Arraiolos. This 5,000-year-old monument was enterprisingly turned into a chapel in the sixteenth century, and today stands in a diminutive square, crowned with a small belfry and cross.

ÉVORAMONTE

The name of Évoramonte came to the fore in 1834 when the Convention of Évoramonte was promulgated here, marking the end of the civil war. The old walled village, some distance away from the newer settlement, is very much a one-donkey, one-street kind of place, but worth the side trip from Évora (28 km or 17 miles) or Estremoz for the views from its castle battlements across miles of sun-baked plains.

MONSARAZ

The fortified border town of Monsaraz, 52 km (32 miles) southeast of Évora, has an eagle's eye view of the Alentejan plain and the Guadiana Valley. Its location and hefty walls that once protected it against enemy attack, seem also to have kept the twentieth century at bay. Monsaraz's military days are over, and it has sunk back into sleepy village life. King Dinis' castle, once a Templars' fort, is now a bullfighting ring. A town of great charm, Monsaraz is slowly adapting to visitors: a few shops and cafés have mushroomed and a few rooms are available to rent.

In Monsaraz, the *Turismo* ((266) 557136 is at the Largo Dom Nuno Álavares Pereira.

HOW TO GET THERE

Buses run from both Évora and Estremoz to Arraiolos. Arraiolos is 21 km (13 miles) north of Évora along the N114-4 and the N370. Continue along the N370 for a further 20 km (12 miles) to reach Pavia.

The Évora-Estremoz bus stops at Évoramonte. By car Évoramonte is 28 km (17 miles) from Évora on the N18.

Évora is the nearest railway station to Monsaraz and a bus service connects the two. Rodoviária Nacional buses run infrequently from Lisbon to Évora and Reguengos de Monsaraz, also connected infrequently by bus to Monsaraz. By car (the best way to travel

here) Monsaraz lies 52 km (32 miles) southeast of Évora. Drivers should leave Évora on the N18-IP2, after 16 km (10 miles) turn on to the N256 to Reguengos de Monsaraz, then follow the signs to Monsaraz.

NORTHEASTERN ALENTEJO

ESTREMOZ AND ENVIRONS

Gleaming white and sturdily fortified, Estremoz stands on a hilltop in the heart of the province's marble-producing region, 194 km (120 miles) east of Lisbon. It was once a strategically important town, and has retained its Vaubanesque fortifications, its battlemented marble keep, and its garrison. With its size and importance having diminished over the centuries, Estremoz seems to have settled into being an agricultural center with a large **Saturday market**, its reputation resting on pottery rather than military strength.

The streets of the old town snake around the ruins of King Dinis' hilltop castle which, together with the palace, was largely destroyed in the seventeenth century when the gunpowder store blew up. Part of the **palace** has been restored to create an exceptional *pousada*. In what remains of the castle is a seventeenth-century chapel dedicated to Queen Isabel, built in the room in which she is said to have died in 1336. It is decorated with *azulejos* that depict the miracle when the alms she was smuggling out to the poor turned into roses. Behind the altar a small chamber is set aside for votive offerings.

The hub of the lower town is the large **Rossio Marquês de Pombal**, a busy tree-shaded square fringed with bars and cafés. It is the scene of the Saturday morning **market**, an enjoyable opportunity to buy pottery or the excellent local cheeses.

In Estremoz the *Turismo* ((268) 333541 is at Largo da República No. 26, near the Rossio, and there is also a kiosk in the Rossio Marquês de Pombal.

Thirteen kilometers (eight miles) south of Estremoz, **Vila Viçosa** was the seat of the Dukes of Bragança, Portugal's royal family from 1442 to 1910, and their vast **Paço Ducal** (Ducal Palace) ((268) 98659 overwhelms the town. Its severe marble façade occupies one entire side of the Terreiro de Paço (Palace

Square), and before it stands a statue of João IV on horseback, the eighth Duke of Bragança but the first to be king. It was here that Jaime, the fourth duke, killed his young wife and her page in front of his entire court in an apparently misguided fit of jealousy. There is a long string of indifferent rooms, some beautiful tapestries, and huge kitchens glowing with hundreds of copper pans. The private rooms are scattered with the personal possessions of the last two kings and their wives. Open from 9 AM to 1 PM and from 2 PM to 6 PM; closed Mondays.

Rainha Santa Isabel ℂ (268) 337025 FAX (268) 332079, 7100 Estremoz, housed in the restored palace overlooking the town and the plain below, is glorious. Guest rooms are furnished in antiques, public areas are marble and sport gold leaf, yet astoundingly, the atmosphere is remains comfortable. The swimming pool is set in a lovely garden with views of the city below. Luxury prices apply.

At significantly more modest prices is the **Residencial Carvalho** ℂ (268) 339370 FAX (268) 22370, Largo da República No. 27,

Vila Viçosa's other famous feature is the **Porta dos Nós** (Knot Gate), a vaunted gateway set in the sixteenth-century town walls. In a Manueline conceit, great ropes and knots have been carved into the stone to create the arched entry. A play on the word *nós* — meaning both knot and we or us — is not accidental. Close by the palace is the **old castle**, the original residence of the Braganças built by King Dinis.

At Vila Viçosa the *Turismo* ℂ (268) 881101 is on the Praça da República.

Where to Stay

If in your entire tour of Portugal you stay at only one *pousada*, it absolutely must be the one in Estremoz. The **Pousada da**

7100 Estremoz. Located in the center of the city, accommodation is better than the inexpensive rates would indicate.

One of several country homes in the region is the beautiful nineteenth-century **Monte dos Pensamentos** ℂ (268) 333166, Estrada da Estação do Ameixial, 7100 Estremoz. Prices are mid-range.

Where to Eat

Under the vaulted and chandeliered ceilings of Estremoz's **Pousada da Rainha Santa Isabel** (see WHERE TO STAY, above), the cuisine is exceptionally even and does not

Monsaraz crowns a craggy hilltop above Alentejo's expansive plains east of Estremoz.

suffer from the state-run uniformity experienced at some *pousadas*. Located in a rather grand house on Estremoz's main square, **Águias d'Ouro (** (268) 333326 in Rossio Marquês de Pombal No. 7, has good regional food and wines, and a particularly warm ambiance. The cheery **Arlequim Restaurant (** (268) 323726, Rua Dr. Gomes de Resende Jr. No. 15, is a favorite with both locals and visitors and has some good dishes that are just a bit out of the ordinary, such as chicken and fruit kebabs. Both are moderately priced.

is 18 km (11 miles) southeast of Estremoz along the N4-IP7 and the N255.

ELVAS

Just 12 km (seven and a half miles) from the border, Elvas is home to the most massive fortress on the whole peninsula, possibly even in Europe, and still maintains a garrison. Its Roman and Moorish defenses were reinforced against Spanish attack, and were further extended during the Spanish Wars of Succession. From these well-preserved

How to Get There

The nearest railway station to Estremoz is at Évora, where trains run from Lisbon's Barreiro station connecting with buses to Estremoz. There is also continuing bus service to Estremoz from the Portalegre train station. Rodoviária Nacional Express buses run infrequently to Estremoz from Lisbon, from Elvas, and from Arraiolos. By road, Estremoz is 44 km (27 miles) northeast of Évora along the N18, which becomes the N4 just before reaching town.

Buses run from Évora to Vila Viçosa, and the express from Lisbon passes through Vila Viçosa en route for Elvas. By road Vila Viçosa

ramparts are views across the countryside and of the ungainly **Aqueduct of Amoreira** that stretches a total of seven and a half kilometers (five miles) across the plain and took close to one hundred years to complete. Elvas also has a gentler side to its character: it is famous for its sugar plums.

Within the walls, steep cobblestone streets are overhung with iron lanterns and wrought-iron balconies brimming with flowers. Overlooking the **Praça da República**, a square paved with diamond-shaped mosaic patterns, is the sixteenth-century **Sé** (cathedral) whose fortress-like design and ferocious gargoyles reflect the military tenor of the town. Of more interest is the **Igreja Nossa Senhora da Consolação** on

Montemor-o-Novo's medieval castle can be seen from afar, high above the Alentejan expanse.

the steeply sloping Largo de Santa Clara. Unremarkable from the outside, it has an octagonal interior with a distinctly Moorish flavor. Blue and yellow *azulejos* line the walls, delicately painted columns support a cupola, and dim lighting creates an exotic air. In the Largo de Santa Clara itself is a rather strange sixteenth-century pimply **pillory** that still has its four iron hooks attached to the capital.

In Elvas the *Turismo* ((268) 622236 is also on the Praça da República.

Where to Stay and Eat

The **Pousada de Santa Luzia** ((268) 622194 or (268) 622128 FAX (268) 622127, Avenida da Badajoz, 7350 Elvas, is one of the modern *pousadas*, its architecture typically Alentejan Moorish with its fountained courtyard and orange trees. It has a fairly large swimming pool, tennis courts, and an unexpectedly good restaurant. Prices are mid-range. The only other real choice is the **Estalagem Dom Sancho II** ((268) 622684 FAX (268) 624717, Praça da República No. 20, has more quaint charm, small but pleasant rooms, and a particularly good restaurant. Inexpensive.

How to Get There

The nearest train station to Elvas is at Fontainhas, four kilometers (two and a half miles) north of the city, where trains arrive from Lisbon, Évora, and Badajoz in Spain. A bus service links Fontainhas with Elvas. Rodoviária Nacional Express buses run to Elvas from Lisbon but involve one or two changes, and also run from Évora and Estremoz. By road Elvas is 44 km (28 miles) east of Estremoz along the N4-IP7.

UPPER ALENTEJO

PORTALEGRE

As the capital of the Upper Alentejo, the bustling city of Portalegre is well served by transportation and is conveniently situated for exploring Marvão, Castelo de Vide, and the towns of Crato and Alter do Chão. Lying 57 km (35 miles) north of Estremoz, it has an older quarter within the castle walls, a world apart from the so-called new town.

There are many fine buildings dating from Portalegre's period of affluence during the sixteenth and seventeenth centuries, which was largely due to its renowned tapestries and silk mills.

A visit to the **Fábrica de Tapeçarias** (Tapestry Factory) ((245) 23283, within the old Jesuit seminary, can be quite interesting, seeing how the painstaking and costly process of translating pictures into tapestries is done. Tours operate Monday to Friday 9:30 AM to 11 AM and 2:30 PM to 4:30 PM. Nearby on the Avenida George Robinson (he was the founder of town's cork factory) stands the **Church and Convent of São Bernardo**, now used by the infantry; a polite request may gain you admittance to the church. The main reason for doing so is to see the wonderfully pompous tomb of the founder, Bishop Jorge de Melo, the work (at least in part) of Nicolas Chanterene.

From here, continue on into the old town, making sure to stroll along the **Rua 19 de Junho**, where elaborate wrought-iron work adorns the houses. This street leads to the somber **Sé** (cathedral) next door to the old seminary that houses the **Museu Municipal**. Here, archaeological finds and sacred art are exhibited along with a more eclectic array of objects. Open from 9:30 AM to 12:30 PM and from 2 PM to 6 PM; closed Tuesdays.

In Portalegre the *Turismo* ((245) 331359 is at Estrada de Santana No. 25.

MARVÃO

Twenty-five kilometers (15 miles) northeast of Portalegre, the well-preserved medieval village of Marvão is nestled some 865 m (2,838 ft) up in the Serra de São Mamede at the foot of a thirteenth-century **castle**. Its sturdy keep offers the best views in the village: you can see across to Spain and, on a clear day, the Serra da Estrela to the north. What in the past made Marvão a crucial military point, these vistas now make for a spectacular stop, as does the *pousada* (see WHERE TO STAY, below).

Visit the **Museu Municipal** in the **Igreja de Santa Maria** close by the castle to see Roman relics, as well as displays of local costumes and culture.

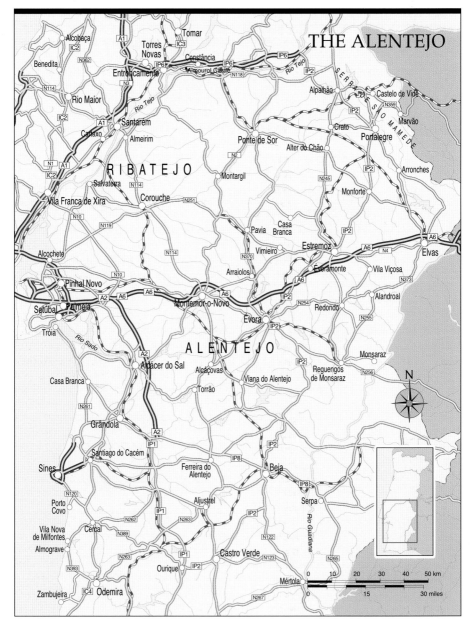

THE ALENTEJO

The *Turismo* ((245) 993104 is on Rua Dr. Matos Magalhães.

CASTELO DE VIDE

Castelo de Vide is a small, mainly sixteenth-century, spa town on the slopes of a wooded hill.

The interesting part of the town is the **Judiaria** (Jewish quarter), which has re-

mained relatively unchanged since the Middle Ages. There is a small thirteenth-century **synagogue** in the Rua da Judiaria that contains some Hebrew stone inscriptions. Traces of fourteenth-century doorways that closed the area off from the Christian parts of town can still be seen, and down the hill at the town center, noble buildings surround the **Praça Dom Pedro V**. Among them are the **Paços do Concelho** in front of which stands a pillory, the eighteenth-century **Church of Santa Maria**, and the **Torre Palace**, now the hospital. The *Turismo* ((245) 901361 is on Rua de Bartolomeu Alvares da Santa No. 81.

WHERE TO STAY

In Portalegre the **Hotel Dom João III** ((245) 330192 FAX (245) 330444, Avenida da Liberdade, 7300 Portalegre, is modern with a swimming pool, but somewhat uninspired. Prices are mid-range. The **Pensão Mansão Alto Alentejo** ((245) 202290, Rua 19 de Junho Nos. 59-63, 7300 Portalegre, close to the cathedral, has clean inexpensive rooms.

In the old town of Marvão, there is the **Pousada de Santa Maria** ((245) 993201/2 FAX (245) 993440, Rua 24 de Janeiro No. 7, 7330 Marvão, which is comprised of three converted old houses, and with traditional Alentejan furnishings. It has magnificent views and mid-range prices. Several places offer private accommodation of varying quality within the town walls; inquire at the *Turismo* for details.

In Castelo de Vide there are two modern hotels that offer all the expected services. The more expensive is the **Hotel Garcia d'Orta** ((245) 901100 FAX (245) 901200, Estrada de São Vicente, 7320 Castelo de Vide. **Hotel Sol e Serra** ((245) 901301 FAX (245) 901337, Estrada de São Vicente, 7320 Castelo de Vide, overlooks a public garden. Both have outdoor swimming pools. The **Pensão Casa do Parque** ((245) 901250 FAX (245) 901228, Avenida da Aramenha No. 37, is a comfortably, old-fashioned pension with low prices.

WHERE TO EAT

In Portalegre, **O Abrigo** ((245) 331658, Rua de Elvas No. 74, is a centrally placed, inexpensive restaurant and serves regional cuisine. **O Cortiço** ((245) 202176, Rua Dom Nuno Alvares Pereira No. 17, is quite lively at night. Moderate.

In Marvão, the **Pousada de Santa Maria** has a restaurant (see WHERE TO STAY, above) that serves fine local dishes at moderate prices. In Castelo de Vide, the best cuisine is at **A Castanha**, the restaurant of the Hotel Garcia d'Orta (see WHERE TO STAY, above).

HOW TO GET THERE

Trains run from Lisbon, Évora, and Estremoz to the Estação de Portalegre, 12 km (seven and a half miles) south of the city, with a bus shuttle service between the station and Portalegre proper. Several Rodoviária Nacional Express buses run into the center daily from Lisbon. By road, Portalegre is 57 km (35 miles) north of Estremoz along the N18-IP2.

Lisbon–Madrid trains stop at the Estação Marvão-Beirâ on the border, about nine kilometers (five miles) north of Marvão and linked to it by bus. Buses also run to the village from Elvas and Portalegre, a quicker option than traveling by train. By car Marvão is 25 km (15 miles) northeast of Portalegre. Drivers should leave Portalegre along the N359 then follow the signs for Marvão.

The nearest train station to Castelo de Vide is also the Estação Marvão-Beirâ, and buses again link the station with the town. By road, Castelo de Vide lies 25 km (15 miles) from Portalegre along the N359 to Marvão, and then the N246-1.

LOWER ALENTEJO

BEJA

The capital of the Lower Alentejo stands surrounded by wheat fields and is the hottest spot in the whole country. As it is 177 km (110 miles) from Lisbon, it could serve as a useful base from which to explore the Lower Alentejo, although accommodations here is largely limited to *pensãos* and the somewhat austere *pousada* **São Francisco** ((284) 328441 FAX (284) 329143, 7800 Beja. Prices are expensive. The best dining in town is at **Os Infantes** ((284) 322789, Rua dos Infantes No. 14.

The **Convento da Conceição** is best known as the home of the seventeenth-century nun Mariana Alcoforado, who allegedly wrote the passionate and scandalously explicit *Love Letters of a Portuguese Nun* to the French Count Chamilly, her supposed lover. There are, however, those who believe that the 1669 French "translation" was in fact the original. Regardless, the convent itself is a fine example of the use, typical of the period, of both Gothic and Manueline styles in a single structure. The cloister and chapter house are both decorated in stunning *azulejos* dating from the fifteenth to eighteenth centuries, some of Spanish origin, others Portuguese. The **Museu Regional** ((284) 323351, is housed here, with its modest exhibits of coins and mosaics from Roman and Visigoth eras, Spanish, Portuguese, and Flemish paintings.

The *Turismo* ((284) 311913 is at Rua Capitão João Francisco de Sousa No. 25, south of the central square.

SERPA

Serene and white, Serpa lies 27 km (17 miles) west of Beja, set amid fertile land famous for its ewe's milk cheese, and traditional mournful songs performed by male choirs that unexpectedly appear in town. In the main square, the **Café Alentejano** is a good place to stop for pastries and coffee, however better food is to be had at the modest **Molhó Bico**, which anyone can direct you to.

Entering the town by the **Porta de Beja**, the first sight of Serpa is impressive: an eleventh-century **aqueduct** runs along part of the castle walls, its slender arches are more graceful than those of the stodgier construction at Elvas. The walls themselves remain largely intact, but as you enter the courtyard you will see a great slab of masonry menacingly poised overhead. It has been maintaining this precarious hold since 1707, when the Spanish blew up part of the fortifications. The castle's **museum** has some prehistoric, Roman, Visigoth and Moorish remains, as well as a rather alarming life-sized tableau of the Last Supper.

The *Turismo* ((284) 544727 is at Largo Dom Jorge de Melo No. 2.

MÉRTOLA

The sleepy little town of Mértola lies 50 km (31 miles) southeast of Beja, overlooking the Guadiana River at its confluence with the Oeiras. A steep, winding road leads up to the ruined **castle** overlooking the small streets and modern town. Down the hill, a converted thirteenth-century mosque is now a unique **Igreja Matriz**. Inside this white-

washed building the ceiling is low and vaulted, and a niche known as a *mihrab*, which indicates the direction of Mecca, is a reminder of its former use.

The *Turismo* ((286) 62573 is at the Largo Vasco da Gama No. 1.

HOW TO GET THERE

Trains from Lisbon's Barreiro station, from Évora, and less frequently from Faro run to Beja. Rodoviária Nacional Express buses run to Beja from Lisbon and Faro. By road, Beja lies 177 km (110 miles) from Lisbon. Drivers should follow the IP1 out of Lisbon and 20 km (12 miles) beyond Grândola turn on to the IP8 to Beja. From Évora, Beja is 77 km (48 miles) along the N18-IP2.

Serpa is served by bus only. The nearest train station is at Beja which is linked to the town by bus. One Rodoviária Nacional Express bus runs daily from Lisbon to Serpa. By road Serpa is 27 km (17 miles) from Beja along the N260-IP8.

The Rodoviária Nacional Express from Lisbon also serves Mértola. By road, Mértola is 50 km (31 miles) southeast of Beja on the N122.

THE COAST

One of the greatest surprises that the Alentejo has is its lovely (and as yet unspoiled) coastline, a combination of cliffs and coves. The waters here are colder and rougher than in the Algarve and it can be windy, but if you like rugged seascapes and don't mind the scarcity of tourist amenities, this could suit you well.

PORTO COVO DA BANDEIRA

In this clean and orderly village 173 km (128 miles) south of Lisbon, neat white cottages with blue trim are laid out along a grid plan, the signature of the Marquês de Pombal, who gave instructions to rebuild the village after the 1755 earthquake. It has the sea on its doorstep, a few cafés, bars, restaurants, and a *pensão*. Just one kilometer (a half a mile) offshore is the **Ilha do Pessegueiro** (Peach Tree Island), fortified during the seventeenth century to protect the village from pirate attack, it contains the remains of a Roman harbor and a sixteenth-century church. The real attraction, however, is the onshore **beach** facing the island, with its campsite, washing facilities, and restaurant.

VILA NOVA DE MILFONTES

This is probably the most popular place on the Alentejan coastline, 17 km (ten miles) south of Porto Covo, and a favorite *Lisboetan* vacation spot at the mouth of the Mira River. The fishing town itself is typically Alentejan in style, surrounded by rolling hills, sandy beaches, and overlooked by a small medieval castle now restored to provide some of the most exclusive accommodation on the coast. Its few hotels and *pensãos* tend to fill up fast during summer months. The *Turismo* can be contacted at ((283) 96599.

ON THE WAY SOUTH

Twelve kilometers (seven and a half miles) south of Vila Nova de Milfontes the coastline becomes more dramatic and rockier at **Almograve**. The beach here is quiet and has a nudist section at the southern end. The village has a smattering of bars and cafés, but little else. Further south, **Zambujeira** offers a similarly dramatic prospect, perched on a cliff above the beach; its lack of accommodation means that you will probably have to limit yourself to a day-trip. The *Turismo* can be contacted at ((283) 61105.

A better possibility for accommodation is the inland town of **Odemira**, an oasis of green in the typically sunburned Alentejan landscape. Overlooking the Mira it is not quite geared to a tourist inflow, but can cope with a few visitors. Follow signs to the *Turismo* where there is information on accommodation here and for the surrounding region. The Odemira *Turismo* can be reached at ((283) 327621.

WHERE TO STAY

In Porto Covo there are a couple of reasonable, if basic, *pensãos*, but Vila Nova de Milfontes has a wider range. Top of the list is the **Castelo de Milfontes** ((283) 96108, housed within the old fort. It offers some exclusive

accommodation and cuisine, but reservations should be made well in advance. Prices are high. Other private accommodation is available through the *Turismo de Habitação* (TURIHAB) scheme at the **Quinta do Moinho de Vento** ((283) 96383 FAX (283) 96383, Milfontes, 7645 Vila Nova de Milfontes, a modern villa close to the beach. In addition there are a few *pensãos* and a modern complex outside the town itself.

Zambujeira has a some basic *pensãos*, but Odemira has more. The **Residencial Rita** ((283) 22423, Largo do Poço Novo, 7630 Odemira, and the **Pensão Paisagem** ((283) 95406 FAX (283) 95442, Avenida das Escolas de São Teotónio, are inexpensively priced.

HOW TO GET THERE

An express bus runs twice daily from Lisbon to Vila Nova de Milfontes, Almograve, and Zambujeira. A local service links Odemira to Zambujeira and there is a more frequent service between Odemira, Almograve, and Vila Nova de Milfontes. A car is by far the best way of getting around this coastal region.

By road, Vila Nova de Milfontes lies 190 km (118 miles) south of Lisbon. Drivers should leave Lisbon along the IP1, turn off shortly before Grândola on to the IP8 and continue along it until just outside Sines, then take the N120 to Vila Nova de Milfontes. To continue on to Almograve, 12 km (seven miles) further south, take the N393 out of Vila Nova then follow the signs. Zambujeira lies 18 km (11 miles) further south along the coastal road while Odemira lies 19 km (12 miles) inland. Porto Covo is 28 km south of Sines, best accessed along the coastal road south of the town. If you happen to be approaching this part of the country from the south, travel along the IC4, which is much more rural than its dominance on the map might indicate. Following the congestion of the Algarve, this route north, essentially an arcade of eucalyptus and pine trees, is literally a breath of fresh air.

The
Algarve

WITH ITS WARM WINTERS, BRILLIANT SUMMERS, and seemingly endless coastline, it was inevitable that this southernmost strip of Portugal should attract visitors from around the world. In fact, it has for centuries: the Phoenicians, the Carthaginians, the Romans all passed through. The Moors managed to retain their hold until 1249, and their legacy lives on in the local place names (Algarve itself is derived from *Al Gharb* meaning the West), in the cuisine, and in the design of the houses, traditionally low with roof terraces and crowned with the latticed chimney tops that have become a symbol of the province.

Unfortunately, the tourist boom of the 1970s resulted in unchecked development, overcrowded beaches, and the destruction of many of the very elements that the tourist industry sought to exploit. During that period, many northern Europeans took advantage of the favorable exchange rate, and made the Algarve their retirement home. With the result that in many areas Portuguese is rarely heard.

Amazingly, villas continue to be built, but now with an eye to attract more of an upscale tourism. Crowds have colonized the coastline between Faro and Lagos, but elsewhere there are still a few spots where one can enjoy the pleasant climate in relative peace.

Spring is a particularly good time to visit, when there are fewer people around. Visitors in late January and February may get to see one of the Algarve's most famous spectacles: groves of almond trees in blossom, with their delicate white flowers and even more delicate perfume.

The more tranquil parts of the province are to be found east of Faro, west of Lagos, and inland where the Monchique and Caldeirão mountains separate the province from the Alentejo.

A large sector of the Algarvan coast is not discussed herein, as no recommendations can be made with any editorial integrity. However, there is no doubt that if you are looking for reliably good year-round weather, beaches, sporting opportunities — including some of Europe's top golf courses — and good tourist facilities, there are plenty of choices available in the resort-filled Faro–

Lagos strip. The simplest and most economical way to vacation here is on a package deal, of which there are many.

EASTERN ALGARVE

ALCOUTIM AND CASTRO MARIM

One of the most enchanting corners of the Algarve is its eastern edge along the Spanish border. The road meanders through the hills along the Guadiana River, passing border towns and villages such as the little river

port of Alcoutim, where whitewashed houses and sleeping dogs lie at the foot of a ruined fourteenth-century castle facing the larger Spanish fortress across the river in Sanlucar. A good spot to unwind from the travails of traveling.

Migratory and wading birds proliferate around Castro Marim, some 40 km (25 miles) south of Alcoutim, where the fertile marshland as far as Vila Real de Santo António is a nature reserve. Castro Marim was the headquarters of the Order of Christ from 1321 until 1334, when it was moved to Tomar. Their castle, along with a fortress built by

Silves OPPOSITE was the Moorish capital of "Al Gharb," whose coastline ABOVE has all the components of the modern beach vacation.

King João IV on a facing hill, was reduced to ruins by the 1755 earthquake. If you are interested in a hike through the nature reserve, stop in at the castle where the *Turismo* is located and information on walks and wildlife is available.

There is a *Turismo* ((281) 531800 at the border with Spain at a spot called Ponte Internacional do Guardiana, Monte Francisco. The one at Alcoutim ((281) 546179 is on Praça da República; Castro Marim's *Turismo* ((281) 531232 is at Praça 1 de Maio.

VILA REAL DE SANTO ANTÓNIO

Just four kilometers (two and a half miles) south of Castro Marim is Vila Real de Santo António, a major border crossing point. The proximity of the popular seaside resort of **Monte Gordo**, three kilometers (two miles) to the west, together with the through traffic makes this a busy place geared to tourism. Its center was built at the command of the Marquês de Pombal, with the same rigid geometry that he applied to Pombaline Lisbon, but here the effect is somewhat soulless. One of the main reasons to visit Vila Real is to take a **boat trip** up the Guadiana or to make a quick foray into Spain (ask at the *Turismo* for details of trips).

It is a surprise to find a little oasis of peace 14 km (nine miles) west of Vila Real at the tiny village of **Cacela Velha**, centered around a fortress and church high on a cliff top and with views looking over the sandspit.

TAVIRA

Tavira is perhaps the prettiest town in the Algarve, unspoiled despite catering to tourists. A mixture of vacation town and tuna fishing port, it is cut off from the sea by the sandy spit. The town occupies both banks of the Séquia River, which is crossed by two bridges, one of them a seven-arched Roman structure. A garden stretches along one bank, complete with bandstand, palm trees, and an ornamental building that houses the morning **market** where fish, local produce, and handicrafts are sold. Behind the gardens there is a long row of seafood restaurants, while elsewhere in the town there are more restaurants, cafés and bars, those on the north

side of the river catering more to tourists and resident expatriates.

Tavira seems over-endowed with churches. The hilltop **Igreja de Santa Maria do Castelo**, contains the tombs of crusading knights including that of Dom Paio Peres Correia, who captured Tavira from the Moors in 1242, but views of the town are best from the ruined castle nearby. The **Igreja de Carmo** with its baroque interior is worth a visit, as is the fine Renaissance **Igreja da Misericórdia**. You may have to ask around for keys to both these places.

The sandbar, known as the **Ilha de Tavira**, has a stretch of beach along its eastern side. During the summer months only, a bus from Tavira will take you to the Praia de Tavira, two kilometers (one mile) out of town, where boats leave frequently for the stretch. Ferries, however, leave from the harbor year round. The beach does tend to get quite crowded in the high season.

Tavira's *Turismo* ((281) 322511 is at Rua da Galeria No. 9.

WHERE TO STAY

Tavira's **Hotel Apartamento Eurotel** ((281) 325041 FAX (281) 325571, Quinta das Oliveiras, 8800 Tavira, is a large and luxurious tourist development by the sea a few kilometers east of Tavira with good leisure facilities. Self-catering apartments and hotel rooms are available, and prices are mid-range, however,

OPPOSITE: The Algarve's eastern flank is still relatively unscathed by the excesses of tourist developments. Its jewel is Tavira which lies near an offshore sand bar. ABOVE: A fresco in the Palácio do Visconde de Estói.

summer months are usually booked long in advance by tour groups. In Tavira itself there are no hotels, and only two of the numerous pensions are acceptable to anyone other than the ardent backpacker. The best is **Marés** ((281) 325815 FAX (218) 325819, Rua José Pires Padinha No. 134, where all rooms have television, telephone and private baths, and are air-conditioned. The other option would be the **Pensão Princesa do Gilão** ((281) 325171, Rua Borda d'Agua de Aguiar, 8800 Tavira, overlooking the river, is particularly popular with the young. Both are inexpensive.

precursor of the modern-day pressure cooker, comprised of two hemispherical copper halves that fit tightly together. *Cataplana* dishes are usually ordered as a main course to be shared by two people.

In Tavira the quayside restaurants offer a good range of very fresh seafood. There is a string of them near the ferry dock, and the least touristic and most recommended is **Marés**, which is associated with the *pensão* of the same name (see WHERE TO STAY, above). Slightly back from the quayside, the **Restaurante Imperial** ((281) 322306, Rua do

The **Pensão do Castelo** ((281) 323942, Rua da Liberdade No. 4, is worth mention. The management is in the process of expanding, perhaps fivefold. The new accommodation will range from guest rooms to suites to multi-room apartments — all equipped with brand new furnishings and appliances. They have vowed to keep prices inexpensive to mid-range. It should be noted that unless the old quarters are renovated, they should be avoided, as now they are at best seedy.

Cais No. 22, serves good seafood at inexpensive prices.

The best restaurants, however, are found about two kilometers (one mile) east of Tavira in the town of Quatro Águas. The top choice for all seafood dishes there is **Portas do Mar** ((281) 321255.

HOW TO GET THERE

The Algarve Line links Lagos with Vila Real de Santo António, stopping at Portimão, Silves, Tunes, Faro, and Tavira. Lisbon trains connect with the Algarve Line at Tunes. There are also plenty of buses linking Tavira with Vila Real de Santo António, Faro, and other towns in the eastern Algarve. At Vila Real

WHERE TO EAT

Something worth sampling during a stay in the Algarve is one of the delicious seafood dishes prepared in a *cataplana*, a Moorish

ferries run to the Spanish town of Ayamonte, en route for Huelva and Sevilla.

By road Vila Real de Santo António lies 51 km (32 miles) from Faro and 23 km (14 miles) from Tavira, along the N125, which follows the coast. If you are traveling directly to Faro, the IP1 highway may be preferable, as the N125 can get painfully congested. The N122 runs north of Vila Real shadowing the path of the Guadiana, passing through Castro Marim, four kilometers (two and a half miles) north of Vila Real, and continuing northward into the Alentejo, passing close by Alcoutim, 40 km (25 miles) north of Castro Marim.

OLHÃO AND THE ILHAS

The town of Olhão, eight kilometers (five miles) east of Faro, is one of the Algarve's major fishing ports, and beyond its seedy outskirts the old section is a maze of Moorish-style houses. Unlike the lacey designs most commonly seen in the Algarve, these square, flat-roofed buildings with stairways on the outside and simple angular chimneys, makes the town distinctive and drew the attention of artists when they explored Cubist themes.

GENERAL INFORMATION

The *Turismo* ((289) 713936 is on the Largo Sebastião Martins Mestre No. 6A.

WHAT TO SEE AND DO

The main attraction is the ferry service to the two nearby islands where (surprising for these parts) it is possible to find enough sand to stretch out on, without feeling that you are in a subway car. Ferries run every hour or so to **Ilha da Armona** (less frequently after September), which has swimming, a few restaurants, some beach huts and a lot of sand, all preferable to the other option, the **Ilha da Culatra**.

Much of the Olhão's daily life centers around the extensive indoor **fish market**, one of the best in the country. Nearby the public park next to the river is the **Parque Natural da Ria Formosa**, a wildlife reserve some five kilometers (three miles) long that encompasses islands, as well as a sandspit, and contains expansive oyster and clam beds.

The bell tower of the baroque **Igreja da Nossa Senhora de Rosário** on the main street affords good views of the unusual townscape, and at the back of it, the **Capela dos Aflitos** is open all hours for women who come to pray for those in danger on the sea.

WHERE TO STAY

The **Hotel Ria Sol** ((289) 705267 FAX (289) 705268, Rua General Humberto Delgado No. 37, 8700 Olhão, has inexpensive rooms,

all with telephones and private baths. Apart from this, there are half a dozen or so *pensãos*, the best is the **Pensão Bela Vista** ((289) 702538, Rua Dr. Teófilo Braga Nos. 65-67. Inexpensive.

HOW TO GET THERE

Olhão is on the Algarve Line, so trains link it to towns in the eastern and western Algarve, as does the local bus service. By road it is eight kilometers (five miles) east of Faro and 43 km (27 miles) west of Vila Real de Santo António along the N125.

OPPOSITE: The brilliantly white Moorish fishing port of Olhão. ABOVE: All along the Algarvan coast, outdoor dining is popular.

ESTÓI AND MILREU

In the little village of Estói, 11 km (seven miles) north of Faro, is the **Palácio do Visconde de Estói**, hidden behind a pink wall. This pink rococo confection is now quite decayed; its clock has stopped at ten minutes to three, and although plans are in the works for restoration, they have been so for a long time. The gardens, with their array of statues in varying degrees of undress, are still carefully tended and open to the public.

Because of its dilapidation, access to the palace itself is prohibited but the views of it from the garden, where statues rise above palm trees, orange groves, magnolias, and exotic plants, make this a very rewarding side trip. The centerpiece is the ornamental staircase, tiled, balustraded and topped with statuary. At its foot an iron grille protects a vaulted and columned chamber containing statues of goddesses surrounded by greenery. The interior walls are decorated with Roman mosaics that were appropriated from nearby Milreu.

Roughly one kilometer (half a mile) west of Estói and just off the road at Milreu are the remains of the Roman town of Ossonoba, built between the first and third centuries and occupied until about the sixth century. A ruined apse stands in a field, once a temple, later used as a church. There are the remains of baths, columns and delicate mosaics of dolphins, prawns, and other forms of sea life. Excavation here is still at a relatively early stage.

Faro's Capela dos Ossos is adorned with skulls and bones from floor to ceiling.

There is a *Turismo* ((289) 842211 in São Brás de Alportel on Rua Dr. Evaristo Sousa Gago No. 1.

WHERE TO STAY

The nearest accommodation is to be found eight kilometers (five miles) to the north of Estói and 17 km (10 miles) north of Faro at the town of São Brás de Alportel. There are rooms to rent here, but many choose to stay at the **Pousada de São Brás** ((289) 842305/6 FAX (289) 841726, Estrada de Lisboa, N2, 8150 São Brás de Alportel, an attractive 1940s villa with views of the Serra do Caldeirão. Its swimming pool and pleasant sun terrace make it a good and comfortable base from which to explore the eastern Algarve. Midrange prices apply.

HOW TO GET THERE

Buses run frequently to Estói from Faro and also to São Brás de Alportel from both Faro and Loulé. By road from Olhão, Estói lies 10 km (six miles) northwest of Olhão along the N2-6; from Faro it is 11 km (seven miles) north along the N2.

FARO

The old walled town and harbor (now a yacht marina) surrounded by street cafés and squares is a setting of great charm, but what was once an attribute has been instrumental in causing the Algarve's capital to swell beyond belief. Sprawling apartment complexes and slick tourist hotels now define the scene.

BACKGROUND

Although the Moors founded what came to be the city of Faro early in the eighth century, its known history reaches back to the time of the Phoenicians and the Carthaginians, whom for both it served as an important center of commerce. By the time the Christians captured the city in 1249 Faro had grown into a prosperous and important port. By the fifteenth century, it had also become a major intellectual center, in which its resident Jewish community, under the lead of Samuel Gacon, produced Portugal's first

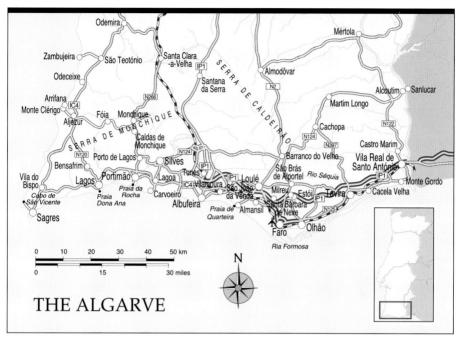

THE ALGARVE

printed works. Following the reconquest the city was rebuilt, and in 1577 it became a bishopric. Its new pride was short-lived: in 1596, during the period of Spanish rule, English troops under the command of the Earl of Essex sacked and burned the city, having first removed 200 valuable books from the Bishop's Palace. These volumes became an important asset of the Bodleian Library in Oxford. Disaster again befell Faro, a consequence of the 1755 earthquake and ensuing tidal waves, but the city was once again rebuilt under the direction of Bishop Francisco Gomes de Avelar.

GENERAL INFORMATION

The *Turismo* ((289) 803604 is at Rua de Misericórdia Nos. 8-12, and there is also a desk at the airport ((289) 818582, which is about six kilometers (four miles) out of town.

WHAT TO SEE AND DO

At the eastern end of the harbor, the eighteenth-century Renaissance archway known as the **Arco da Vila** leads into the old walled town from the Jardim Manuel Bivar. The Rua do Municipio will bring you to the **Largo da Sé**, a cobbled square surrounded by elegant

buildings. Amongst them stands the **cathedral**, a baroque-style structure of no great interest, other than for the **Capelo do Rosário** with its seventeenth-century *azulejos*. There is also a somewhat bold, if incongruous red Chinoiserie organ. Behind it, the two-storied cloister of the sixteenth-century **Convento de Nossa Senhora** is now the **Museu Arqueológico**, which has an excellent collection of Roman, pre-Roman, and Moorish relics. Some Roman statues on display were unearthed at nearby Milreu, and one room is set aside solely for the reconstituted Roman mosaic of Neptune that was unearthed in Faro in 1968. Open from 9 AM to noon and from 2 PM to 5 PM; closed weekends.

Leaving the walled town by the Arco do Repouso, look in at the **Igreja de São Francisco** to see that very Portuguese combination of gilt-covered woodwork and blue and white azulejos. In the Praça Alexandre Herculano, the **Museu Etnográfica Regional** ((289) 827610, provides an insight into local culture with models of houses, reconstructed interiors, paintings, and photographs of Faro before the tourist explosion of the 1970s. Open from 9:30 AM to 6 PM; closed weekends.

North of the harbor in the Largo do Carmo, behind the grand baroque façade of the **Igreja do Carmo**, lurks the gruesome nineteenth-century **Capelo dos Ossos**, a chapel whose walls are constructed with layers of skulls and bones of monks. The cemetery adjoins.

Needless to say, the primary reason most people visit Faro is to bask in the sun. **Praia de Faro**, the town's closest beach, is a stretch of white sand on the Ilha de Faro. Both ferries and buses run to the island and during warm months, service is frequent.

WHERE TO STAY

Hotel Eva ((289) 803354 FAX (289) 802304, Avenida da República No. 1, 8000 Faro, is generally held to have the best accommodation in town. There are some rooms in this modern hotel on the harborfront that overlook the sea and others that face the old town. It provides plenty of amenities including a rooftop swimming pool, hairdressing salon, bar, restaurant, and disco. Prices vary from mid-range to expensive.

The English-run **Casa de Lumena** ((289) 801990 FAX (809) 804019, Praça Alexandre Herculano No. 27, is an old townhouse decorated with antique furniture, and has a popular bar and restaurant. Its prices are mid-range. The **Pensão Madalena** ((289) 805806, Rua Conselheiro Bivar No. 109, 8000 Faro, is inexpensive, friendly, and efficiently run.

For luxury accommodation in the area, the choice is **Hotel La Réserve** ((289) 999474 FAX (289) 999402, Estrada de Esteval, Santa Bárbara de Nexa, 8000 Faro. Situated 12 km (seven miles) west of Faro on a huge private gardened estate, independent apartments equipped with all amenities, as well as an outdoor swimming pool and tennis courts are offered at luxury prices.

WHERE TO EAT

Restaurante Cidade Velha ((289) 827145, Rua Domingos Guieiro No. 19, is the classiest place in town to dine. It is in an eighteenth-century house close to the cathedral, offering local and international cuisine (the crab cakes are particularly good). Prices are

moderate, and reservations are essential in high season. **Dois Irmãos** ((289) 823337, Largo do Terreiro do Bispo, is old by Faro standards, as it started life in the 1920s. It serves seafood, particularly *cataplana* dishes, and it is inexpensive.

Justly considered home to the best dining in the Algarve, **La Réserve** ((289) 999234 is the restaurant of the above-named hotel. The kitchen is a bit globe-trotting with its Nordic and tropical influenced dishes, but the point of departure is always the supremely fresh seafood. An extensive wine list accompanies. Expensive.

HOW TO GET THERE

International and domestic flights from Lisbon and Porto arrive at Faro airport (see GETTING TO PORTUGAL, page 271 in TRAVELERS' TIPS), six kilometers (four miles) west of the town. A bus shuttles between the airport and the town center, and taxis are plentiful. The Algarve Line links Faro by rail to Lagos in the west and Vila Real de Santo António in the east. Buses link Faro with all the main towns in the Algarve and various express services, including Rodoviária Nacional Express, run between Lisbon and Faro.

By road, Faro is 300 km (196 miles) southeast of Lisbon along the IP1, and 52 km (32 miles) from Vila Real de Santo António, also along the IP1, or the local route N125.

FROM FARO TO LAGOS

This stretch of coastline is jam-packed with resorts and tourist villages; it has the highest concentration of package vacation destinations in the Algarve. **Vale do Lobo**, 16 km (10 miles) west of Faro, has a huge and luxurious vacation village with its own sports facilities including golf courses. Moving down-scale, neighboring **Praia de Quarteira** has long shed its image of a small fishing village, while nearby **Vilamoura** is one of the largest tourist developments in the Algarve, boasting two 18-hole golf courses.

Albufeira lies 36 km (22 miles) west of Faro, a onetime cliff-top fishing village that now seethes with tourists. Its **old town**, however, has retained some of its charm, where the narrow streets are lined with white-

OPPOSITE: The marina at Vilamoura and Portimão's café-lined waterfront. OVERLEAF: Praia da Rocha, the "Rocky Beach" west of Faro is a favorite of Algarve sun worshippers.

washed houses and crossed by Moorish arches, gaily-painted boats still line the fishermen's beach, and there is a morning fish market. The main beach is framed by jagged cliffs and reached by a tunnel carved through the rock.

West of Albufeira is a sweep of rock-sheltered beaches where development is characteristically intensive. The relatively small resort of **Carvoeiro** is more pleasant than others, but its beach quickly gets over-crowded during the peak season. Continuing westward, the large fishing town of

Portimão is notable only for its shopping and the proximity of the delightful **Praia da Rocha**. This, along with the **Praia Dona Ana** (nearer Lagos), is one of the most-photo-graphed Algarvian beaches, unusually framed by strange yellow rock formations but, once again, spoiled by the crowds.

Again, most visitors come here to enjoy the outdoor activities—whether beachfront or café—which exist in abundance. Bars and restaurants are self-evident, but for informa-tion regarding water and other sports, inquire at the local *Turismos*.

The *Turismo* in Quarteira ((289) 389209 is on the Praça do Mar, in Albufeira ((289) 585279 on Rua 5 de Outubro. In Carvoeiro ((282) 357728, it is found on the Praia do

Carvoeiro; while in Portimão, the *Turismo* ((282) 419131 is on Avenida Zeca Afonso. Praia da Rocha ((282) 419132 has its own at Avenida Tomás Cabreira.

LAGOS

One of the most elegant resorts is Lagos, a harbor town that has retained a great deal of charm, probably more so than any other along this stretch of coastline. Yes, it is an-nually besieged by tourists, but for the most part, its fervent clutch on to its small town definition has been successful. Lagos stands as the only place in Portugal that, although quite expanded, after a ten-year absence, did not seem to me to have changed tremendously.

Perhaps its greatest saving grace in mod-ern history (and even ancient as well, for that matter), is that Lagos proper, although adja-cent to some of the regions best beaches, does not literally have an ocean front. The town faces the Rio Bensafrim, and its fishing har-bor, main marina, and the Meia Praia (the top local Atlantic beach) are across the river. Even the train station is on the far side of the foot bridge. This is not to give the impres-sion that either Lagos or its beaches are inac-cessible. Merely to say that perhaps due to its topography, the rampant, ill-conceived mass development that infected the entirety of the Algarve coast east of Lagos, and that continues all the way to the Spanish border, has, by and large, not attacked Lagos.

GENERAL INFORMATION

The *Turismo* ((282) 763031 in Lagos has re-cently been relocated and is no longer in the center of town, but rather at the entrance on Rua Projectada at N120, Sitio de São João.

WHAT TO SEE AND DO

Lagos remains a town that, along with the natural hedonism of the region, does value its historical past — and no visit here would be complete without a look at the early eigh-teenth-century **Igreja de Santo António**, the interior of which shimmers with its baroque gilt carvings. Adjoining the church is the **Museu Regional** with a minor, but interesting archeological exhibit, as well as a much more generalized, if occasionally strange, collection.

Another curiosity is the bizarre **statue of King Sebastião** in the Praça Gil Eanes, commemorating the ill-fated crusade against the Moors that he led from Lagos in 1578. In an attempt to capture the essence of the messianic cult that grew up around King Sebastião (whose body was never found), the sculptor, João Cutileiro, has depicted him as a bewildered spaceman. No amusement is to be derived from a visit to the **Mercado de Escravos**, in the Praça Infante Dom Henrique. The original building, which was destroyed in the 1755 earthquake, dated from the fifteenth century and was the site of the first slave markets held on the European continent. The building is now used for temporary art exhibits, and little mention is made of its past use.

But without question, you've come to Lagos for sun and fun, both of which are almost constant year round. The closest **beach** is Meia Praia, where along its four-kilometer (two-and-a-half-mile) sandy stretch, you will find some easygoing beach cafés good for both eating and drinking, as well as outfits that rent water sports equipment. Without crossing the footbridge, and following Avenida dos Desobrimentos to the south, you will come upon a string of somewhat less crowded beaches and coves. If you're interested in **scuba diving**, contact the Blue Ocean Divers ((282) 782718, a PADI®-certified operation that offers a range of scuba dives and snorkeling "safaris," as well as training courses.

WHERE TO STAY

Most agree that the preferred place to stay is **Hotel de Lagos** ((282) 769967 FAX (289) 769920, Rua Nova da Aldeia, 8600 Lagos, with its indoor and outdoor swimming pools, tennis courts and a golf course, a complete gym and health club and on and on. Prices are generally expensive, although somewhat discounted out of the (broad) high season. For a less expensive stay, the **Pensão Marazul** ((282) 769749 FAX (282) 769960, Rua 25 Abril No. 13, 8600 Lagos, offers immaculate accommodation includ-

ing private bath, telephone, and television at mid-range prices. Although the entrance to the pension is on the central pedestrian street, they have sea-view rooms at no additional charge.

WHERE TO EAT

Restaurants and cafés are everywhere, but despite the plethora, some do stand out. Ask around for the latest sushi restaurant; they're coming into their own, and considering the freshness of the fish and seafood here and in

Portugal in general, it's astounding it has taken this long.

Dom Sebastião ((282) 762795, Rua 25 de Abril No. 20, is along the main pedestrian street, but despite its location, it hasn't fallen to catering solely to tourists. Well, less than elsewhere. Real Portuguese food at moderate prices is what's on the menu. **O Galeão** ((282) 763909, Rua da Laranjeira No. 1, leans a little more toward continental cuisine, but still local fish and seafood dishes are the basis of its kitchen. Overall prices are moderate, but you might want to take the plunge and order a Lobster Thermidor.

Along with its dozens of world-class golf courses, the Algarve also boasts well-preserved historical sites.

INLAND

LOULÉ

About 16 km (10 miles) northwest of Faro, Loulé is something of a craftwork center, with numerous shops that sell locally produced baskets, lace, leather, and metalwork. You can see some of its craftsmen at work in the **Art Gallery and Handicraft Center** close by the castle. The restored medieval **castle** now houses the *Turismo* ((289) 463900 as well as the **Museu Municipal**, which has some archaeological exhibits. The thirteenth-century **Igreja Matriz** in the Largo da Matriz is worthy of a brief visit, a Gothic-style building with a tiled interior looking on to the evocatively-named **Jardim dos Amuados**— Sulky People's Garden.

SILVES

Like Xelb, Silves was the Moorish cultural and political capital of the Algarve, and during the twelfth century it was famous for its great beauty and prosperity. Marauding Crusaders were largely responsible for the city's downfall in 1189, however the Moors regained control two years later. By the time the Christians retook control, there was not much to speak of.

Today, Silves has some riverside cafés and restaurants, but there are few vestiges of its bygone glory other than the heavily restored **Castelo dos Mouros**, whose red sandstone ramparts still dominate the town. Apart from the views from the walls, the most interesting features in the castle are the huge vaulted cisterns that stored water during the sieges of the *Reconquista* period when Moorish strongholds resisted Christian forces.

The red sandstone **Sé** was founded in 1189, then rebuilt in 1242. Although the structure has undergone extensive repair work over the years, it has retained its Gothic simplicity. In it are tombs believed to be those of Crusaders killed during the *Reconquista*. At the eastern edge of the town along the N124 stands one of Portugal's most prized

The Castelo dos Mouros in Silves stands on a hill blanketed with almond groves and orange orchards.

The Algarve

monuments, the sixteenth-century **Cruz de Portugal** (Cross of Portugal), a white sandstone cross with a lacey outline that bears the image of the crucified Christ on one side and his ascent on 'the other.

In Silves, you can find the *Turismo* ((282) 442255 at Rua 25 de Abril.

CALDAS DE MONCHIQUE

The roads running inland from Portimão and Silves meet at Porto de Lagos, where N266 continues north along the Arade valley, climbing into the wooded **Serra de Monchique**. This mountain range divides the Algarve from the Alentejo and provides a cool retreat from the busy coastline, while remaining within easy day-tripping distance of the beaches. The road leads to the little spa town of Caldas de Monchique which, apart from the advent of a modern bottling plant and spa, has hardly changed since the nineteenth century. The town is set in a ravine some 22 km (14 miles) northwest of Silves. It has a faded charm with some unusual *pensãos*.

Many of the buildings date from the nineteenth century when the town enjoyed great popularity, particularly with the well-to-do Spanish. A remnant of this heyday is a mock-Moorish casino, now a **craft center** in a shaded square alongside cafés and restaurants. Today the thermal waters (said to be good for rheumatism and respiratory problems) can be taken at the modern spa. Perhaps just as therapeutic would be a walk through the hilly gardens, replete with eucalyptus, above the main square.

MONCHIQUE

The N266 continues to climb northward for some seven kilometers (four miles) from Caldas de Monchique to the town of Monchique, where low whitewashed houses lie high up in the *serra*, overlooked by the ruined Franciscan monastery of **Nossa Senhora do Desterro**. Marvelous views reward those prepared to make the climb to it. The town itself has several craft shops but few buildings of individual interest other than its **Igreja Matriz**, which has a Manueline doorway surrounded by carved ropes

twisted and knotted into five points above the arch.

In Monchique, the *Turismo* ((282) 911189 is in the Largo dos Chorões.

FÓIA

One of the most spectacular panoramas in the whole country is to be had at Fóia, eight kilometers (five miles) west of Monchique. Here the highest point in the *serra* is marked by an obelisk and an unsightly television transmitter, with views from Portimão to the

Cabo de São Vicente. There are a few shops, a *pensão*, and a hotel here, as many organized tours of the Algarve make stops.

WHERE TO STAY

Loulé has a few *pensãos* and hotels, the **Loulé Jardim Hotel** ((289) 413094/5 FAX (289) 463177, Praça Manuel d'Arriaga, 8100 Loulé, being the preference. Its traditional building, quite luxuriously furnished, has two bars, a restaurant, and a swimming pool. Mid-range.

Residents of inland Monchique OPPOSITE and Silves ABOVE do brisk business with tourists through the summer months.

The Algarve

At Caldas de Monchique, the **Albergaria do Lageado** ((282) 912616, 8550 Monchique, has small rooms, a garden with a pool and a patio, a restaurant, and a bar. Inexpensive.

Set in woods a few kilometers outside Monchique, the **Estalagem Abrigo da Montanha** ((282) 92131 FAX (282) 93660, Corte Pereiro, Estrada de Fóia, has views down to the coast. Mid-range.

WHERE TO EAT

Loulé has several bars and places to eat including a couple of French restaurants. The best kitchen and most elegant ambience, although not overly formal, is to be found at **O Avenida** ((289) 462106, Avenida José da Costa Mealha No. 13. The house specialty is *cataplana*; prices are moderate.

At Silves there are bars and cafés at the riverside with outdoor seating in the warm weather. **Marisqueira Rui I** ((282) 442682, Rua Comendante Vilarinho No. 23, serves good, inexpensive, and popular food.

Caldas de Monchique has several small restaurants.

HOW TO GET THERE

There are frequent buses between Faro and Loulé. Silves is served by the Algarve Line that links it with major towns in the province, Silves is also linked to Portimão, and Portimão has bus service to Monchique.

To reach Loulé by road from Faro, a distance of 20 km (12 miles), take the N125 until São João da Venda where you turn on to the N125-4. To reach Silves from Loulé, 47 km (29 miles) away, head out of Loulé along the N270 then continue along the N125 to Lagoa, where you can follow the signs north to Silves. Caldas de Monchique lies a further 22 km (13 miles) north of Silves along the N124 as far as Porto de Lagos, then north along the N266. Monchique is a further seven kilometers (four miles) north along the N266.

ODECEIXE TO SAGRES

Along the Algarve's west coast, on the provincial border with the Alentejo, the Moorish-style village of Odeceixe lies three kilometers (two miles) from **the Praia de Odeceixe**.

This sandy cove is sheltered by high cliffs. There is good surfing here, and except during the peak summer months, it still tends to be a quiet spot. In the village you will find several cafés and restaurants, as well as a few of the houses have rooms to rent.

Seventeen kilometers (10 miles) further south along the coastal road, the village of **Aljezur** huddles below a ruined castle, and with accommodation in the form of private rooms and a *pensão* it makes a convenient spot from which to visit the sandy beaches of **Monte Clérigo**, eight kilometers (five miles) to the northwest and **Arrifana**, 10 km (six miles) southwest, both more peaceful than Odeceixe.

A further 45 km (28 miles) south along the coast is Europe's most southwesterly point, the **Cabo de São Vicente**, a lonely exposed promontory 75 m (246 ft) above the crashing waves. For hundreds of years this was a shrine to Saint Vincent, whose martyred body is said to have arrived by boat in the twelfth century, guided by ravens who continued to keep watch over his grave until he was removed to Lisbon. Now all that stands here is a powerful **lighthouse** and the ruins of a sixteenth-century **Capuchin convent**.

Six kilometers (four miles) east is **Sagres**, where Prince Henry founded the School of Navigation, the powerhouse of the Voyages of Discovery. It was here that navigation was taught and voyages were plotted. The English attack under the command of Sir Francis Drake, followed by the ravages of the 1755 earthquake, ensured that nothing remains of the school. The major point of interest is the **Fortaleza do Belixe**, believed to have been built on or near the site of the school, and itself rebuilt after the earthquake. The fortress is actually not in Sagres itself, but on further west on the precipice of the continent. It is now an annex of the *pousada*. The fourteenth-century chapel can no longer be visited, as its foundation has eroded beyond the point of safety. Quite impressive is the **rosa de ventos** — the wind compass — made of stones set into the ground on the plateau overlooking the sea. Excavated earlier this century, it measures 43 m (141 ft) in

Weather-beaten rock formations contrasted with stretches of white sand beaches are emblematic of the Algarvan coastline.

The Algarve

diameter, a strange construction that seems to date from the time of Henry the Navigator. Today its radial lines are traced with moss.

Small as it is, Sagres offers several **water sports**. For boat trips, evening fishing trips that include dinner on board, or for the truly adventurous, shark fishing expeditions, contact Sagres Estrela-do-Rio on their mobile phone ((91) 340642, or at the Bar Moby Dick (282) 624442. For scuba diving, contact Scubado (/FAX (282) 624821, or call their mobile phone (96) 738960.

In Sagres the *Turismo* ((282) 624873 is on Rua Comandante Matoso.

WHERE TO STAY

In Sagres, the **Pousada do Infante** ((282) 64222/3 FAX (282) 64225, 8650 Sagres, is a modern building built in Algarvian style perched on a cliff overlooking the port. It has a swimming pool and tennis courts. Mid-range prices apply. It also has an annex, the **Fortaleza do Belixe** ((282) 624124, in the fort: the rooms are comfortable and the views spectacular. A natural stone patio that barely hangs on to the coast, presents a calm utterly incongruous with today's Algarve. Breakfast is served here, the setting sun can be watched from here. Prices are mid-range, and guests have use of the facilities at the *pousada*.

Highly recommended is the **Hotel da Baleeira** ((282) 624212 FAX (282) 624425 E-MAIL hotel.baleeira@mail.telepac.pt WEB SITE www.sagres.net/baleeira, 8650 Vila de Sagres, which overlooks the bay and has such features as a saltwater swimming pool, a tennis court, and direct access to the beach. Prices are moderate, but rise with the ambient temperature.

A more moderate and extremely pleasant option is the **Pensão Residência Dom Henrique** ((282) 620000 FAX (282) 620004, Praça da República, 8500 Sagres. All rooms have private baths and satellite television, and some have expansive sea views. The *pensão*'s restaurant has recently been closed.

WHERE TO EAT

Clearly, there is always the *pousada* for lunch and dinner, where the cuisine is fairly standard fare. It should be noted that, quite un-

fortunately, the restaurant at the Fortaleza do Belixe annex has downgraded its services to simple and somewhat overpriced meals.

In Sagres itself, the best restaurant is on the same road that leads to the *pousada*. **Vila Vehla** ((282) 624788, has a typical seafaring Portuguese menu that adds a continental flair and even offers a few vegetarian dishes. Although they are open seven days a week, it is only for dinner; prices are moderate. In Vila do Bispo (the town next over), there are two interesting restaurants that serve typical Algarvian dishes, which naturally

contain the freshest of fish. Near the municipal market is **A Eira do Mel** ((282) 639016, and in the center of town, you will find **Correia** ((282) 639127. Both are inexpensive.

HOW TO GET THERE

There is a frequent bus service from Lagos to Sagres, and several times a day buses run from Lagos to Aljezur via Sagres.

To reach Sagres and the Cabo de São Vicente from Faro by car, take the N125 to Lagos then follow the signs to Vila do Bispo, where you take the N268 to Sagres. For Aljezur and Odeceixe, take the N125 from Faro as far as Lagos, then continue northward along the IC4. Drivers from Lisbon should leave the city on the IP1, branching off to the N263 to Odemira then continue south along the N120-IC4 to Odeceixe. To proceed to Sagres and São Vicente, turn off the IC4 on to the N268.

OPPOSITE: Red sandstone cliffs reign over the beaches from Albufeira to Faro. ABOVE: The stone compass purportedly used by Henry the Navigator.

Travelers'
Tips

GETTING TO PORTUGAL

BY AIR

TAP Air Portugal, Portugal's national airline, offers a variety of fares and discounts, and can arrange reasonably-priced car rentals to coordinate with your flight and travel plans. TAP Air Portugal can be contacted in New York ((212) 661-0035 TOLL-FREE (800) 221-7370 FAX (212) 867-3275 at 521 Fifth Avenue, and in London ((071) 839-1031 FAX (071) 839-3682 at 19 Lower Regent Street.

TAP flies from New York, Newark, Boston, Toronto, and Montréal to Lisbon, with connecting flights from Los Angeles. TWA, reachable in the United States at TOLL-FREE (800) 221-2000 flies nonstop from New York to Lisbon on their continuing flight to Barcelona, and offers combined packages. Air Canada TOLL-FREE (800) 776-3000 also flies to Lisbon, with departures from Montréal and Toronto.

TAP and its subsidiary airline, LAR, operate an internal network of services linking the main Portuguese airports with regional ones.

In Britain both TAP and British Airways operate direct flights from London to the main Portuguese airports of Lisbon, Faro, and Porto, and TAP also runs flights from Manchester and Dublin to Lisbon, and from Birmingham to Faro.

There are slews of package vacations to Portugal and therefore numerous charter flights (many of which you can book without taking the entire packaged deal). Charter flights from North America almost invariably fly to Lisbon, whereas those departing from Great Britain are primarily destined for Faro in the Algarve, although there are also a few that go to Lisbon and Porto. This makes it possible to pick and chose, however some (but certainly, not all) discount travel agencies are less than scrupulous, and checking them out prior to committing to a nonrefundable ticket is advised. (Many years ago, it was only through my capacity for ferocious argument that I was "awarded" the return voucher of a round-trip ticket I had purchased in New York. Unfortunately, I was not so ferocious in my preliminary investigations.)

BY TRAIN

All international rail connections run through Spain and France. Although there is a daily overnight sleeper train that departs from Madrid at 10:35 PM and arrives in Lisbon around 9 AM. If you are connecting from Paris, you should probably consider the TGV/Rapido Sud Expresso route that travels from Paris to Biarritz and Irun in Spain, where after

changing trains, you continue on to Lisbon via the Basque region and Northern Spain and Portugal. Leaving Paris at 4 PM will have you arrive the following morning in Lisbon at 11:25 AM. This route passes through numerous Portuguese cities, including Aveiro, Porto, and Coimbra, where you might consider jumping off in one direction or the other.

If you are traveling by rail from London, be forewarned that the *Chunnel* service arrives in Paris at the Gare du Nord, and the train for Lisbon leaves from either Paris Montparnasse or Paris Austerlitz, both of which require crossing to the opposite side

Lisbon remains a blend of cosmopolitan bustle and traditional festivities. Streets, such as the Rua de São Paulo, happily change their demeanor for the feasts.

of the city, which can be done either by the metro or taxi.

If, however, you plan to start your journey from Madrid, there is one train that departs Madrid Charmatin at 10:35 PM and arrives in Lisbon at 8:40 AM the following morning. This is a *Talgo* with dining and sleeper service.

A few other *avisos*. Unless you have an Interail or Eurorail card, train fares tend not to be significantly cheaper than airfares, and although you will be passing through some rather scenic countryside, mostly you will

vices from London's Victoria Coach Station to Coimbra, Lisbon and the Algarve, and the journey spans a grueling three days. Further information is available from Victoria Coach Station, London ((071) 730-0202.

BY CAR

For Britain-based travelers who intend to bring their own cars to Portugal from England, you have the option of taking the Channel Tunnel or a ferry of your choice, and then driving through France and Spain. The

be doing so during the night. Also, please note that rail links are continually being renovated, with the obvious goal of reducing travel time. Along with scheduling changes, this may likely entail routing changes, so contact the Portuguese *Turismo* in your home country prior to departure, or be certain to verify the specifics at the station of your departure.

BY BUS

There are international bus services from London and Paris, although these can be more expensive than charter flights (even before calculating in the cost of food and discomfort). National Express operate ser-

drive from Calais to Lisbon is 2,125 km (1,320 miles), so it would be wise to plan at least two overnight stops en route. There are two possibilities for cutting down the driving time: you could take the ferry from Plymouth to Santander in northern Spain, which still leaves you with a 970-km (600-mile) drive to Lisbon (see following section for details); or you could drive to Paris, where you can put your car on the Motorail bound for Lisbon at the Gare d'Austerlitz, and yourself on the Sud Express. You will be reunited with your car one day after your arrival. For details regarding this motorail service contact the SNCF (the French national railway company) ((071) 409-3518 at 179 Piccadilly, London W1V 0BA or at any French railway station. Information is also available on the French national railway's WEB SITE WWW .sncf.com.

An increasingly popular option is to fly-drive, and some good deals are available through travel agents and the airlines. There is no question that driving is one of the best ways to explore Portugal, as it affords you the freedom to roam without prescribed schedules. It is not, however, ideal for the nervous or novice driver. See also BY CAR, page 276, and DRIVING under GETTING AROUND, page 277 for details about car rentals.

BY SEA

The only direct ferry service to Portugal is from Santander, Spain, so once again, if you are starting out from Britain, you will have to make a transfer. Brittany Ferries runs a service that transports cars and their passengers from Plymouth to Santander. The ferry itself takes approximately 24 hours to reach Santander and currently sails twice weekly from Plymouth. From Santander it is an 800-km (500-mile) journey to Porto, or a 970-km (600-mile) journey to Lisbon. For further details contact Brittany Ferries ((0705) 827701 or (0752) 221321 at The Brittany Centre, Wharf Road, Portsmouth PO2 8RU. Reserve well in advance.

ARRIVING

TRAVEL DOCUMENTS

American, Canadian, Australian, British, New Zealand, and Japanese, citizens need only a valid passport to enter Portugal, while other European Union citizens need only a national identity card. Other Commonwealth citizens and British nationals living overseas need a visa. British, Irish, American, Canadian, Australian, New Zealand and Japanese citizens, as well as citizens of certain European countries may stay for up to 90 days. The procedure for extending your stay in Portugal is fairly straightforward (see STAYING ON, page 293), but you are not permitted to work in Portugal while staying as a tourist.

CUSTOMS

As Portugal and Spain are both members of the European Union, all of their shared borders are open, and thus all legal crossings are accessible 24 hours a day. This is so regardless of whether or not you carry a passport of an European Union member nation.

Duty-free allowances are the same as in other European Union countries. There are no restrictions on the amount of money you can bring into the country, but you are not allowed to take out more than 100,000 escudos or foreign currency to the value of 500,000 escudos unless it can be proved that you brought in at least the same amount.

EMBASSIES AND CONSULATES

American Embassy ((21) 727-3300 FAX (21) 726-9109, Avenida das Forças Armadas, 1600 Lisbon.
Australian Embassy The closest Australian embassy is in Paris ((33.1) 40 59 33 00 FAX (33.1) 40 59 33 10, 4 rue Jean Rey, 75015 Paris.
British Embassy ((21) 392-4000 FAX (21) 392-4188, Rua São Bernardo No. 33, 1200 Lisbon.
British Consulate ((22) 618-4789 FAX (22) 610-0438, Avenida da Boavista No. 3072, 4100 Porto.

Donkeys are still a dominant factor of the rural work force, while sunning backpackers have also begun to penetrate the scene.

273

Canadian Embassy ((21) 347-4892 FAX (21) 347-6466, Avenida da Liberdade No. 144-3, 1250 Lisbon.

South African Embassy ((21) 353-5041 FAX (21) 353-5713, Avenida Luís Bivar No. 10, 1050 Lisbon.

TOURIST INFORMATION

For general information outside Portugal contact one of the Portuguese Tourism offices.

Austria ((1) 513-2670 FAX (1) 512-8828, Stubenring 16/3, A-1010 Vienna.

Belgium ((2) 230-9625 or (2) 230-5250 FAX (2) 231-0447, Rue Joseph II No. 5, Boite 3, 1040 Brussels.

Canada Ontario ((416) 921-4925 FAX (416) 921-1353, 60 Bloor Street West, Suite 1005, Toronto M4W 3B8; or Québec ((514) 282164 FAX (514) 49914, 500 Sherbrook Street West, Suite 940, Montréal H3A 3C6.

England ((071) 494-1441 FAX (071) 494-1868, 22-25a Sackville Street, London W1X 1DE.

France ((1) 56 88 30 80 FAX (1) 56 88 30 89, 135 Boulevard Haussmann, 75008 Paris.

Germany ((21) 184912/4 FAX (21) 132-0968, Kreuzstrasse 34-3, 40210 Dusseldorf; or ((69) 234094 FAX (69) 231433, Schäfergasse 17, 60313 Frankfurt am Main; or ((30) 882-1066 FAX (30) 883-4851, Kurfürstendamm 203 W, 10719 Berlin.

Italy ((2) 795228 FAX (2) 794622, Largo Augusto 3, 20122 Milan; or ((6) 320-3443 FAX (6) 361-3163, Via Flaminia 56, 00196 Roma.

South Africa ((011) 484-3487 FAX (011) 484-5416, Fourth Floor, Sunnyside Ridge, Sunnyside Drive, Parktown 2193, Johannesburg.

Spain ((91) 522-9354 FAX (91) 522-2382, Gran Via 27 No. 1, 28013 Madrid; or ((93) 301-4416 FAX (93) 318-5068, Calle Bruc 50, 08010 Barcelona.

Switzerland ((1) 241-0300 or 241-0309 FAX (1) 241-0012, Badenerstrasse 15, 8004 Zurich.

United States ((212) 354-4403 FAX (212) 764-6137, 590 Fifth Avenue, Fourth floor, New York, New York 10036-4704; or ((202) 331-8222 FAX (202) 331-8236, 1900 L Street NW, Suite 310, Washington DC 20036.

IN PORTUGAL

Virtually every town has its tourist office or *Turismo*, an invaluable source of local and regional information. It's a good idea to make a beeline for it as soon as you reach a town as staff there can supply you with a map of the town, lists of hotels, advice on transportation, and can help with *pousada* bookings or any questions you may have. Even in the remotest of towns, a member of the staff may speak English, often remarkably well. *Turismos* are centrally located and signs with the *Turismo* symbol — a white T on a blue background — will lead you through even the most labyrinthine of ancient towns. Opening hours are generally from 9 AM to 7 PM Monday to Saturday, but this can vary, and in smaller towns it is more likely to be from 10 AM to 5 PM Monday to Saturday, with a lunch break that could be any time between noon and 2:30 PM.

If you are after information beyond the scope of a local tourist office, try one of the main city branches. Try the **ICEP** (Investimentos, Comércio e Turismo de Portugal) in Lisbon ((21) 346-3681 at Palácio Foz, Praça dos Restauradores, 1200 Lisbon; in Porto ((22) 205-7514 at Praça Dom João I No. 43, 400 Porto; and in Faro ((289) 803604 at Rua da Misericórdia Nos. 8-12, 8000 Faro. For not quite round-the-clock toll-free information in Portuguese, English, French, or Spanish ranging from questions regarding museums and hotels to those about hospitals and police stations, while in Portugal call TOLL-FREE (800) 296296. Hours to call are from 9 AM to midnight Mondays through Saturdays, and 9 AM through 8 PM on Sundays and holidays.

If you have access to the Internet, here are three web sites that make for good starting points: www.portugal.org, www.icep.pt, and www.turismo-portugal.com.

Other web sites of interest are: www .pousadas.pt, which, as no doubt you've guessed, offers information on all of Portugal's *pousadas*. Somewhat less self-evident is www.maisturismo.pt, which presents an array of hotels throughout the country, along with direct contact links. Please do note that the listing is not comprehensive, although it may lead you to believe it is. The organization publishes a large glossy book that is more informative (and heavy to carry along with you), but at 5000$ (or about US$26), it might well not be worth its weight.

GETTING AROUND

BY AIR

TAP operates regular services between the major Portuguese cities — Lisbon, Porto, and Faro, as well as to Madeira and the Azores. Reservations can be made by contacting ((21) 841-6990 FAX (21) 841-6540. Portugália ((21) 840-5849 FAX (21) 849-1307 also services the same destinations.

BY TRAIN

Portugal has quite an extensive rail network, with services that range from the slick commuter lines to a slow regional service stopping at all stations on the route. Fares are inexpensive, though the faster the service, the more it costs, and reservation fees (often obligatory on the express services) add substantially to the ticket price. There are discounts for senior citizens, students, and children. Tickets must be bought before boarding, either from a travel agent or from the station ticket office where, regardless of the hour, you will almost invariably find long lines. On routes other than the main intercity lines, trains often turn out to be slower than buses. Added to that, train stations are sometimes a bus ride away from the towns they serve.

The *regionais* network covers most of the rural areas where stations can sometimes be quite far from town; the *directos* and *semi-directos* are slightly faster trains, but still quite leisurely. More efficient express trains run

the Lisbon–Coimbra–Porto and Lisbon–Faro routes, and there is a fast electric rail link from Lisbon's Cais do Sodré station to Cascais, Estoril, and other places along the Costa do Sol. The fastest and most luxurious of all the trains is the *Alfa* express that runs between Lisbon and Porto.

Other commuter lines leave from Lisbon's Cais do Sodré and Rossio stations, while trains to the north and east run from the Santa Apolónia Station. To travel south from Lisbon or to the Alentejo, you need to get to the Barreiro Station, which involves a ferry

crossing from the landing station just west of the Praça do Comércio (the rail ticket includes the cost of the ferry).

BY BUS

The national bus company, Rodoviária Nacional (RN), runs services throughout Portugal, and there are some smaller private companies such as Mundial de Turismo and Rodonorte that cover specific routes or regions. This is probably the best form of public transportation for touring the heart of the country, and it is undoubtedly the cheapest.

OPPOSITE: Fishermen mend their nets along the Beira coast. ABOVE: On the plains, windmills have been restored for nostalgia.

Turismos can furnish you with timetables and details of where to pick up your bus.

BY TAXI

The most easily identifiable taxis are those with green roofs and black bodies, whereas the beige-colored ones found in many cities and towns can blend into the background. In towns and cities the cost is metered, but elsewhere the fare is calculated by the kilometer and you should check the cost before taking the cab. Everywhere, even in Lisbon and Porto, prices are very reasonable, and if there are a few of you sharing it can work out to be more economical than other forms of transportation. A surcharge of up to 50% for baggage over 30 kg (66 lbs) is imposed, and between 10 PM and 6 AM there is a 20% surcharge. It is usually quite easy to find a taxi except at lunchtimes, when taxi drivers, like the rest of the populace, take a long lunch break.

BY THUMB

There is no law against hitchhiking in Portugal, but few people do it and you should be aware that Portuguese drivers may be wary of stopping for you as their insurance policies do not cover hitchhikers. Although Portugal has an extremely low crime rate, women—whether traveling alone or in pairs or more—should not consider hitchhiking.

BY CAR

Although nothing beats the freedom of traveling by car, driving in Portugal can have its harrowing moments. The quality of the roads and highways has improved tremendously over the years, as has the clarity of the signs. Unfortunately, the same cannot be said about the Portuguese mode of driving. Be careful, try to anticipate the madness, and keep your cool. As when traveling anywhere in Europe, it works out to be considerably less expensive to arrange your car rental before you get to Portugal. Once there, however, rates do compare reasonably well with other European countries. If you are booking your flight with TAP, they can arrange a good value car rental to fit in with

your travel plans. All the major international car rental companies do business in Portugal but I highly recommend contacting Auto Europe TOLL-FREE IN THE UNITED STATES (800) 223-5555 TOLL-FREE IN PORTUGAL (800) 811932. This is a very well-run outfit based in Maine that arranges rentals throughout Europe at unbeatable US rates. They have toll-free numbers in most countries that connect you directly with their agents who are on call 24 hours a day; and they are extremely indulgent when it comes to last minute reservations and changes (which can be made from Europe without any penalties). In the event of a problem regarding the rental car (which is to say, not necessarily your driving), they will act as an intermediary with the Portuguese agency.

At 160$ (approximately 85¢) per liter, fuel costs are quite high by American, and even by British, standards. The tolls on the *autoestradas*, however, are significantly lower than in other European countries, although they do add up.

DRIVING

The roads in Portugal are improving all the time. European Union money is helping to pay for improvements and new roads keep appearing: be sure you get as up-to-date a map as possible. In the northeast, once renowned for its isolation and rough tracks, some of the roads are now better and smoother than those around the more heavily populated areas or the much-visited Algarve.

However, in the mountainous areas there are lots of blind bends and getting stuck behind a slow-moving farm vehicle can greatly slow you down. If you're traveling through this kind of terrain, you should take into consideration the unpredictable when calculating your driving time. To get an idea, consult some of the brochures about *pousada* vacations, as they sometimes have charts indicating the distances and estimated driving times between various *pousadas*.

The really bad news is that Portugal has Europe's worst record for road accidents, and whether as a driver or a pedestrian it will soon be excruciatingly apparent why. Portuguese

Vilamoura in the Algarve is one of the largest tourist complexes in Europe. The marina has more than 1,000 moorings.

drivers have an absence of road sense as well as a blatant disregard for traffic law. Worse, they seem to know no fear, so beware of bends and what may come hurtling around them on the wrong side of the road. The best advice I can give is to drive defensively and not to get involved in a war of nerves with a Portuguese driver. On that note, if you need emergency services call (115. In addition, emergency telephones dot the route along the *auto-estradas*, as well as most national roads.

Both American and Canadian driver's licenses are valid in Portugal, however, if you're driving your own car, nationality plates and a green card from your insurers as third-party insurance is compulsory. You are required to carry in your car a red warning triangle which, in the case of an accident or breakdown, is to be placed at least 50 m (164 ft) before the site. British and American automobile clubs cooperate in a reciprocal assistance scheme with the Portuguese Automobile Club — Automóvel Clube de Portugal (ACP). The head office ((21) 318-0100 FAX (21) 318-0227 WEB SITE www.acp.pt is at Rua Rosa Araújo No. 24, 1250 Lisbon, and there are branches in most cities including Porto, Aveiro, Braga, Coimbra, and Faro.

Continental rules of the road apply, and the international sign system is used. On highways (*auto-estradas*) the speed limit is 120 kph (74 mph); in towns and other built-up areas it's usually (60 kph (37 mph) unless otherwise marked; out of town other than on highways it's 90 kph (56 mph). Be especially careful in towns and villages, as children often play at the edge of the road and some of Portugal's large canine population choose to sleep on it. In rural areas beware of suddenly coming upon ox- or horse-drawn carts or one of the many slow and unroadworthy vehicles.

The wearing of seat belts is compulsory. The legal alcohol limit is below 0.5 grams per liter. Penalties for driving while over the limit include heavy fines payable on the spot in escudos, confiscation or suspension of your driver's license, and/or a prison term, in accordance with your blood-alcohol level.

At a road junction where both roads are of equal size, traffic approaching from the right has priority. Extreme caution should be exercised in traffic circles: generally speaking, you must yield the right of way to traffic already in the circle, however, occasionally incoming traffic has the right of way. Signs should indicate what is correct, but as always, observe and then err on the side of caution. Pedestrians have priority at zebra crossings, but if they depend on that rule being observed they risk their lives. As a driver, observe it, as a pedestrian, don't trust it. When driving, always indicate your intention to the driver behind well in advance, and then make absolutely sure that it is safe to switch lanes, turn, or stop before doing so.

Parking in the cities can be difficult, especially in Lisbon, Porto, Coimbra, and on and on. You have to park facing the same direction as the traffic flow on that side of the road, but the main problem is actually finding somewhere to park legally. Vehicles do get towed away, so if you want to play safe, use the multilevel garages. If you leave your car overnight, however, it will prove to be very expensive. To avoid this unnecessary expense, move your car back onto the street in the evening when meters are no longer in effect and parking spots magically appear. Without question, the best solution is to stay in a hotel with private parking and abandon your car for the duration. I cannot overemphasize this advice. The annoyance

Travelers' Tips

of a car in the main cities can well destroy your visit, and when choosing your hotel, the availability of parking, whether free or not, should not be taken lightly.

A further note. In all major cities and towns that attract tourists, unemployed men perform an unsolicited service. Whether you want/need it or not, you will be led to an empty parking spot, and more often than not, poorly directed into it. Whether or not the spot is free-of-charge, whether or not it is after-hours for the meter, you will be expected (*de facto* required) to pay for this service.

international levels; above US$160 for a standard double. Some of the best bargains and nicest surprises are to be found among the *residencials* and *pensãos*, which have fewer amenities than hotels, often serving only breakfast. *Estalagems* are inns rated between four and five stars; *albergarias*, also inns, are four-star accommodation. In the tourist resorts, apartment hotels, always a good family option, are rated between two and four stars, motels are given either two or three stars, and tourist villages are divided into luxury, first class, and second class. Standards

The manner of these "parking attendants" ranges from intimidating to threatening, particularly at night (and particularly as a woman traveling alone), and on several occasions I have complained to the local police.

ACCOMMODATION

There are quite a few different kinds of accommodation to choose from in Portugal, and some of the most delightful are not necessarily the most expensive. Hotels are given a one-to five-star rating, based on price and type. Those in the deluxe (five-star) category are on a par with luxury hotels anywhere, and in Lisbon, Porto and the major Algarve resort hotels the prices are very much at

on the whole are very good and even the least expensive accommodation is usually immaculately clean. In terms of price, the star ratings (in the index) translate generally to one star: US$30 and up, two star: US$60 and up, three star US$90 and up, four star: US$120 and up.

The institution of a state-managed network of hotels known as *pousadas*, similar in kind to the Spanish *paradors*, was one of the better innovations that materialized during Salazar's dictatorship. These are strategically positioned throughout Portugal

OPPOSITE: Converted into a luxury hotel, this restored nineteenth-century palace overlooks the Tagus. Guests find York House ABOVE has more Portuguese flavor than its name suggests.

and provide ideal accommodation for those wishing to explore the country. Some locations have been chosen purely for their scenic beauty, some because they are in a zone of historical interest, while others are converted palaces, castles, convents or monasteries. There are over 40 in all and it is possible to plan a thorough tour of the country and stay only at *pousadas*. They are classified into four groups: B, C, CH, and CHL (in ascending order of quality and price). Peak-season prices vary from US$75 to US$150 for a double room; while not cheap, state subsidies assure that they are excellent value. Expect a cordial welcome, professional service, and refined traditional cuisine. A justified criticism that is occasionally heard is that the service and even the cuisine, although

formal, can be "impersonal" or "institutional." You can book through the Portuguese tourist offices but beware of making last-minute cancellations as money has to be paid up-front and you will lose at least the cost of the first night. If you are traveling any time other than during high season, accommodation in *pousadas* can often be found on the spot, or if you are on the road and can project your itinerary a few days in advance, call to be sure.

Other, perhaps even more interesting accommodation can be found through what is generally known as the *Turismo de Habitação* (TURIHAB) scheme under which people open their homes to guests, offering bed and breakfast accommodation. These guesthouses are particularly predominant in the

offer only a few rooms and as the scheme in general, and many homes in particular, are becoming better known, you may find yourself disappointed. As these are private homes, along with high standards, it is the personal touch that has many guests making reservations for their return the following year while they are still packing their bags. Breakfast is included in the price, and it is sometimes possible to have main meals at an additional charge by prior arrangement. A booklet called *Turismo No Espaço Rural Guia Oficial* is available for purchase at Portuguese tourist offices in most countries, and it has photos together with details of hundreds of houses. If you are considering staying at a few (and I cannot recommend doing so strongly enough), this is an investment you should definitely make.

In terms of price, the star ratings translate generally to one star: US$50 and up, two stars: US$75 and up, three stars US$100 and up, four stars: US$120 and up. Thus, when a hotel is described as inexpensive, the price will be US$50 or less (this category includes pensions, which can run much lower, particularly in the off-season); mid-range indicates US$51 to US$120; and expensive, over $120. The few instances when luxury is specified, the price will be in the vicinity of US$185 or more. As everywhere, prices are progressively getting more expensive in Portugal, and as the European Union becomes more homogenized, this trend will only become more pronounced.

Minho province, and compensate for the general lack of other accommodation in the region. They are classified into three categories: TURIHAB, which are manor houses (some quite grand) or houses of recognized architectural value; *Turismo Rural*, which are houses typical of the area and situated in or near a town; and *Agroturismo*, which is farmhouse accommodation. Prices vary although these are privately owned houses they are registered with the Direcção-Geral do Turismo, which requires that they conform to certain standards. In general, reservations need to be made at least three or four days in advance either directly with the owners or through travel agents, *Turismos*, or the owners' associations, and a deposit is required. It should be noted that most houses

All accommodation prices vary according to the time of year. The most expensive time is during the high season (June to September), while the cheapest period is from November to the end of March, with the exception of Christmas and Easter holidays. If you are planning your visit in the peak season and have strong ideas about where you would like to stay, you are strongly advised to reserve in advance, and if you want to stay in any of the *pousadas*, the advice is that much stronger.

When the time comes to check out, there should be no unexpected surcharges, as most establishments display the room prices,

Port grapes are grown along the valley of the meandering Douro River, which runs from the Spanish border to Porto and the Atlantic Ocean.

inclusive of taxes and service charges, in the lobby and also on the door of each room. In addition, cheating and manipulation of any sort is just not the Portuguese way. Wherever you check in you will be asked for your passport. This is usually kept long enough for reception to fill out the obligatory registration form, in which case you can usually pick up your passport before going out in the evening. (You are, however, advised not to carry you passport with you on the street unless you will absolutely be needing to use it.) Some places prefer to hang on to it during the first night of your stay.

Breakfast, unless you are staying at one of the luxury hotels, is usually very simple — fresh bread, rolls, jams, and plentiful supplies of coffee or tea. More and more, cheese, ham, and yogurt are also served, and at a some of even the mid-range hotels, a more extensive buffet including cereals and eggs is offered. The breads are invariably delicious, the coffee often less so.

Hotel information and booking services can also be found on the Internet at the WEB SITE www.maisturismo.com, however do note that listings include only those hotels that are part of the organization and it is by no means exhaustive. If you already know the hotel where you want to stay and it is included, the service provides a convenient way to make reservations.

EATING OUT

The long Portuguese lunch is a respected tradition, and thus most places — shops, museums, churches — shut down around this time, so there's little choice but to join in and enjoy. Lunch is anytime between 12:30 PM and 3 PM while dinner tends to be between 8 PM and 10 PM (although in major cities, it's becoming chic to dine even later).

At a *confeitaria*, a *pastelaria*, or *salão de chá*, you can enjoy light, inexpensive food — sandwiches, omelets, simple meals — or afternoon teas and pastries in a relaxed café atmosphere. In the cities, art nouveau coffee houses are an institution and are ideal places for a drink, reading a paper, meeting friends, and best of all, people watching.

The *cervejaria* is more than just a beerhouse as its name might indicate. Most serve food, some have quite extensive menus, and shellfish is often a popular snack. They tend to be busy places, good on atmosphere, easy on the pocket, and similar to the *tabernas*, which are generally older drinking establishments where a variety of wines as well as beer are served. You will not find the same choice of eating places in the smaller towns and villages, but remember that where there's a *pousada* there's an acceptable restaurant, and that you never have to be a registered guest to eat there, nor even to drink at its bar.

Portions, especially in northern restaurants, are typically huge. It is, however, quite acceptable for three people to share two main courses, or even for two people to share one.

Bread, butter, and some tasty appetizers — olives, sardines, Russian salad, croquettes, or cheeses — might be placed on your table while you are perusing the menu. You will be charged for them, but may decline when they are served.

Restaurant prices have been divided into three categories: Expensive, Moderate, and Inexpensive. Rather broadly speaking, these definitions should be assumed to indicate approximately and respectively: US$75, US$50, and US$30 for dinner for two. Wine is not included in this calculation, and a midday meal, even at a rather upscale restaurant is almost invariably less expensive than dinner. A 15% tip is included in all restaurant tabs (and assumed in the prices here), but often something more is expected. In no way should you feel obliged to pay extra, however if you find the service exceptional, consider adding at least 5% to the total.

RECREATIONAL ORGANIZATIONS

Portugal's temperate climate is ideal for a vast array of participative sports, and the following organizations can be provide detailed information on available facilities and opportunities:

Fishing Federação Portuguesa de Pesca Desportiva ((21) 314-0177, Rua Eca Queiros No. 3, 1200 Lisbon.

Golf Federação Portuguesa de Golfe ((21) 867-4658, Rua Almeida Brandão No. 39, 1200 Lisbon.

The Marches Populares on Lisbon's Avenida da Liberdade.

Horseback Riding Federação de Equestre Portuguesa ((21) 352-5676, Avenida Duque de Ávila No. 9, 1000 Lisbon.

Scuba Diving Federação Portuguesa de Activadades Subaquátiques ((21) 840-6153, Rua Manuel Cardosa No. 39, 1200 Lisbon.

Tennis Federação Portuguesa de Ténis ((21) 419-5244, Estádio Nacional, Caxias, 2480 Oeiras.

Cycling Federação Portuguesa de Vela ((21) 364-7324, Doca de Belém, 1300 Lisbon.

FADO HOUSES

Fado music is not only for the tourists: it has a serious Portuguese following. If you'd like to hear some you should take visit one of the many *fado* houses of Lisbon, the most authentic of which are to be found in old neighborhoods such as the Alfama and in the Bairro Alto district. There is a cover charge or entrance fee, and you can either arrive early for a meal — which can be excellent — or drop in after dinner time and just have a drink (see WALLOW IN *FADO*, page 12 in TOP SPOTS).

In the early evening many of these places are filled with bus loads of tourists who come to eat and listen to a little music, so it is a good idea to make reservations in advance if you want a meal. However, after about 11 PM the big parties tend to leave, tables are cleared, and the atmosphere changes from that of restaurant to drinking club. This is also when the music really takes off and often continues on nonstop until dawn. Aficionados take their *fado* very seriously, and talking during the performances is not at all appreciated.

SPAS

Portugal has an amazing number of spas — about 45 in all — which are said to have therapeutic properties for a wide range of ailments that include liver, kidney, allergic, gastric, circulatory, and respiratory problems. The spas are well-patronized, and the better-known ones tend to have excellent treatment rooms and hotels set in restful surroundings with plenty of leisure facilities (see ELIMINATE THOSE EVIL HUMORS, page 16 in TOP SPOTS).

Most are open from May to October, some for longer. Brochures are available from tour-

ist offices and further information is also available through the Associacão Nacional dos Industriais de Águas Minero-Medicinais e de Mesa ((21) 794-0574 FAX (21) 793-8283, Avenida Miguel Bombarda No. 110, 1050 Lisbon.

BASICS

TIME

There is no time difference between Portugal and Great Britain and Ireland. On the last Sunday in March the clocks are moved one hour ahead of Greenwich Mean Time and on the last Sunday in October the clocks are put back an hour. To calculate the time in the United States and Canada, subtract five to eight hours (Eastern Standard to Pacific time). Australia is eight to 10 hours ahead of Portuguese time; New Zealand is 12 hours ahead.

ELECTRICITY

The local current is 220 volts (a few remote areas still have 110 volts). The outlets take continental European plugs with two round prongs. Visitors from the United States will need both a plug adapter as well a voltage converter for their appliances. It should be noted that many new models of razors, irons, hairdryers, and even portable computers have internal automatic transformers, and only require a plug adapter. Visitors from Britain will only need an adapter.

WATER

The water throughout Portugal is safe to drink. However, if you are prone to minor stomach upsets from a change of bacteria, it's a good idea to stick to bottled water, which you can buy anywhere.

TOILETS

Toilets can be found in museums, railway and metro stations, and generally in the town centers. Look out for the sign *Senhoras*, which means Ladies, or *Homens*, which means

---

Lisbon's young scene is much the same as in other European capitals.

Gentlemen. If an attendant is on duty you should leave a tip, and in some places there is a charge of a few escudos. As usual, it can save you possible anguish if you carry a small supply of toilet paper or tissue around with you.

WEIGHTS AND MEASURES

Like most countries, Portugal uses the metric system. If you are used to pounds and ounces, feet and inches, pints and quarts, you may need to make some quick calculations. Rather than a list of the exact conversion formulae, the following are some rough conversions that you can do in your head rather than with a calculator.

First, measurements: there are two and a half centimeters to one inch, so to convert inches to cm you multiply by 2.5; one meter is just over a yard; one kilometer is six-tenths of a mile, so a mile is a little over 1.6 km. When it comes to buying food and drink you may find it useful to know that 125 grams is approximately a quarter of a pound, that 500 grams is roughly one pound, and that one kilogram is 2.2 lbs. With regard to liquid measures, a liter is just over two American pints and just under two English pints. In reverse, an English pint is just over half a liter and an American pint just under.

To convert temperatures from Celsius to Fahrenheit, double the Celsius temperature and add 32.

OPENING HOURS

Beware the lunch break. If you're planning a tour of the country don't forget that everything — shops, churches, museums, tourist offices, and most of the banks — closes for lunch, otherwise you may find your schedule disrupted and let yourself in for some unnecessary disappointments.

If you're visiting some of the more out-of-the-way churches and other historical buildings, remember that some are kept permanently closed and you may have to ask someone living nearby for the key. In general—but this is very general—churches are open from 7 AM to 1 PM and again from

The Miradoura de Santa Luzia gives a bird's-eye view of Lisbon's Alfama district.

4 PM to 7 PM. Museums and galleries are closed on Mondays and public holidays, while palaces and some other buildings shut on Tuesdays. Opening hours for weekdays and weekends are roughly from 10 AM to 5 PM but often closing between 12:30 PM and 2 PM for lunch, so always try to check in advance. Government offices are usually open from 9 AM to midday and from 2:30 PM to 5:30 PM.

Shops are usually open from 9 AM to 1 PM and from 3 PM to 7 PM. Monday to Friday, from 9 AM to 1 PM only on Saturdays, and are closed on Sundays. However, in the big towns and cities there are now shopping centers and supermarkets that stay open from 10 AM to midnight seven days a week.

HOLIDAYS

Major public holidays in Portugal are as follows:
January 1   New Year's Day
April 25   Liberation Day
May 1   May Day
June 10   Camões Day
August 15   Assumption Day
October 5   Republic Day
November 1   All Saints' Day
December 1   Independence Day
December 8   Immaculate Conception
December 25   Christmas Day
   Movable holidays are:
Shrove Tuesday   February or March
Good Friday and Easter Sunday   March or April
Corpus Christi   June
   Regional holidays include:
In Lisbon   13 June is Saint Anthony's Day
In Porto   24 June is Saint John's Day

MONEY

The monetary unit is the escudo, which is divided into 100 centavos. The escudo is denoted by the $ sign, which appears after the number of escudos and before the number of centavos, thus 20$50 = 20 escudos and 50 centavos. It should be noted that in most daily transactions, the centavo has become virtually obsolete, and prices are generally rounded to the nearest 10 escudos. You may occasionally hear one thousand escudos referred to as a *conto*. Escudos are issued in coins

of five, 10, 20, 50, 100, and 200; and notes are issued in denominations of 500, 1.000, 5.000, and 10.000 escudos (note that in Portugal, a period is used instead of a comma to separate thousands).

Travelers' checks are accepted by many hotels and shops but at a poor exchange rate. For better rates go to a bank. Opening hours are 8:30 AM to 3 PM and they are generally closed on weekends, but you may find one open on Saturdays in the main tourist areas. In some of the smaller towns banks sometimes shut at lunchtime. Airport exchange

offices remain open until 11 PM and in Lisbon the exchange at the Santa Apolónia train station and a couple of banks around the Praça dos Restauradores are also open late.

Eurocheques supported by a Eurocheque card are widely accepted, and an ever-increasing number of places now take major credit cards. Obviously the smaller the restaurant or the smaller the town, the less likely it is that you will be able to use either, so don't rely too heavily on them if you are traveling outside the cities and larger towns. You will be better off exchanging money in Portugal than buying currency at home and taking it with you, and often you will get a better exchange rate if you use your credit card to get money, though not in small amounts.

Travelers' Tips

For best exchange rates and supreme convenience, forget the travelers' checks and rely *solely* on your ATM card. I emphasize this only because I am always surprised to find that tourists are reluctant to trust this simple, efficient, and cheap method of exchange. In Portugal, ATM machines that are hooked up to international networks are to be found everywhere. They are generally in service 24 hours a day, seven days a week, but service can be reduced on weekends. You will receive bills in local currency and your account will be debited at the international trading rate, which is significantly more advantageous than the rate offered by banks, and certainly than that offered by hotels. Your personal bank may charge a nominal service fee, and thus making small daily withdrawals is not advised. Check with your bank for specifics.

COMMUNICATION AND MEDIA

MAIL

Post office (*correio*) opening hours vary from place to place, but in general they are open from Monday to Friday, from 8:30 AM or 9 AM to 6 PM, and some of the smaller ones shut for lunch (12:30 PM to 2 PM). In the major cities some stay open until late evening and a few are open on Saturdays until midday. A variety of transactions take place in the post office but if you only want to buy stamps, go to the window marked *selos* (stamps), or use the coin-operated (and easy to use) vending machines. Alternatively, if you are just sending some postcards or letters, tobacco shops sell stamps and are up on the correct postage.

Mail within Portugal takes between one and three days to reach its destination and deliveries are from Monday to Friday with a second delivery only in the main cities. Mail to other European countries takes roughly one week, and to other countries between one week and 10 days. Main post offices have telex and fax services available to the public.

If you want mail sent to you during your stay in Portugal and don't know in advance where you will be staying, you can have it sent to any post office if it is marked *Posta Restante* and has the address of the branch from which you wish to retrieve it. You will need your passport for identification when you go to collect the mail, and a small fee is charged for each item you receive.

TELEPHONES

Portugal was for a long time notorious for its inefficient telephone service. Happily, this is absolutely no longer the case. Both direct local and international calls can be made easily and quickly from any telephone.

Telephoning from your hotel room or from a bar usually incurs quite a substantial surcharge. Public telephones either are equipped to accept 2$, 5$, and 25$ coins, or Credifone phonecards, which are sold at tobacco shops and newspaper kiosks and come in denominations of 50 and 120 units. These cards can be used in telephones throughout the country, and it's a good idea to carry one. Both local and international calls can be made from all public telephones and using them is straightforward. Some telephones are equipped with magnetic swipes for use with credit cards. To place an international call, you must first dial 00, followed by the country code, city code (dropping the initial 0), and then desired number.

If you have an account with one of the US carriers such as Sprint® or MCI®, this can be the most economical way to make international calls. Carriers have local toll-free numbers, and then their own uncomplicated procedures. They are also useful for making collect calls, which do not require your having an account with them. Ask your carrier for their Portugal contact number before leaving home.

Telephone calls can be made at most post offices, which also have telegram and fax services.

A word about modems and hotels. Most hotels have telephone jacks that use the standard American modular plug. Some, however, have made accessibility to the plug impossible. (No, not even moving the bed will prove of any help.) In addition, many systems still function on "pulse" dialing, so be sure your access software has an option for this. Similarly, be sure you can add a prefix to get an outside line. In some cases, I have

Kiosks selling international newspapers can be found throughout Lisbon.

found an outside line was still inaccessible directly through my modem, and I have had to connect by dialing on the phone keypad, then continuing the connection with my modem/computer. Obviously, doing such entails the use of a dual adapter and a few practice rounds to get the timing right. Then there are other times when nothing works. One further *aviso*: the number of stars your hotel is rated does not necessarily correspond with the expected efficiency of their telephone system. My experience is that *pousadas* are the most difficult.

RADIO AND TELEVISION

Radio broadcasts can be heard in English, French, and German during the summer on the RDP, while Program Two, which is predominantly a classical music station, has English broadcasts for tourists in the morning and evening. Radio Algarve is an English-language station that has the news in English in the morning and early evening. The BBC World Service can be picked up, and Radio Canada International and the Voice of America can be heard at various times of day. Signals are often best in the early morning and in the evening.

There are two government-run television channels: RTP 1, which goes on the air at 9 AM, and RTP 2, which doesn't start up until 3 PM. They broadcast a strange mix of programs, with Brazilian soaps being the national favorite, and American, British, and Australian series brought in and subtitled. Hollywood movies, also subtitled, are often aired during the evenings and overnight, but as they are generally not top-rate, it may only be insomniacs who appreciate their broadcast. Satellite dishes are a growing trend and so televisions in some of the higher grade hotels can offer an array of stations that generally include CNN, the BBC, SkyNews, and Eurosport.

NEWSPAPERS AND MAGAZINES

Among the most widely-read local dailies is *Diário de Notícias*, which has an entertainment guide that is particularly useful for tourists, whether or not they understand Portuguese. Also good for entertainment listings is *Sete*,

a weekly that comes out Wednesday afternoons and also carries a television and radio guide.

Major European newspapers and the Hague edition of the *International Herald Tribune* are usually available on the day of publication from newsstands, hotels, and bookstalls in the major cities and tourist resorts, as are European editions of *Time* and *Newsweek*. Some smaller cities receive delivery one day after publication, and most don't receive any delivery. There are locally-produced English language magazines that primarily serve the expatriate community, such as the *Algarve Gazette* and the fortnightly *Algarve News*. The ICEP publishes the useful *What's On in Lisbon*.

ETIQUETTE

Portuguese society is quite formal and good manners are considered important. It is polite to shake hands with anyone you are introduced to, and with anyone who has been particularly helpful, whatever the service performed. In a formal situation people do not address one another by their first names but by their title and surname. For a man this is *Senhor*, for a woman *Senhora*, sometimes *Dona*, while doctors, lawyers, civil servants, and other professionals are addressed by their titles. If in doubt, elevate.

It is considered impolite to talk loudly in public, although loud music and horrendously noisy motorbikes don't seem to bother anybody. Yawning in public is frowned on; *com licença* is the useful equivalent of "excuse me." If you want to say, "I'm sorry," it's *desculpe*.

To attract a waiter's attention, *faz favor* (please) is the way to do it. It is appropriate to say thank you for everything, even if it's a service you're paying for: if you're a man, the word *obrigado*, while a woman would say *obrigada*. Greet people with *bom dia, boa tarde*, or *boa noite* (according to time of day) and after bidding them good-bye, it is polite to turn to say a final good-bye before you're out of sight.

The Portuguese are fastidious about their dress and appearance. Women regularly visit the hairdresser, and everyone, regardless of means, presents himself well. If you are in doubt as to how to dress, dress up rather than down for the occasion. It will be appreciated.

And finally, there remains the question of undress. Topless sunbathing for women is quite common among the Portuguese as well as the tourists and is the fashion on many Algarve and Lisbon coast beaches, and in fact, the practice is taking on throughout the country. Sunbathing bottomless (regardless of gender) is another matter and is actually illegal. However, if you're in search of the all-over suntan, there are a few beaches in the Algarve and the Costa Azul where it is unofficially accepted.

TIPPING

A service charge of 15% is included in restaurant bills, but a tip of around 10% will be appreciated, and generally speaking, will have been well-earned. In hotels the service charge is also included in the price, but it is appropriate to tip for particular services. The porter who carries your luggage should be tipped about 100 to 200 escudos per bag, and it is usual to leave a tip of about 100$ (70¢) per day for the chambermaid. In clubs, tip the waiters about 10% and cloakroom attendants about 100 escudos.

Taxi drivers should get about 10% of the fare, maybe more if it's a short journey, while tour guides should be tipped closer to 15%. Coat check attendants should be tipped about 50$ (30¢) as should the ushers in theaters and cinemas. Barbers and hairdressers are usually tipped about 10%.

It may all sound like a bit of a pain, but these services are usually well performed and the tips are considered part of the wage, which is generally much lower than it would be for a similar service at home.

HEALTH

Visitors do not require any inoculations to visit Portugal, and certificates are only needed if you are traveling from a country where there is an epidemic. Medical treatment at Portuguese state hospitals is free to visitors from the United Kingdom and other countries that have a reciprocal medical agreement with Portugal, but it is nevertheless advisable to take out medical insurance

coverage. Visitors from the United States and Canada are not entitled to free treatment. They should check if any current insurance policies cover them for medical treatment while traveling, and if not are advised to take out specific insurance cover.

For minor ailments go to the nearest pharmacy (*farmacia*). You will find that many pharmacists speak English and can give you reliable advice. Certain drugs are available on prescription only, however restrictions are often less stringently enforced here than elsewhere. Pharmacies are open during normal

shopping hours and are usually closed for lunch, but there is always one in each neighborhood that is open at any given hour, and a list of those on this special duty is displayed on the door of every pharmacy.

For more serious problems you can always ask hotel reception to call you a doctor, though this might cost you more than finding one yourself. Lists of English-speaking doctors are available from *Turismos*, as well as from the embassies and consulates. In case of emergency, from anywhere in the country, telephone (115 or go to the nearest hospital or health clinic. All principal residential

With its aquarium, concert arenas, and art pavillions, the Parque dos Nações on the site of Expo '98 is a place to experience contemporary Portugal.

areas have one or the other that provides 24-hour emergency service. As many doctors and surgeons are trained in the United States and the United Kingdom, communicating in English is rarely a problem. The standard of treatment is generally good, though some smaller hospitals might lack complete nursing and diagnostic services.

There is a small British hospital ((21) 395-6057 in Lisbon at Rua Saraiva de Carvalho No. 49, 1250 Lisbon, staffed by British-trained and English-speaking staff. It sees outpatients but has no emergency department.

EMERGENCIES

The emergency or SOS 24-hour telephone number is (115. The main hospital in Lisbon for dealing with accidents is the São José Hospital ((21) 886-0131 at Rua José António Serrano. It also has a 24-hour emergency dental service. It is difficult to get a private room in a state hospital, so if you desperately want one you will probably have to go to one of the very expensive private clinics.

SECURITY

The crime rate in Portugal is relatively low, the major problems being tax evasion and drug trafficking. However, as in any country where there is poverty, there is some theft, mostly in the cities and in places popular with tourists. So, don't leave belongings in your car for all to see, observe the usual rule about keeping your travelers' checks and slips separately, and hang on to your handbag, especially in crowded places.

Police here are armed with pistols, which rarely get used. If you need to attract a policeman's attention, you should address him as *Senhor Guarda*. The Guarda Nacional Repúblicana patrol the highways and their main occupation seems to be stopping vehicles (particularly trucks) to inspect documents.

Women traveling alone should not be particularly concerned, and no more than the usual city caution need be observed. Although there is no documented evidence of any danger, hitchhiking is absolutely not recommended for women.

WHEN TO GO

Portugal's temperate climate makes the period between April and November a good time to visit. The peak season runs from July to September, and for those not restricted to the standard academic or work calendar, lower prices and fewer tourists make the spring and autumn months ideal times to visit.

The Algarve, however, has a pleasant climate throughout the winter, although for

some people's taste (particularly golfers), it can get too hot during July and August. To convert temperatures to Fahrenheit, double the figure quoted and add 32.

WHAT TO TAKE

Traveling light is always a good idea, especially if you plan to take some souvenirs home with you. As to what clothes to pack, I recommend taking a sweater or jacket as the evenings, even in summer, can be cool, and also one somewhat formal outfit if you intend to dine in some of the finer restaurants. Like elsewhere in Europe, the Portuguese have taken to dressing down and jeans are to be seen everywhere, however, dressing fastidiously is still considered appropriate in certain settings, and it's best to reciprocate. Sightseeing in Lisbon and the hilly north most definitely requires sensible shoes. Another important accessory if you are traveling around the north, particularly off-season, is an umbrella as there are often sudden and heavy cloudbursts. The weather can get raw in this parts, so a leather jacket or the equivalent is also a good idea.

STAYING ON

United States citizens do not need a visa prior to entering Portugal. At your point of entry your passport will be stamped, allowing you a stay of sixty days. If you are interested in staying on, you may apply for a permit at the local police station or contact the Serviço de Extrangeiros e Fronteiras (Foreigner's Service) for no more than an additional thirty days. Australian citizens are now required to apply in advance for a tourist visa for a stay of no longer than ninety days. If your original visa is for less than ninety days, you too may apply for an extension. Neither Americans nor Australians can stay in Portugal for longer than ninety days in any six-month period. Applications should be made a few days before your time is up, in case of bureaucratic delay. In Lisbon the Serviço de Extrangeiros e Fronteiras ((21) 714-1027 is at Rua Conselheiro José Silvestre Ribeiro No. 4, 1600 Lisbon.

PORTUGUESE FOR TRAVELERS

If you have a knowledge of Spanish, or even French or Italian, you will find it a great help in reading Portuguese. It will be of little use, however, in understanding the spoken word, for the pronunciation of Portuguese is very different. A phrase book is always a useful piece of travel equipment, but the best way to prepare yourself for your visit (other than by taking Portuguese lessons) is to get hold of a rudimentary Portuguese course book that is backed up by audio cassettes; there's no substitute for hearing the spoken language. The Berlitz method is not bad as a superficial introduction to the grammar and spoken language. The BBC's *Get By In Portuguese* booklet and accompanying cassettes

also present an acceptable introduction. A little goes a long way, and there will be times when it will come in handy. If you do get totally stuck, French can sometimes prove useful as it is taught in the schools. Many people do speak Spanish — in fact, some do quite well — but immediately setting off in the language is often taken as an insult. My rule of thumb is always, through some locution or other, first ask permission before rattling on in Spanish, or in English for that matter. You will also find that English is quite broadly spoken, even in remote spots, and often extremely well.

PRONUNCIATION

The pronunciation of Portuguese is very difficult, and as people tend to speak quickly, attempting to pick it up also proves difficult. While the spelling and grammatical structure is quite similar to Spanish, there are major differences in pronunciation. Here are a few pointers.

When a word ends in a, e, o, m, n, or s, the stress falls on the penult; other words carry the stress on the last syllable. The exception to this rule is when an acute accent is placed on the syllable to be stressed — eg., *está, rápido*.

Some vowels are pronounced nasally — that is, through the nose and mouth simultaneously as if they were followed by an ng as in *cunning*. These include vowels with a tilde (~) over them, or those that are followed by m or n. Thus:

ão is pronounced somewhere in between aw and owrg;

on sounds like ong in *long*;

un or *um* is like oo in *mood* followed by ng;

in or *im* sounds like the e in *me* and is nasalized.

Most consonants are similar to English, but there are exceptions:

c is pronounced s as in sit before e and i but hard (k) before a, o, and u;

ç is pronounced as in French, s as in sit;

ch is pronounced sh, as in *push*;

h is always silent;

j is soft, like the s in *pleasure*;

lh is pronounced ly, as in *slowly*;

nh is pronounced ni;

Flags from sundry nations mark the international flavor of the Parque dos Nações.

s is soft at the beginning of a word or after a consonant, but when it occurs between two vowels it is pronounced "z" — as in *zoo*, and at the end of a word or before *c, f, p, q* and *t* it is sh;

x is sh, but before a vowel it is pronounced z — when between two vowels it is pronounced s;

z at the end of a word is pronounced sh.

VOCABULARY

Numbers

1	*um*
2	*dois*
3	*três*
4	*quatro*
5	*cinco*
6	*seis*
7	*sete*
8	*oito*
9	*nove*
10	*dez*
11	*onze*
12	*doze*
13	*treze*
14	*catorze*
15	*quinze*
16	*dizasseis*
17	*dezassete*
18	*dezoito*
19	*dezanove*
20	*vinte*
21	*vinte e um*
30	*trinta*
40	*quarenta*
50	*cinquenta*
60	*sessenta*
70	*setenta*
80	*oitenta*
90	*noventa*
100	*cem*
200	*duzentos*
500	*quinhentos*
1,000	*mil*
2,000	*dois mil*
100,000	*cem mil*
1,000,000	*um milhão*
2,000,000	*dois milhões*

Calendar

Sunday	*Domingo*
Monday	*Segunda-feira*
Tuesday	*Terça-feira*
Wednesday	*Quarta-feira*
Thursday	*Quinta-feira*
Friday	*Sexta-feira*
Saturday	*Sábado*
January	*Janeiro*
February	*Fevereiro*
March	*Março*
April	*Abril*
May	*Maio*
June	*Junho*
July	*Julho*
August	*Agosto*
September	*Setembro*
October	*Outubro*
November	*Novembro*
December	*Dezembro*
Spring	*Primavera*
Summer	*Verão*
Autumn	*Outono*
Winter	*Inverno*
day	*dia*
week	*semana*
month	*mês*
year	*ano*

Time

morning	*manhã*
noon	*meio-dia*
afternoon/evening	*tarde*
night	*noite*
today	*hoje*
yesterday	*ontem*
tomorrow	*amanhã*
what time is it?	*que horas são?*
now	*agora*
later	*mais tarde*

Key Words and Phrases

yes	*sim*
no	*não*
none	*nenhum(a)*
much, very, a lot (of)	*muito/a*
please	*por favor(se) faz favor*
thank you	*obrigado* (if said by a man)
	obrigada (if said by a woman)
thank you very much	*muito obrigado(a)*
don't mention it	*de nada*
OK/that's fine/it's good	*ésta bem*
hello	*olá*
good morning	*bom dia*
good afternoon/evening	*boa tarde*
good night	*boa noite*

good-bye *adeus*
welcome *seja benvindo*
excuse me *com licença*
I'm sorry *desculpe*
see you later *até logo*
well/good *bem*
beautiful *belo/a*
how? *como?*
how are you? *Como ésta?*
how many? *quantos/as?*
what? *que?*
when? *quando?*
who? *quem?*

here *aqui*
there *ali*
near *perto*
far *longe*
left *esquerda*
right *direita*
straight on *em frente*
hot *quente*
cold *frio*
big *grande*
small *pequeno*
open *aberto*
closed *fechado*

why? *porquê?*
where? *onde?*
where is? *onde é?*
how much is it? *quanto custa?*
I understand *comprendo*
I don't understand *não comprendo*
I don't know *não sei*
can/may I...? *posso...?*
I want/I would like *quero*
do you have? *tem?*
do you sell? *vende?*
I don't speak Portuguese *não falo Português*
do you speak English? *fala Inglês?*
he/she/it is/you are *ésta*
there is/there are *há*
this/this one *éste(a)*
that *esse(a)*

new *novo/a*
old *velho*
cheap *barato*
expensive *caro*
money *dinheiro*

Places and Things
bakery *padaria*
beach *praia*
boarding house *pensão*
bookshop *livraria*
bridge *ponte*
bus station *estação de autocarros*
bus or tram stop *paragem*
butcher *talho*

Just some faces in the crowd.

cake shop *pastelaria*
cathedral *catedral/sé*
church *igreja*
cigarette *cigarro*
cigar *charuto*
city *cidade*
convent *convento*
dry cleaner *limpeza a seco*
grocer *mercearia*
harbor *porto*
lane or alley *travessa*
market *mercado*
monastery *mosteiro*
mountain *serra*
palace *paço*
pharmacy *farmacia*
police station *esquadra*
post office *correio*
restaurant *restaurante*
river *rio*
street *rua*
square *largo/praça/campo*
tourist office *Turismo*
tower or keep *torre*
train station *estação de comboios*
viewpoint *miradouro*

On the road
bus *autocarro*
regular gasoline *gasolina normal*
super *gasolina super*
unleaded *sem chomo*
fill it up, please *encha ó depósito, por favor*
oil *óleo*
diesel *gasóleo*
water *água*
petrol station *bomba de gasolina*
tire *pneu*
lights *luzes*
brakes *travões*
spark plugs *velas*
accident *acidente*
Diversion *desvio*
Stop *alto*
Slow down *devagar*

In the Hotel
room *quarto*
single room *um quarto simples*
double room (twin beds) *um quarto com duas camas*
with a double bed *com cama de casal*
with a bathroom *com banho*

without a bathroom *sem banho*
shower *chuveiro*
soap *sabonete*
towel *toalha*
toilet paper *papel higiénico*
laundry *lavandaria*
key *chave*
registration form *ficha*

In the Post Office
stamp *selo*
letter *carta*
postcard *postal*
parcel *encomenda*
airmail *via aérea*
general delivery/poste restante *posta restante*

In Emergencies
doctor *médico*
nurse *enfermeira/o*
sick, ill *doente*
pain, ache *dor*
fever *febre*
I am allergic to *sou alérgico à*
I have toothache *doem-me os dentes*
help *ajuda*
I am diabetic *sou diabético*

In Restaurants
breakfast *pequeno almoço*
lunch *almoço*
tea *lanche*
dinner *jantar*
menu *lista/ementa/carta*
fixed-price menu *preço fixo*
wine list *lista dos vinhos*
(to summon waiter: *faz favor!*)
bill, check *conta*
glass *copo*
pepper *pimenta*
salt *sal*
sugar *açúcar*
bread *pão*
butter *manteiga*
sandwich *sandes*
mineral water *água mineral*
carbonated water *água com gás*
still water *água sem gás*
fruit juice *sumo de fruta*

The festivities go on at the Festa de Santo Antonio in Lisbon.

milk *leite*
ice *gelo*
coffee with milk *café com leite*
tea *chá*
beer *cerveja*
draught beer *imperial*
red wine *vinho tinto*
white wine *vinho branco*
rosé wine *vinho rosado*
cheese *queijo*
olives *azeitonas*
mixed vegetable salad *salada mista*
green salad *salada verde*
meat *carne*
beef *carne de vaca*
lamb *cordeiro*
mutton *carneiro*
ham *fiambre*
veal *vitela*
chicken *frango*
turkey *peru*
rabbit *coelho*
liver *iscas/fígado*
kid *cabrito*
goat *cabra*
kidney *rim*
tripe *tripa*
beef steak *bife*
rare *mal passado*
medium *normal*
well done *bem passado*
fried *frito*
roasted *assado*
stewed *estufado*
boiled *cozido*
baked *no forno*
grilled *grelhado*
smoked *fumado*
fish *peixe*
crayfish *lagostim*
sardines *sardinhas*
prawns *gambas*
clams *ameijoas*
red mullet *salmonetes*
tuna *atum*
lobster *lavagante*
sole *linguado*
swordfish *peixe espada*
crab *santola*
squid *lula*
octopus *polvo*
vegetables *legumes*
beans *feijões*

peas *ervilhas*
cabbage *couve*
potatoes *batatas*
mushroom *cogumelo*
onion *cebola*
garlic *alho*
rice *arroz*
fruit *fruta*
apple *maçã*
orange *laranja*
peach *pêssego*
pineapple *ananás*
plum *ameixa*
figs *figos*
watermelon *melancia*
strawberries *morangos*
apricots *alperces*
almonds *amendoas*
pears *pêras*
dessert *sobremesa*
ice cream *gelado*
cake *bolo*
rice pudding *arroz doce*
caramel custard *pudim flan*

WEB SITES

As you have noticed, whenever available, web sites and e-mail addresses have been listed within the text. Here are some additional interesting sites with (at times, somewhat esoteric) information on Portugal. The World Wide Web is ever-expanding, and of course, becoming ever more entangled. So if you are at the beginning of your research, your best bet is to use a "multi-search engine," and start by searching such categories as "Portugal," "Portuguese tourism," "Portuguese culture," "Portuguese language," etc. Two very reliable multi-search engines are: www.dogpile.com and www.mamma.com.

www.portugal.com calls itself "the gateway to Portuguese culture, community, people and business." This is the official site of the Portuguese tourist office and although helpful, it could be much better.

www.well.com/user/ideame/portugal.html is infinitely more useful as it is a catalogue of home pages that relate to Portugal, each of which is well linked to other sites.

www.tntmag.co.uk/ This is a British on-line 'zine comprised of nonprofessionals' articles on their personal travels. There are quite a few interesting ones on Portugal and the slant is refreshing.

www.ipl.org/youth/hello/portuguese is a listing within the Internet public library's site and it has wonderful connections that primarily lead to sites on Portuguese language and history. This area and its links are by no means just for kids.

www.capecodaccess.com/provincetown .html offers an interesting presentation of Portuguese history and culture in New England, and highlights the annual festival on Cape Cod.

www.patherfinder.com/travel/TL/ portugal/poeat.html is *Travel and Leisure*'s specific region on Portugal within the vast Time, Inc. web site. Its main focus is on Portuguese cuisine.

www.ultranet.com/~olmckey/food.htlm This is a site that features information on Portuguese food and even includes recipes from some of the most renowned restaurants in Portugal.

www.home.ici.net/customers/rufus/Fado/ FadoSounds.html This is a wonderful site that allows you to taste excerpts from the best *fadoistas* (as long as you have Real Audio Player®, which can be downloaded from the site). It gets even better when you link to the guitar section.

www.eunet.pt/Lisboa/p/ouvir/fado/ letras.html For true devotees: here is where you'll find the lyrics to several *fado* songs, all of course, in Portuguese.

Recommended Reading

ANDERSON, JEAN. *The Food of Portugal.* London: Robert Hale, 1987.

BIRMINGHAM, DAVID. *A Concise History of Portugal.* Cambridge: Cambridge University Press, 1998.

BOXER, C.R. *The Portuguese Seaborne Empire* 1415–1825. London: Hutchinson, 1977.

BRIDGE, ANN and SUSAN LOWNDES. *The Selective Traveller in Portugal.* London: Chatto & Windus, 1963.

CAMÕES, LUÍS VAZ DE. *The Lusiads.* London: Penguin, 1985.

FIGUEIREDO, ANTONIO DE. *Portugal: Fifty Years of Dictatorship.* London: Penguin, 1975.

GARRETT, ALMEIDA. *Travels in My Homeland.* London: Peter Owen, 1987.

GIL, JULIO (text) and CABRITA, AUGUSTO (photographs). *The Finest Castles in Portugal.* Lisbon: Verbo, 1988. *The Finest Churches in Portugal.* Lisbon: Verbo, 1988. *The Loveliest Towns and Villages in Portugal.* Lisbon: Verbo, 1991.

INSIGHT TEAM OF THE SUNDAY TIMES. *Insight on Portugal — The Year of the Captains.* London: André Deutsch, 1975.

KAPLAN, MARION. *The Portuguese: The Land and Its People.* London: Penguin, 1991.

MACAULAY, ROSE. *They Went to Portugal.* London: Penguin, 1985.

MODESTO, MARIA DE LOURDES. *Traditional Portuguese Cookery.* Lisbon: Verbo.

DE OLIVEIRA MARQUES, A.H. *History of Portugal.* New York: Columbia University Press, 1972.

PESSOA, FERNANDO. *Poems of Fernando Pessoa.* Translated and edited by Edwin Honig and Susan M. Brown. New York: Ecco Press, 1986, and Canada: Penguin Books, 1986. *The Book of Disquiet.* Translated by Alfred MacAdam. Boston: Exact Change, 1998. *Fernando Pessoa & Company: Selected Poems.* Translated and edited by Richard Zenith. New York: Grove / Atlantic, 1998.

PROPER, DATUS C. *The Last Old Place: A Search Through Portugal.* New York: Simon & Shuster, 1992.

READ, JAN. *The Wines of Portugal.* London: Faber, 1987.

SARAMAGO, JOSÉ. *Blindness.* Translated by Giovanni Pontiero. New York: Harcourt Brace & Company, 1998.

SUBRAHMANYAM, SANJAY. *The Career and Legend of Vasco de Gama.* Cambridge: Cambridge University Press, 1997.

SMITH, ROBERT C. *The Art of Portugal 1500–1800.* London: Weidenfeld & Nicolson, 1968.

Quick Reference A–Z Guide
to Places and Topics of Interest with Listed Accommodation, Restaurants and Useful Telephone Numbers

The symbols ⑤ FAX, ⑦ TOLL-FREE, ⑥ E-MAIL, ⑳ WEB-SITE refer to additional contact information found in the chapter listings.

Photo Credits:

David Borigot: Pages 48 and 119.

Alain Evrard: Pages 15, 19, 26 *bottom*, 31, 33, 35, 40, 42, 43, 44 *bottom*, 45, 49, 51, 62 *top and bottom*, 64 *top and bottom*, 78, 80, 81, 83, 84, 89, 107, 115, 117, 131, 133, 270, 271, 282, 284, 287, 291, 292, 295 and 297.

Bruno Barbier: Pages 3, 6 *left and right*, 11, 12, 22, 23, 25, 26 *top*, 29 *bottom*, 30 *top*, 32, 42, 44, 58 *top and bottom*, 66, 73, 76–77, 82, 88, 93, 97, 98, 114, 121, 123, 130, 135, 136, 146, 149, 153, 154, 155, 156, 158, 159, 161 *top and bottom*, 169 *left and right*, 170, 171, 172, 173, 175, 176, 177, 179, 180, 181, 185, 187, 195 *top and bottom*, 196, 197, 211, 214, 215, 223, 224, 233, 237, 238, 247, 248 *top and bottom*, 249, 250, 272, 273, 274, 280, 288, Back Cover *top and bottom*.

Hoa Qui: Pages 61, 63, 70, 75, 90, 99, 108, 111, 113 *bottom*, 116, 127, 139, 143, 145, 151, 182, 183, 190, 228, 229, 230, 232, 234, 244, 255 *top and bottom*, 264, 267, 275 and 277.

Nik Wheeler: Cover, Pages 4, 5 *left and right*, 7 *left and right*, 10, 13, 17, 18, 21, 27, 28, 29 *top*, 30 *bottom*, 34, 37, 39, 46, 47 *top and bottom*, 50, 52, 53, 55, 59, 60, 65, 67, 68, 69, 72, 74, 79, 85, 86, 87, 92, 100, 101, 103, 104, 109, 148, 193, 198, 201, 202 *left and right*, 205, 206, 209, 213, 216, 219, 226, 227, 245, 246, 251, 256–257, 258, 259, 260, 262, 263, 266, 268, 269, 278, 279, Back Cover *middle*.

SIPA: *A Luwkowicz:* 125. *J. Nicolas:* 141–142. *Jaap Bournan:* 252. *JPH Ruiz:* 113 *top*, 134. *Marc Cinello*: 186.